EVERY. DAMN. DAY.

EVERY.
DAMN.
DAY.

THE MORNING HERO'S GUIDE TO BUILDING A 5-STAR LIFE

JARVIS LEVERSON

THIN LEAF PRESS | LOS ANGELES

EVERY. DAMN. DAY.: The Morning Hero's Guide to Building a 5-Star Life. Copyright © 2025 by Jarvis Leverson. All rights reserved. No part of this publication may be reproduced, distributed, or transmitted in any form or by any means, including photocopying, recording, or other electronic or mechanical methods, without the prior written permission of the author, except in the case of brief quotations embodied in reviews and certain other non-commercial uses permitted by copyright law. The contributing authors maintain all rights to use the material inside the chapter he or she wrote for this book.

Disclaimer—The advice, guidelines, and all suggested material in this book are given in the spirit of information with no claims to any particular guaranteed outcomes. This book does not replace professional consultation. Anyone deciding to add physical or mental exercises to their life should reach out to a licensed medical doctor, therapist, or consultant before following any of the advice in this book; anyone making any financial, business, or lifestyle decisions should consult a licensed professional before following any of the advice in this book. The authors, publisher, editors, and organizers do not assume and hereby disclaim any liability to any party for any loss, damage, or disruption caused by anything written in this book.

Library of Congress Cataloging-in-Publication Data
Names: Leverson, Jarvis, Author
Title: EVERY. DAMN. DAY.: The Morning Hero's Guide to Building a 5-Star Life.
LCCN: On File

ISBN 978-1-968318-32-1 (hardcover) | 978-1-968318-31-4 (paperback)
ISBN 978-1-968318-30-7 (eBook) | 978-1-968318-33-8 (audiobook)

Productivity, Success, Professional Development, Personal Transformation
Cover Design: 100 Covers
Interior Design: Dindo Sanguenza
Editors: Nancy Pile, Dhanliza Cellona
Thin Leaf Press
Los Angeles

THIN
LEAF

To my wife and best friend, Jane… the original Morning Hero.

When I was stuck, unhappy, and unfulfilled, you lit the fire in me to keep going, to believe again, and to fight for a bigger life. This book would not exist without your patience, your unwavering support, and your love. While raising two kids and being a rockstar wife and mother, you stand as the ultimate example of what it looks like to play the game of life all out.

NOTE FROM THE AUTHOR

I am convinced reading this book will change your life. The book alone has massive value. And for those who really want to get a head start transforming your life, you can get going right away. Before you dive into this book, I want to give you some tools.

Along with this book, I've put my entire life's work into one place so you can accelerate your transformation. Scan the QR code below to unlock:

- **The Quick Start Guide** – Your step-by-step blueprint to begin winning your mornings immediately.
- **The Win the Day App** – This is the command center for your greatness. This app will gamify your life so you can WIN. Every. Day.
- **The Zero Calendar / 5-Star Planner (Free Download)** – Plan your day with precision and intention.
- **The Morning Hero Method Course (Free)** – Install the foundational habits that change everything.
- **The 30-Day Morning Hero Challenge** – Build unshakable consistency and momentum alongside other heroes.

This isn't about me selling you anything. Everything here is free and I don't hold anything back. My only "payment" is seeing you live a fully charged life… and then spreading the word, so together we can build a movement of Morning Heroes across the world!

Don't just read this book. Activate it. Scan the code. Step into your greatness. And let's win… EVERY. DAMN. DAY.

CONTENTS

Introduction xi

Part I: The Birth of a Hero xvii

Chapter 1: Sleepwalking Through Life 1
Chapter 2: The Birth of a Hero 13

Part II: The WINNING Formula 25

Wake Up Early 27
Chapter 3: The Battle of Your Life 29
Chapter 4: Take Back Your Power 41
Chapter 5: The Cost of Comfort 55
Chapter 6: Power Down to Power Up 67

Intentions 77
Chapter 7: Vision 83
Chapter 8: Goals 95
Chapter 9: Level 3 Intentions: Actions 115
Chapter 10: Level 4 Intentions: Schedule 131
Chapter 11: The Morning Practice 145

No Days Off 155
Chapter 12: The Power of Consistency 157
Chapter 13: Program Your Autopilot 167
Chapter 14: Accountability Is Everything 177

Part III: The Cheat Codes 187

Chapter 15: Heart Rate 191
Chapter 16: Eat Right 213
Chapter 17: Read 225
Chapter 18: One Big Action 235
Chapter 19: Spread Joy 257

Part IV: Your Hero's Journey 275

Chapter 20: It's Your Turn 277
About the Author 299
Acknowledgments 301

INTRODUCTION

Winter Is Coming

If you've ever watched an episode of Game of Thrones, then you've heard the ominous warning: Winter is coming. In nearly every scene, someone utters those three chilling words. It's more than a seasonal reference... it's an existential threat. A dark, looming storm that represents danger, urgency, and the slow, creeping demise of humanity. It kept the characters on edge, constantly aware that something fierce and unforgiving was always approaching.

Well... our winter is here.

Not in the form of ice or snow, but in the form of distraction. In the form of endless dopamine hits and mind-numbing entertainment. We're living in a time where our greatest threat isn't a mythical White Walker... it's the glowing screen in our hand. Social media. Notifications. Streaming platforms. It's a blizzard of noise, stealing our time, our attention, and slowly eroding our purpose.

This isn't just a poetic metaphor. It's our reality, and it's happening all around us. We are living in the storm, and most of us don't even realize we're buried under it.

The opening scene of the movie Idiocracy captures this perfectly. A rocket ship crashes into a man's living room, but he's too consumed with his TV to even notice. He's slumped in a chair just two feet from the screen, which is playing multiple shows at once. That chair is his entire world. It has a built-in soda dispenser, speakers, and even a toilet. He never has to stand. Never has to move. He's become a useless blob, a mute zombie, soaked in flickering lights and forgotten dreams.

The man emerging from the rocket is a time traveler sent from the future to save humanity from becoming exactly that: brain-dead couch potatoes with no ambition and no connection to real life.

That movie came out in 2006. And yet, here we are.

Technology has lulled us into complacency. With a few taps, you can have a Big Mac delivered without leaving your couch. With a few swipes, you can date, work, shop, and socialize… without ever stepping outside. And now, thanks to AI, we're at the point where you don't even need to think. ChatGPT can write your emails, respond to your texts, and even call someone using your own voice. We're hurtling toward a future where machines think for us, and we just sit back and consume.

It's starting to feel a little too much like The Matrix, isn't it? A future where we're plugged into simulations, living fake lives through virtual experiences while our physical selves slowly waste away. It's not science fiction anymore. It's reality. We are becoming a generation of spectators… watching life happen on screens while slowly forgetting how to live it ourselves.

We used to be builders, creators, inventors. Now, we're scrolling. Watching. Consuming. Numbing.

And it's killing us.

Bronnie Ware, a hospice nurse who spent her career with people on their deathbeds, once asked each of her patients a powerful question: What is your biggest regret in life? The #1 answer, over and over again, was this: I wish I had followed my dreams.

EVERY. DAMN. DAY.

That's the real tragedy. Most people never pursue their purpose. They settle. They coast. They watch. They binge. They numb themselves from the guilt of knowing that deep down... they were called for more.

I believe every single person was created with a divine purpose. We each carry a unique gift, a special promise only we can fulfill. Maybe someone reading this was born to cure cancer. Maybe someone was born to bridge the wealth gap or create a new technology that will advance mankind. But what happens if they never pursue it? What if they never rise? Not only do they rob themselves of a meaningful life... they also rob all of us.

In his book Can't Hurt Me, David Goggins tells a story about a recurring dream. In it, he dies and reaches the gates of heaven. The gatekeeper doesn't show him the life he lived, but the life he was supposed to live. A life of greatness, achievement, and impact. And then he says to Goggins, "You didn't kill anyone, you didn't do anything evil... but you didn't become the man you were created to be. We're letting you in, but we're disappointed in you."

To Goggins, that wasn't heaven. That was hell.

I couldn't agree more.

Heaven is knowing you lived full out. That you said yes to your calling. That you gave the world every ounce of your potential. Hell, on the other hand, is the guilt of knowing you left greatness on the table. That you played small. That you gave in to fear, distraction, or laziness.

That kind of disappointment is unbearable. It leads to depression, addiction, and a reliance on anything... drugs, alcohol, food, entertainment... to numb the pain of not living the life you know you were meant to live.

And here's the truth: We're at a crossroads.

We can either keep drifting toward distraction and regret, or we can wake up. We can take control of our time, our energy, our focus, and start building lives that we're proud of. Lives full of purpose. Lives full of power.

I believe you were called for something bigger. And I believe this book found you at the exact moment you needed it most.

You are not here by accident.

There is a specific blessing over your life. A calling with your name on it. There are lives only you can touch, solutions only you can bring, a legacy only you can leave. And if you don't step fully into your greatness, the world misses out.

Don't let that happen.

Let this be the moment you draw the line in the sand. The moment you say, enough is enough. The moment you rise. The moment you answer the call.

What to Expect

In this book, you will be challenged to wake up from your sleepwalker state and step into a new identity of a Morning Hero. A Morning Hero is someone who wakes up every day with passion, purpose, power, and productivity! They are the producers who get more done by 7 a.m. than most people can accomplish in an entire day!

This new identity of being a Morning Hero will be your secret weapon. It will protect you from being lulled into a mediocre life, a life of comfort and regret as your dreams and highest potential go unfulfilled.

EVERY. DAMN. DAY.

This isn't just a book... it's a blueprint. A roadmap to help you reclaim your time, rewire your habits, and reignite your life with purpose.

It's broken into four parts, each designed to walk you step by step through your transformation from chaos to clarity, from coasting to conquering.

Part 1: The Birth of the Hero is where it all begins... with my personal story. You'll see how I went from burnout and rock bottom to building a life of intentional success. This section isn't about me... it's about showing you what's possible when you stop living on autopilot and start living with purpose.

Part 2: The WINNING Formula gives you the core framework that powers everything. These are the foundational habits... Wake up early, Intention setting, and No days off... that will unlock your consistency, energy, and productivity. It's the operating system of a Morning Hero.

Part 3: The Cheat Codes is where we level up. You'll discover simple, powerful hacks to upgrade every area of your life... health, relationships, mindset, and more. These aren't just nice ideas. They're battle-tested strategies that have helped thousands of people win their day before 9 a.m.

Part 4: Your Hero's Journey brings it all together. You'll create your custom blueprint to apply these systems to your life, with clarity on your goals and the accountability to follow through. This is your invitation to rise up, own your greatness, and become the Hero you were born to be.

Now that you know where we're headed, let's start at the beginning.

Because before I could teach any of this... I had to live it.

I'll see you in Part 1: The Birth of the Hero... the moment everything changed.

Take Action

- Scan the QR code to watch the Quick Start video on becoming a Morning Hero so you can Wake up and WIN starting tomorrow morning!

PART I
THE BIRTH OF A HERO

CHAPTER 1
SLEEPWALKING THROUGH LIFE

"Most people die at 25 and aren't buried until 75."

— Benjamin Franklin

Sleepwalkers

The average person wakes up already behind. They open their eyes, grab their phone, and let the world rush in before they've even taken a breath. Scroll. Swipe. Tap. Comparison. Noise. Email. Anxiety. They roll out of bed, not because they're ready to lead the day, but because the day has already gotten ahead of them. They move through their morning half-awake, half-distracted, and completely reactive.

And then? They spend the rest of the day putting out fires they didn't start, chasing tasks they didn't choose, and wondering why they feel stuck, scattered, and silently disappointed with where their life is going.

They are Sleepwalkers. Not literally asleep, but not truly awake either.

Sleepwalkers look alive. They have jobs, schedules, meetings, goals. Some even have six-figure incomes, nice homes, good intentions, and gym memberships. But inside, they're drifting.

They move through life in loops: wake up late, rush to catch up, react all day, escape into alcohol, food, and distractions, then repeat. They say things like, "Things are just crazy right now." "I just don't have enough time." "I just need to get through this week." "Once things slow down, I'll get back on track." They are stuck in a vicious cycle of low-level living where the only thing they look forward to is weekends or vacations… fleeting moments of relief from the pressure of their everyday lives.

Their life becomes nothing more than sporadic peaks of happiness connected by long periods of coping, numbing, and pretending to be happy. They live in survival mode. Their eyes are open. They are moving around. They are busy. They are going to work, taking the kids to practice, cooking dinner, and going to church. It looks like they are awake, but they aren't. They are sleepwalking.

Sleepwalking, or somnambulism, is a sleep disorder that happens during the deepest stage of sleep… what's called slow-wave sleep (non-REM stage 3). The body is active, but the mind is asleep. People appear awake… eyes open, walking around… but they're not conscious. They can perform basic routines like dressing, eating, or even driving, but have no memory of it later. They are completely operating on muscle memory… routines that have been burned into the subconscious so that they can literally do them even if their eyes were closed.

And that's how people live their lives. In a half-sleep state. To themselves and everyone around them, they can maintain the illusion that they are living… but they are just acting out pre-programmed routines that have been hard-coded into their autopilot. They are doing a lot, but not going anywhere.

They are asleep to their power. Asleep to their purpose. Asleep to the life they were meant to live. They are sleepwalkers.

And I know this… because I used to be one.

The Fall from Grace

On the outside, I was living the dream. I was the #1 sales rep in my division for a Fortune 500 software company. I had a beautiful girlfriend and we lived in a beautiful downtown condo with with floor-to-ceiling windows overlooking the ocean. Everything seemed perfect, but it wasn't. I was running on fumes, going through the motions. It felt like I was on a hamster wheel, just running furiously in place.

Even though I had more than most people could ever dream of, I started to feel unsettled. Things just started to feel mundane and I grew more and more unhappy. I just kept thinking, "There has to be more to my life than this." The things that I thought would make me happy, didn't. Even though my life was ok… I still didn't feel satisfied or fulfilled. The only time I felt alive was when I was out drinking with friends… so that's what I did.

I chased fleeting moments of happiness to fill the growing void. A drink after work turned into two, then three, then an entire evening spent numbing myself. Weekends became an endless pursuit of self-indulgence. Parties, late nights, anything to avoid sitting alone with the uncomfortable truth: I wasn't happy.

I was sinking deep into a pit of self-sabotage. I ignored the gym. I stopped eating well. I avoided hard conversations with my partner. I slacked off at work. All the habits that had once made me successful were now working against me, pulling me further into a cycle of self-destruction. I felt stuck. And when you feel stuck, the easiest way to cope is to escape even more.

High-functioning people often disguise their self-sabotage as rewards. Maybe it's a bottle of wine after a long day, hours scrolling on social media, or eating trashy food because "you've earned it." But these habits aren't rewards; they're coping mechanisms. They're attempts to escape the anxious feeling that you want more out of life.

And that's who I had become... someone who knew there was "more" for me, and I wasn't living up to it. And guess what? That guilt sent me deeper into the downward spiral. The numbing got worse. The coping got stronger. The escaping became more intense. I didn't realize it then, but looking back, I was suffering from an "upper limit problem."

The Upper Limit

According to Gay Hendricks, in the book The Big Leap, we all have an internal thermostat that defines our "upper limit."

A thermostat controls the temperature of a room. When the room gets too cold, it kicks the heat on to bring the room back up to the set temperature. When it's warm, it turns on the A/C to cool the room back off. Because of the thermostat, the room will always stay within 1 or 2 degrees of the temperature setting.

We have an internal thermostat that controls the temperature of our lives. It determines the level of success, happiness, and love that we are comfortable experiencing. The problem is, this thermostat is usually set early in life based on our past experiences, upbringing, and beliefs about what we deserve. It becomes a subconscious limit dictating how much good we allow ourselves to have.

When things get better than what we believe we're "allowed" to have, the thermostat kicks in to bring us back to what feels familiar. It's not conscious or intentional... it's automatic. And for me, when I reached that pinnacle of success, when I had the money, the career, the penthouse, the relationship... it triggered my thermostat. My life was "too good," and deep down, I didn't believe I deserved it. So without realizing it, I started to sabotage myself to bring everything back down to my set point.

At first, it was subtle. I started going out more, telling myself I deserved to celebrate, to let loose after all the hard work. But one drink turned into several. A night out turned into a pattern. Before I knew it, I was staying out late every night, waking up hungover, and dragging myself into work. The sharp, focused energy that had made me a top performer was gone. I started missing deadlines, losing clients, and eventually, my performance dropped.

The thermostat doesn't let you stray too far from what feels safe, whether that's in success, relationships, or happiness. And for me, my comfort zone was built on the belief that I had to struggle to succeed. The idea that life could be easy, that I could live a big life felt foreign… unrealistic even. So when I reached that high point, my mind went to work finding ways to create struggle again. And little did I know that it would all come to a climax during one of our team meetings.

The Team Meeting

It was rare to catch everyone from the sales team in the office at the same time. You were actually encouraged to not be in the office. You should be out in the field, visiting clients, conducting sales presentations, scouting your territory, and prospecting new business. This actually made it pretty easy for me to hide away and pretend like I was working. But once a month, we would have a mandatory team meeting. Everyone had to be there, and we would all review the "scoreboard."

The scoreboard showed all of the sales reps ranked in order according to their sales numbers. It was on a big 65-inch digital screen as soon as you walked into the conference room. It was huge, it was bright, and it was the main attraction of the meeting. In fact, the entire meeting was just a big pep rally to celebrate the people at the top of the board and to get everyone else fired up. If you were at the top of the board, it was a big deal.

I had spent an entire year at the top of that board. These meetings were usually just the Jarvis show. People would say sarcastically, "I wonder who's going to be at the top this time?" knowing that it was going to be me. It had really just become a formality. But this time was different. As soon as I walked in the room, the rankings were staring me in the face. Twenty-five names were sitting there up on the screen. There were actually more than 25 reps, but that's all that could fit on the screen. Usually, it was the rookies that were ranked so far down that their names didn't appear on the screen. But that was to be expected. All of the seasoned reps usually fought for spots 2 to 25, while my name was cemented in position number one. But not this time.

My name didn't occupy any real estate on all 65 inches of that screen. My name was so far down on the list that it didn't even show up! I could see people whispering to each other and then turning back to look at me as I sunk down low in my seat. Maybe there was a mistake and someone forgot to put my name on the list. Or maybe they created a whole new category for me. Maybe I was on a completely different list altogether. A list for the ultra-achievers.

But no, this was no mistake. I ranked dead last on the entire team. I could no longer hide. I could no longer fake it. I could no longer pretend. Numbers don't lie.

The embarrassment and shame were more painful than when I had broken my shoulder playing high school football. I kept a stoic face during the whole meeting. My eyes halfway filled with tears. I just sat there kind of dazed, almost in a trance. I snapped out of it just as the meeting was ending.

I remember one of my friends coming up to me saying, "Hey, man, is everything alright?" I put on a smile and made up some lame excuse, "Yeah, I've got some really big deals in the works and they just haven't landed yet. Don't worry, I'll be back on top as soon as they go through!" But the reality was, I had no deals. I wasn't going to be back at the top anytime soon. And that's when my boss looked over at me and said,

EVERY. DAMN. DAY.

"Jarvis, could you swing by my office after the meeting?" Oh shit, I knew what that meant.

The Green Mile

I'd been in my boss's office many times. Most of the time, we had our feet kicked up on his desk, talking about what we were going to do together over the weekend or having a glass of his special scotch that he kept hidden in his desk for special occasions.

But the sound in his voice this time was different. I knew there would be no feet kicked up. No scotch celebrations. His voice had a tone that I had never heard from him before. It was almost like he was mourning. That walk from the conference room to his office was like walking The Green Mile. If you're not familiar with The Green Mile, it refers to the long walk that a death row inmate takes from their jail cell to their execution chambers. It's a death march. They know what's about to happen and they have a long, slow walk to contemplate everything in their life, make amends, and come to terms with their expiration. Expiration is just another way of saying they are about to die.

I would imagine that the worst part of being on death row is the buildup. The knowing what's about to happen. I'd much rather not know that I'm about to die. Just make it quick and painless, like getting hit by a bus. One minute I'd be happy-go-lucky, and the next minute I'd wake up in heaven with my grandmother. That's how I'd want to go.

But the "green mile?" I'd imagine that's worse than the actual execution. Every step contemplating your life. All things you did, didn't do, could've done differently, regrets, disappointments, mistakes, failures. Emotional and mental pain is far worse than physical pain. And that's what the "green mile" is. It's purposefully and intentionally done to kill the inmate's spirit before they kill their body.

And there I was, walking my own "green mile." I knew exactly what we were walking to his office to do. It was my execution chamber. With every step, I had an opportunity to reflect on how I failed to live up to the expectations that everyone had of me and how I was letting everyone down.

The Golden Child

When I was growing up, I was always "the gifted one" in the family. I played just about every sport you can think of. My mom was a single mother raising a rambunctious black boy on the West Side of Chicago. Her name is Sweetie (yes, the name on her birth certificate is actually Sweetie!) and it's a very fitting name for her. She is as sweet as can be! She did everything she could to keep me on the straight and narrow, so she kept me busy! From baseball to football to basketball and wrestling and track and Taekwondo, you name it, I did it all.

It was her way of keeping me off the streets. There's no future for a young black boy on the West Side of Chicago. Chicago is consistently ranked among the most dangerous cities in the US. On my block, there were two other boys that were the same age as me. We did everything together. We took the bus to school together, played kickball in the streets together, hung out at each other's houses on the weekends. We were the three amigos. One of the boys started getting involved in gangs and was shot in the head from a rival gang our freshman year of high school. The other boy started breaking into people's homes and got sent to jail.

And that's the expected outcome for young black boys in Chicago... either dead or in jail. The only difference between me and the other two amigos was that they didn't have a mother like mine.

She never had the opportunity to go to college. After she graduated from high school, she went right into working for an insurance company as a claim processor. She was a whiz with numbers. She could calculate percentages and fractions faster than anyone. She always said that she should have been an accountant. That was her calling in life, and she missed out on it so she could work and take care of me. She put her dreams on hold to make sure that I had every opportunity to excel in life.

I remember a conversation that she had with my father. They were talking about how they never had the opportunity to travel to Europe. My dad said, "Don't worry, Sweetie, Jarvis is going to take care of us. He's going to take us to all the places that we've never been to." Even though she had good intentions, that put a lot of pressure on me. Maybe that's why I fell so hard. Because I knew there was so much on the line and I couldn't handle it. Now, I had to face the fact that I wouldn't be able to live up to her expectations of me. I wasn't living up to my potential, the potential that she worked so hard to preserve. I wasn't going to be able to spoil her like she deserved from all of the sacrifices that she made for me. That walk was torture.

Running Away

We got to his office and he got straight to the point. He said, "Jarvis, this hurts me to say this, but management feels that you are no longer a good fit for the team."

There it was, the dagger in my heart. But I did what every weak-minded person would do. I made excuses. I said, "You know, I have to be honest, I haven't been passionate about the job anymore. That's why I've been disengaged. I'm ready for my next challenge."

It was all a lie. It was my ego talking. Rather than me facing the fact that I was failing, I just lied to him... and myself... by saying that I was done with the job and ready to quit. The funny thing is that he wasn't actually going to fire me. He was just voicing his concerns and was going to offer some extra support to get me back on track. But at the time, I was filled with such overwhelming guilt that I actually wanted to "fire myself" so that I wouldn't feel that shame from being at the bottom of the board. I was running from my problems.

I still remember that long drive home like it was yesterday. The guilt was weighing heavy on me. The shame was unbearable. The disappointment was overwhelming. I started sinking into a hole. A dark pit of despair. My first thought was to just numb myself from the pain. I wanted to just forget about everything.

That's exactly what I did. I stayed out all night partying with friends, pretending like I didn't just lose my job. Pretending like everything was OK. Wearing the mask of happiness when I was empty on the inside. But that mask is temporary. Eventually you have to face reality.

When I finally came home, I had some explaining to do with my girlfriend. "Where was I?" "Why was I not answering my phone?" "Who was I with and what was I doing with them?" I wasn't prepared to answer these questions, so I did what I do best… I ran.

I walked in the house and I spoke first. "Babe, this isn't fair to you. I haven't been the boyfriend that you need. It would be better if I wasn't in your life."

She didn't deny that what I was saying was true. She was hurting just as much as I was, and it wasn't fair to her. She didn't deserve my behavior. So I packed up a duffle bag and walked out of the house.

Where was I going to go? What was I going to do? I didn't have any of those answers. All I knew was that I didn't have any excuse for my behavior, and rather than try to come up with more lies to justify it, I just needed to leave.

She, being the rock that she is, didn't make much of a fight. She was totally blindsided. She was totally hurt, but she didn't show it. She had too much pride for that. I knew that after saying our goodbyes, she wouldn't call or text me again. I would be saying goodbye forever. Goodbye to our beautiful home. Goodbye to our beautiful life. Goodbye to the potential of our beautiful babies.

Everyone thought that I was crazy. Hell, even I thought that I was crazy. I couldn't explain it to anyone. No one could understand. "Jarvis, you did what? You quit your great-paying job… and then quit your amazing relationship… and then threw some clothes into a beat-up duffle bag and walked out of your penthouse without having plans of where you're going to go or what you're going to do?"

The three months that followed were a blur. I bounced around, living with different friends until I wore out my welcome. Eventually, there were no more friends to lean on, so I had to face the music and retreat back to Chicago. San Diego had officially chewed me up and spit me out. At that point, my mom had moved in with my aunt to help take care of my sick grandfather, so I moved in with them. Every room in the house was taken, so I had to claim a spot on the couch.

There I was, sleeping on my aunt's couch at 35 years old. You can imagine the blow to my ego. I had vowed that I would never end up back in Chicago, but I had no other options. I was homeless and hopeless.

☐ **Reflection**

- Where in your life do you feel like you're just going through the motions?
- What "coping mechanisms" do you turn to to escape the stresses of life? What impact have they had?
- If an outsider watched a day in your life, would they say you're sleepwalking through your life or fully alive?

☐ **Take Action - Take Back Control**

- Right here... right now, close your eyes and take three long deep breaths.
- Ask yourself one simple question: *"What do I want for my life?"*
- Then ask yourself, *"What would I have to start doing or stop doing for this to happen in my life?"*
- Write down your answer on paper. That one intentional step is how you start breaking the autopilot cycle.
- Scan the QR code for a guided meditation to help you uncover the grand purpose and calling in your life.

CHAPTER 2
THE BIRTH OF A HERO

"The two most important days in your life are the day you are born and the day you find out why."

– Mark Twain

LinkedIn

So there I was, settling into my new reality. That reality was that I had no job, no girlfriend, no more money, no hope, no dream, no plan, no purpose. I was just existing.

One day, I was lying on the basement couch, scrolling on my phone, and I got a notification from LinkedIn. LinkedIn tries to keep you posted about all the updates from everyone in your network. Every time someone gets promoted or something notable happens in their career, it will send you a notification so you can acknowledge and celebrate them.

On this one particular day, I was laid up on my aunt's couch, and I got a notification that said, "Go congratulate Eric on his new job promotion!" I thought to myself, "Eric? I haven't seen him since college."

Eric was my lab partner at the University of Illinois. When you join the computer engineering program, you get assigned a lab partner. It's kind of like a buddy system. You and your lab partner take all the same classes, do the labs together, turn in homework assignments together. You essentially go through the program together and get the same grades. Eric and I both graduated and went to work for tech firms. We were on the exact same trajectory in life. We were both smart, good-looking, with business savvy.

It had been over 15 years since I had last seen him. So there I was, lying on the couch, getting notified that he just got a promotion. Part of me didn't want to click that notification. I didn't want to see him doing better than me. But the other part of me was curious to see exactly how well he was doing. I clicked it and waited with a nervous tension.

As his profile page slowly loaded, it felt like the early days of the internet when the pages would load line by line. His page finally loaded, and I quickly scanned it to find his new job title. It took a second or two for my eyes to refocus to be able to read the small font on my phone. And then, I saw it.

Sitting right up under his gorgeous picture with his chiseled cheekbones and perfect hair was his new job title. It read, "Chief Technology Officer." I sat there stunned for a second. I rubbed my eyes and squinted, hoping to get a better read. Maybe I'd misread that, so I went back over it again.

"Chief Technology Officer." This was no mistake.

Eric was now sitting in the C-suite. I sat there in shock as I tried to digest the gravity of what I was reading. This guy and I had been on the same path in life with all the same skills, attributes, and talents, and now he was sitting in the C-suite while I was homeless and helpless, living on my aunt's couch.

EVERY. DAMN. DAY.

Then I did what every normal, emotionally stable person would do. I stalked his social media. I checked out all his photos on Facebook, and it looked like he had an amazing life. He had a beautiful wife and kids. An amazing home. They had a boat, and he was an active member of the community, giving to charities and serving on several boards of directors for nonprofits. It was like someone was twisting the dagger that was pierced into my heart.

Eric was living his life to his full potential; meanwhile, I was a useless waste of space. It was like the Lord was showing me what my full potential was. I saw exactly what I could have been amounting to in life. It was the first time that I felt the pain of the potential gap.

The Potential Gap

Every one of us is born with a unique set of talents, skills, abilities, and life circumstances to produce something meaningful while here on this planet. Now, let's imagine that you plotted your full potential on a graph.

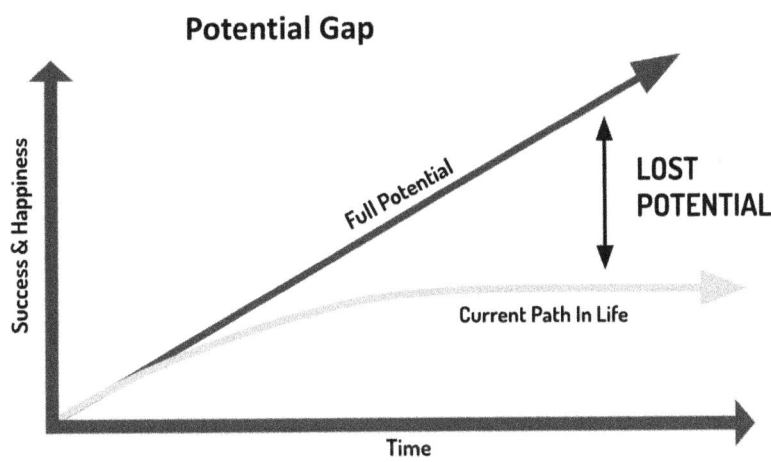

That straight line is you living up to your full potential. If you take full advantage of all of your talents, skills, and opportunities, and maximize your production in life, you would be operating on that line.

But what happens to most people is that they start coasting. They start settling for less than what they are fully capable of. They take their foot off of the gas. They get comfortable and start operating at half speed. This is represented by the curved line. This creates a gap between the person that you were created to be (your full potential) and the person that you settled to be (your current path). That's the potential gap.

And the bigger that gap is, the bigger the disappointment that person will carry when they realize that they were meant for far more in life than what they settled for. More money, more impact, more love, more contribution, more fun, more friends, more fitness, more fulfillment.

People who settle are setting themselves up for a life of resentment and regret. And that's what I was facing on the couch that day when I saw Eric playing the game of life all out while I had sunk into low-level living. I was staring at all my lost potential, and that stung bad.

Quite honestly, it pissed me off. I wasn't pissed at Eric. I was actually proud of him. I was pissed at myself for wasting away my potential. That was the moment that changed my life forever.

I decided that I was going to close that gap. I decided that I was going to live up to my full potential. The world didn't deserve a half-speed Jarvis. I had a moral obligation to stop playing small and go all out!

Moral Obligation

The moment that we realize that we could be doing more, I believe that it's our moral obligation to do more. I believe that it's our duty to fulfill the promise that was placed in us by the Creator. There will be a person born on this earth whose purpose is to cure cancer. They were gifted with all the skills, connections, abilities, tools, resources, intellect, and opportunities to do the unthinkable and solve a problem that has plagued humans since the beginning of time. This person will be ordained to elevate the entire human species. But imagine if they just coasted through life doing the bare minimum and didn't fully pursue their full, God-given potential. Imagine if they settled for a life of less than. A life of comfort and self-indulgence.

Imagine if they never lived out the purpose of their life. Not only will they disappoint themselves, they will also disappoint the entire human species. Millions of people will continue dying every year, and the entire world will continue to suffer. Not only do they lose, we *all* lose. It's their moral obligation to push for their full potential so we can all benefit from the role that they were placed here for.

I realize that this is an extreme example. Not everyone has a purpose as monumental as curing cancer, but we all have a job to play in this universal experience called life. Your unique design does matter. The business that you are supposed to start does matter. The people that you are supposed to impact do matter. The lives that you are supposed to touch do matter. The charities that you are supposed to support do matter. The initiatives that you are supposed to carry out do matter.

In a row of a million dominoes, every single domino matters. If one of those dominoes is off, then the whole line stops. Every single domino needs to play its role and fall perfectly in line for the entire operation to work properly.

The moment that you realize that you have a greater purpose and have greater potential and that you aren't carrying out the vision that the Creator had for your life, you have to realize that you are breaking the grand design. It's like trying to put a puzzle together with missing pieces. You are a missing piece to the grand puzzle, and we all suffer from missing the piece that you were supposed to provide.

That was my breaking point: The moment that I realized that I had more in me. I had more to produce, more to provide, more to give. The Lord gifted me with too much talent, too many resources, too much skill, too many people in my corner to waste away living a mediocre life. It was time for me to get off that damn couch and answer the calling that was placed on my life!

We all have our own proverbial "couch." Your couch is that moment where you stopped growing and started coasting. It's the day you got comfortable and stopped pushing for more. It's a quiet prison. A prison of "less than." A prison of mediocrity.

For me, it was the day the Lord showed me Eric's success and whispered, "This should be you." Then he punched me in the gut and screamed, **"GET YO ASS OFF THAT COUCH!"**

Maybe you're stuck on your couch. Maybe you've settled. Settled for a job you hate. Settled for a relationship that drains you. Settled into a body that no longer reflects the power inside you. But deep down, you know that you were made for more.

And if that's true, then I'm going to tell you the same thing God told me: **GET YO ASS OFF THAT COUCH!** How dare you fade into the background when the world is starving for your greatness? How dare you dim your light when someone out there is counting on your shine?

It's time to stand up, stretch, and be the HERO that you were called to be!

The Morning Hero Is Born

After seeing Eric living on the straight line… thriving, winning, becoming everything we once dreamed about, it lit a fire inside of me. Not a flicker. A blaze. That was the day I made a vow to myself: Never again will I settle for less than who I was called to be.

EVERY. DAMN. DAY.

That night, I made a decision that changed everything. I decided I was going to wake up at 5 a.m. the next morning to start building Jarvis 2.0. No more sleepwalking through life. No more watching someone else live the life I was meant to have. I was done settling for just "ok."

At that time, I didn't have a job that I had to wake for, so I was getting up around 7 a.m. or 8 a.m. So 5 a.m. was a stretch! I assumed that I'd probably sleep through my alarm… but I set it anyway.

That next morning, the wilding thing happened. I woke up at 4:57 a.m… three minutes before my alarm! And for the first time in my adult life, I tasted something I didn't even know I'd been starving for:

Peace.

Pure, unfiltered, uninterrupted peace. There were no dogs barking. No kids crying. No phone buzzing. No text messages. No breaking news. No notifications trying to hijack my soul. It was just… silence.

I pulled out my journal and started writing. I didn't even know what I was writing at first. I just started dumping thoughts onto the page. But soon, those thoughts became ideas. Ideas became strategies. And strategies became a blueprint. It turned into the blueprint for the next phase of my life. That morning, I crafted a business plan. I mapped out my day. I listed my top 3 priorities and completed the biggest one on that list. Then I went to the gym. By the time I got back home and looked at the clock, it was still only 7 a.m.! The house was silent. The world hadn't even woken up yet. And I had already crushed the day!

That was the first time in my life I felt like I had won the day! And get this: The day hadn't even started for most people. I had already WON before the day even began! That morning, I felt like a superhero. It was like I had discovered special powers to defeat the day! Just like how Cyclops can shoot a laser from his eyes, my superpower was destroying the chaos from the day!

I woke up the next morning and did it again... I was up 3 minutes before my alarm, I got clarity in the silence, started mapping out an action plan for my newly created goals, knocked off the top 3 items from that list, then hit the gym and was back by 7 a.m... all before the family even woke up.

Every **MORNING**, I would do this practice and turn into a HERO and then dominate the day. Each **MORNING**, I would become a HERO... and that's how the **MORNING** HERO was born.

I discovered one of the greatest lessons in life...

If you WIN the morning, you will WIN the day. And when you WIN each day, you start to string together WINNING weeks. WINNING weeks turn into WINNING months and WINNING years. You build a WINNING life, starting with every single morning.

And that's what it means to be a **MORNING**HERO. They WIN every morning, allowing them to WIN every day and step firmly into their full purpose and power and potential!

The Come Back

After becoming a Morning Hero, my life transformed dramatically! I rebuilt my business, this time in real estate. I got off that damn couch and moved back to San Diego, quickly making a name for myself selling office and retail spaces in downtown.

I was the first person in the office at 7 a.m. every day... even before the janitors! By the time the next person walked into the office, I was already done with all of my lead generation activities and halfway done with my day. The owner of the brokerage was so amazed at how effective I was at taking charge of the day that he asked me to host a workshop for the company to teach all of the other agents how to "WIN the morning like a Morning Hero." That year, four of the agents who attended my workshop made it to the wall of fame, which celebrates the highest producing agents. They all said that their success was directly attributed to what I taught them in that workshop; How to WIN every morning and WIN every day.

Since then, I started sharing this message on bigger stages, coaching thousands of high producers at companies like Google, Keller Williams, Accenture, and Bank of America to help them double their production at work and in life by becoming **MORNING HEROES** and winning every single day!

But it wasn't just about having success at work. I also got into the best shape of my life. Every morning started with a workout, and my body began to mirror my mindset: strong, lean, and disciplined.

But that wasn't even the most miraculous part. Because as I became a better version of myself, something even greater happened. I reconnected with the love of my life.

See, back when I was spiraling, I lost the love of my life. She saw me unravel. She saw me drift. She saw the light leave my eyes. And eventually, my self-destruction pushed us apart.

But something amazing happened. As I rebuilt me, I started attracting everything I had lost, including her. We reconnected and today, she is my wife and my best friend. We have the most amazing marriage on earth! And now, with two kids, our bond is stronger than ever.

Every morning, I wake up with purpose, with passion, and with people I love. All of it, all of it, started with that one 5 a.m. That one decision to stop wasting my potential and start building the man I was born to become.

I didn't become a Morning Hero just for me. I had to become one for the people around me. For my wife. For my children. For everyone counting on me.

Becoming a Morning Hero got me off that couch. It got me out of a mediocre existence and back in my full potential. It reset my thermostat and stopped my downward spiral of self-sabotage.

It took me from homeless and helpless to speaking on stages around the world, helping thousands of people reclaim their true purpose and power.

Becoming a Morning Hero reignited my life. And it will reignite yours too!

Become a Hero

Now, it's your turn to become a Morning Hero. This isn't just about my comeback story... it's about yours too! It's about you living in your full power. It's about you not falling victim to mediocrity. It's about you not being satisfied with just living an average life. A life on the curved line. You weren't built for average. You were built for greatness!

This book... this moment... it's your couch moment. Your wake-up call. In the next several chapters, I'm going to show you exactly how to do what I did, how to reclaim your peace, your power, your productivity. I'm going to walk you step by step through the W.I.N.ing formula, which is a three-step morning routine that will catapult you into outrageous success and deep, lasting happiness.

EVERY. DAMN. DAY.

This isn't just a new habit. This is a new identity. Being a MORNING HERO isn't just something you do; it's a lifestyle you live. And the world is waiting on you to activate it.

This is the daily framework I used to rebuild my life and the same framework that has transformed thousands of other lives around the world. It's based on the acronym W.I.N. and I'm going to make a prediction. Once you start W.I.N.ing your mornings, you will WIN your days and build a WINNING life!

Let's go, HERO!

☐ **Reflection**

- Right now, if we were to plot out YOUR potential graph, would it be a straight line or has it flattened out?
- What would it look like if you were operating in your full potential in all areas? (Health, Career, Relationships)
- Who suffers when you settle for living less than what you are capable of?

☐ **Take Action - Get Yo A$$ Off That Couch!**

- Write down **one area of your life** (career, health, relationships, finances, impact) where you've been coasting.
- Then write one sentence that declares: *"I refuse to settle. I am committed to closing the gap in this area of my life!"*
- *Scan the QR code to join the free Morning Hero community and leave a post with your declaration statement above. By declaring your intentions publicly, you deepen your commitment and tell the universe that you mean business!*

PART II
THE WINNING FORMULA

WAKE UP EARLY
I
N

CHAPTER 3
THE BATTLE OF YOUR LIFE

"The greatest enemy of progress is not stagnation, but false progress."

– Sydney J. Harris

Your Biggest Enemy

I remember when I got my first Nintendo gaming system in 1987. It came with a game called Super Mario Brothers. The object of the game was to progress through each of the levels, overcoming little obstacles and challenges along the way so that you could save the princess who was captured in a castle.

At the end of each level, you had to defeat the "boss" of that level. Each boss had some unique special power that made them difficult to beat. Some bosses had special weapons that shot fireballs, and other bosses could freeze time. It might take a few attempts (or a hundred), but eventually, you could beat the boss and continue the journey to the next level.

I remember when I finally got to the castle to face the boss of all bosses, Bowser. Bowser wasn't like any other character of the game. He was bigger, faster, with more weapons and crazy superpowers. He could disappear out of thin air just as you were about to attack him and then reappear standing behind you. I remember thinking, "This isn't fair! I can't even hit him! How the hell am I supposed to beat this game?" I stayed on that level for weeks, trying to defeat the big, evil bossman Bowser!

Each day after school, I would race home and fire up my Nintendo gaming system and spend hours playing that game. I must have died over a thousand times. I was determined to defeat Bowser. It seemed impossible. Every time I jumped, he'd hit me with a fireball. Every time I threw a fireball, he'd disappear. He had an answer for every attack. I started to feel like the game was unbeatable.

Then my mom got me a Super Mario strategy book. It was a magazine that had all the secret strategies to defeat each level in the game, including the final level with Bowser. I remember it like it was yesterday. I spent some time learning the strategy and then fired up the game. It was like all the stars aligned. I was just in flow. A magical force took over my fingers and guided every movement, every strike, every blow, every fireball until I hit him with the final blow that knocked him out, and the princess came running out of the castle. I had finally done it! I defeated the big bad boss!

In the game of your life, it's no different. There is a big, bad, evil boss that's standing between you and your proverbial princess (your goals, dreams, happiness, and success). That evil villain is called the whirlwind. And just like Bowser, there is a strategy to beat it.

The Whirlwind

From the time your eyes open in the morning till the time they close at night, the whirlwind is everything pulling and demanding your attention. From social media to family obligations, breaking news, needy clients, work fires, kids crying, dogs barking, cars breaking down, appointments,

EVERY. DAMN. DAY.

notifications, interruptions, group chats, Slack messages, and a dozen fires you didn't plan for... it's all part of the whirlwind.

It's sneaky. It doesn't show up all at once... it builds, slowly and silently. It feels urgent. It feels necessary. But make no mistake: the whirlwind's goal is to keep you distracted. It's the daily chaos that pulls you away from your purpose.

The whirlwind isn't evil in the cartoon villain sense... it's evil because it pretends to be important. It masquerades as productivity. But it's not. It's motion without meaning. This is your biggest enemy. It keeps you busy but unproductive. It gives you the illusion that you're doing something, when in reality, you're just spinning in circles.

This is what happens to most people in life. They spend their days managing their whirlwind, putting out fires, reacting to messages, solving problems that don't actually move them forward. And then they go to bed feeling exhausted and empty. They were busy all day... but they didn't actually do anything. They didn't progress. They didn't do the work that matters. And then they wake up and do it all over again. And again. And again. Days turn into weeks. Weeks turn into months. Months turn into years. And before you know it, a whole decade has gone by.

You haven't become the person you imagined you'd be. You haven't created the life you said you wanted. You've just been managing life instead of designing it. That's the dangerous thing about the whirlwind... it's not loud. It's not dramatic. It's slow and steady. It numbs you into complacency.

At best, you coast through life... unfulfilled. At worst, the disappointment turns into bitterness. Resentment. Depression. Addiction. Escape. You start coping instead of growing. You start numbing instead of living. You start shrinking instead of rising.

That's the damage of the whirlwind. It leaves so many people feeling like they're stuck on a treadmill. Running hard. Going nowhere. They get to the end of the year with nothing to show for it. They make resolutions but never follow through. They have dreams but never take consistent action. And when they reflect, they're not proud. They're frustrated.

Not because they're not capable. Not because they're not smart. But because the whirlwind always wins. Unless… you learn how to beat it.

So what's the secret to defeating the whirlwind? It all comes down to this: if you want to defeat the whirlwind, you have to wake up before the whirlwind!

It sounds simple, but it's not. That's because most people wake up "just in time."

Just in Time

Most people wake up "just in time" to get ready for work. Or "just in time" to deal with family. Or "just in time" for their first obligation of the day. That was me for most of my life. I had it down to a science! My alarm was set for 7:30 a.m. I knew that each time I hit the snooze button, it would give me an additional nine minutes of sleep, so I would snooze twice, giving me an extra 18 minutes of sleep. Then I'd race to the bathroom for an 8-minute shower, which gave me 12 minutes to throw on my clothes, allowing me 10 minutes to grab a quick bite to eat. Then another 7 minutes to grab my things and run out the door, so that I could sit in traffic for 27 minutes on my way to the office, which then gave me 7 minutes to put my things down, grab a cup of coffee, and get to the conference room at 8:59 a.m. "just in time" for our 9 a.m. team meeting.

I got up "just in time" to start dealing with the chaos of the day. And that's exactly what my entire day would be… chaos. All day long, I would be fighting fires, dealing with issues, and reacting to everything that the whirlwind threw my way. My day felt frantic, unorganized, almost like I was trapped inside of a swirling tornado and I was just holding on for dear life.

By the end of the day, I felt like I deserved a reward just for surviving the day. The "rewards" usually took the form of some take-out food or a glass of wine. It was my treat to myself for putting up with all the madness from the day. It was my way of escaping from the whirlwind. Little did I know that this negative rewards system was killing me, literally and figuratively.

Not only was it killing my health, it was also killing my productivity. It was killing my relationships, it was killing my ambition, it was killing my spirit. Eventually, it's what landed me homeless on my aunt's couch where I had to restart my life. My "just in time" approach to life was eating away at my life.

It's the way most of the world operates. We wake up at the last possible second, leap into action, and spend the entire day responding to whatever life throws at us. There is no time to breathe. No time to think. No time to be intentional. We are living our lives from behind… always catching up, always out of breath, always reactive.

The problem with waking up just in time is that you immediately give your power away. From the very first moment of your day, your time, energy, and attention belong to someone else. You don't own your morning, your job does. You don't control your time, your inbox does. You don't choose your mood, social media does. You're not leading the day, you're reacting to it.

Imagine a pilot who shows up to the plane "just in time" for takeoff. No time for a systems check. No time to walk the plane. No time to review the flight plan. Would you want to be on that plane? Of course not.

But that's how most of us live every single day. We wake up just in time, skip the most important systems check of all... our own mental, emotional, and spiritual alignment... and then wonder why we feel like we're flying blind.

This "just in time" approach will keep you stuck in a vicious loop of exhaustion and self-sabotage. To understand how this works, you must first understand the concept of the Joy Tank.

The Joy Tank

Imagine that you have a joy tank. Your joy tank determines your happiness level. The more joy you have in the tank, the more energetic and happy you feel about life. When your tank is high, you feel on top of the world, like everything is going in your favor! The birds are chirping, the sun is shining, and you've got a permanent smile on your face. Conversely, if the tank is low or empty, you feel depleted, exhausted, crabby, and grumpy. You feel like the weight of the world is on your shoulders, and it's just pressing you down to the ground.

Here's the thing about your Joy Tank... every day it starts out only half full. That's right. It's automatically at 50% as soon as your eyes open, and as you progress throughout the day, the whirlwind of your life gradually drains joy from your joy tank little by little. You start the day with the kids jumping into your bed and climbing all over you? Now, your tank goes from 50% to 45% full. Get a stressful email? Now, your joy tank is at 35%. Have a troubling meeting? Now, it's down to 25%. Your joy tank is probably on 0% before your workday is done. If it's an extra stressful day, you probably dip into the negative digits!

So then what happens? When your joy tank gets close to zero, your instinctual reaction is to immediately do something that gives you a quick fix of joy. And what is that normally? Maybe a cheeseburger, maybe 15 minutes of mindless scrolling on social media, or maybe a drink of alcohol or psychedelic substances to "relieve a little stress."

When your joy tank gets dangerously low, your body goes into a state of shock and says, "Quick! We need to get a boost of joy. What can we do immediately that will bring us instantaneous fulfillment?" And for most of us it is nothing but bad, self-sabotaging, self-destructive habits that give us the most immediate boost of joy. Sugar. Scrolling. Wine. Weed. Netflix. Whatever your poison is, your body goes searching for it. That's why at the end of a long, hard day, we lean on these vices because we are searching for quick ways to refill an empty joy tank.

Breaking the Self-Sabotage Loop

And this unconscious behavior of refilling an empty joy tank is what sabotages all of our progress in life. We make a little progress. We lose a few pounds. We have a productive day, and then all of a sudden… WHAM! We have a knee-jerk reaction to a negative joy tank, and we are stuffing our face with a slice of pizza with our favorite drink in front of an entire season of *Game of Thrones*.

This constant "on again, off again" cycle keeps us at the exact same place in life, making a little bit of progress and then destroying that progress with a self-sabotaging reward system, until we get to the end of our life and we realize that we didn't live up to our full potential. Little did we know that we were stuck in the self-sabotaging loop, suffering from the daily depletion of our joy tank.

Now, imagine a different scenario. When you wake up, your joy tank starts the same way at about half full. But instead of waking up "just in time" to deal with the whirlwind which immediately starts draining your joy tank, you wake up to a calm, peaceful environment. One in which there is nothing that immediately demands your attention. You have time, space, and energy to work on yourself. You start filling your joy tank with things like meditating, praying, writing your goals, brainstorming new business ideas, and doing some exercise. Each of these things makes a little deposit of joy into your tank, and by the time you finish these self-serving habits, your joy tank has been boosted from 50% all the way up to 100%!

Now, you go throughout your day vibrating at a higher frequency. You have brighter and better energy. Your mood is much better, so you handle the stress of the day in a more calming manner. Things that would normally stress you out now don't stress you out anymore. The whirlwind has no effect on you. That stressful email would have normally drained your joy tank by 10%, but now, it doesn't even make a dent. You flow throughout your entire day with your joy tank taking minimal damage.

You get to the end of your day at 5 p.m., and instead of your joy tank being at zero, your tank is actually at about 75%. It's practically still full! You come home with much brighter energy, in a better mood, and with a more joyful spirit. Most importantly, instead of desperately looking for a "quick fix" of joy to replenish your tank (which is usually self-sabotaging, self-defeating habits), you don't need a boost at all. And since you have so much more joy still left in the tank, you pour that joy out to everyone around you. Your joy tank literally "runneth over." You have a brighter spirit with your family. You're more engaged. You're less moody and irritable. You're more lively and enjoyable to be around.

In both scenarios, the whirlwind was the same. The only difference is how you started the day. In one instance, you started the day right into the whirlwind and felt drained, defeated and depleted before the day even ended. In the other case, you started the day filling your tank first, and by the time the day was over, you still had a lot of joy left over.

When you start the day filling your tank first, not only do you go throughout the day spreading that joy like wildfire, but by the end of the day, you also don't have an insatiable need to find joy from outside sources that don't serve you.

If you can grasp this one concept, it will change everything for you.

When you start the day filling your joy tank, you tend to fill it with positive, self-serving habits like meditation, prayer, journaling, brainstorming, planning, organizing, and exercise. However, when you end the day trying to refill an empty joy tank, you usually lean on negative, self-sabotaging, mind-numbing, goal-shattering habits that keep you dissatisfied, unhappy, and filled with guilt and resentment.

Start the day filling your joy tank instead of ending the day filling your joy tank.

This one little shift will change your life forever.

But your joy tank doesn't just determine your happiness. According to the law of attraction, it will also determine all of your success in life.

Law of Attraction

According to the Law of Attraction, you attract whatever vibrates at the same frequency as you. So when you're operating at a low frequency… tired, irritable, sluggish, crabby, frustrated, or just plain negative, you start drawing in people and situations that match that exact energy. It's like tuning your life to a station called "Everything Goes Wrong FM."

But when you move through your day with high energy… positive, vibrant, joyful, enthusiastic, and upbeat, that becomes your frequency, and you begin to attract more of the same. Uplifted energy brings uplifting outcomes. It's not magic. It's alignment.

That's where the saying "When it rains, it pours" really comes from. People think bad luck just piles on all at once. But it's not that the Universe is out to get them. What actually happens is this: one bad event knocks them into a negative state, and that negative state becomes a magnet for more negativity.

On the flip side, when you're walking through your day radiating light and joy, good fortune starts chasing you. Suddenly, you get a surprise call about a job opportunity. A check shows up in the mail. You hit every green light. A prospect you've been pursuing suddenly reaches out. That's not luck. That's the Law of Attraction working in real time.

Your joy level is your frequency, and the world responds to whatever signal you're putting out. That's why it's so critical to start each day by filling your joy tank, because it sets the tone for what you attract in your work, your business, your relationships, and your life.

But here's the catch: you can't raise your vibration if you're waking up just in time to survive the day. You need at least one intentional hour to take control of your energy and set your frequency. That's what we call your Power Hour, and it will become the most powerful hour of your entire day.

☐ Reflection

- Are you currently waking up "Just in Time" to deal with the Whirlwind?
- At the end of most days, is your joy tank full, half-empty, or completely drained?
- What self-sabotaging habits do you turn to when your joy tank hits empty? (Be honest… "vegging out" on your phone or TV, sugar, wine, weed, toxic people?)
- Imagine your life five years from now. Would you be satisfied if you continued to keep going in the same trajectory that you're on?

☐ Take Action

- Say this out loud: *"I refuse to let the Whirlwind diminish my power. From this day forward, I will own my days instead of my days owning me!"*
- *Scan the QR code to join the free Morning Hero community and leave a post with your declaration statement above. By declaring your intentions publicly, you deepen your commitment and tell the universe that you mean business!*

CHAPTER 4
TAKE BACK YOUR POWER

"When everyone else is thinking it's time to sleep, I'm thinking it's time to get ahead of the competition."

—Kobe Bryant, The Mamba Mentality

The Power Hour

After my life crashed and burned, I dove headfirst into personal development. I devoured every book I could find on how humans unlock their full potential. I read autobiographies of the world's most extraordinary individuals… Elon Musk, Kobe Bryant, Michael Jordan, Bill Gates, Oprah Winfrey, Tony Robbins… you name it. I was obsessed with discovering their secret sauce. I wanted to reverse engineer their lives and extract the formula for success.

As I studied their habits, routines, rituals, mindsets, and behaviors, I started noticing a pattern. Kobe Bryant would wake up at 4 a.m. to hit the gym for two hours before team practice. Tony Robbins would head down to the beach to meditate and pray for an hour before returning home to have breakfast with his family. Warren Buffett would spend his early hours reading annual reports before heading to McDonald's for his sausage McMuffin and coffee. Each of them had different routines, but one thing was always the same: they all carved out at least one hour of undistracted alone time every morning to focus on themselves before engaging with the world.

No phones. No emails. No social media. No noise. Just one sacred hour to work on their goals, their health, their mindset… their mission. Before the chaos of the day swept in, they claimed that first hour for growth, clarity, and power.

And that's why I call this sacred time the Power Hour. Because what happens during this hour sets the tone for everything that follows.

There's no one-size-fits-all formula for how to use this hour. But there is one non-negotiable rule: it must be undistracted alone time. That means no phone. No emails. No notifications. No reacting to the world.

This hour isn't for scrolling or checking in. It's for tuning in. It's not for engaging with the outside world. It's for reconnecting with your inner world.

The Phone Booth

Have you noticed that Clark Kent must go into isolation in order to transform into Superman? He goes into a phone booth where something magical happens, and then he emerges as the superhero that we know him to be. Prior to him going into isolation, he was just a nerdy little reporter who was pretty useless against any evil villain. But that same nerdy reporter went and hid himself in a phone booth in order to put on his cape.

Your morning Power Hour is your proverbial "phone booth," where you're hidden and untouchable from the outside world. It's where you strap on your cape and gain your superpowers to emerge as your HERO self, ready to defeat the evil whirlwind and save the day for everyone.

You can't serve others until you first serve yourself. That's why you have to wake up before everyone else so you don't feel like you're ignoring people. You don't have to fight your brain from wanting to respond to email or address people's needs because no one is awake yet. You have time to adequately establish your superpowers before they need you.

These hours are a guilt-free zone where you can focus on yourself without anyone else needing your attention. While they are sleeping, you are up, preparing your mind, body, and soul so you can show up powerfully for them later. If you wake up and they are already up, then you will jump right in and start addressing their issues. That's why you have to wake up before your family, before emails start coming in, and before social media gets active. You have to beat the world to save the world.

The First Domino

If you line up a row of dominoes, each one can knock down another that's 1.5 times its size. So a 1-inch domino can topple a 1.5-inch domino. That one knocks over a 2.25-inch domino. Then 3.375 inches. Then 5 inches. If you keep this going, by the time you reach the 20th domino, it would stand nearly 1,500 feet tall which is taller than the Empire State Building!

And here's where it gets crazy... all it takes is that first tiny push on the 1-inch domino to eventually bring down a structure the size of a skyscraper. That's the power of leverage. You don't need brute strength or superhuman effort. You just need to know how to line up the dominoes to deliver the biggest force with the least amount of effort.

See, life is full of Empire State Building-sized goals. We want to make more money, get in better shape, take our families on dream vacations, start nonprofits, raise our kids into kind, powerful, confident humans. Big goals. Massive ones. But here's the truth: trying to knock them all down at once is overwhelming and exhausting. Imagine you, tiny little you, trying to push over the Empire State Building. People would look at you like you're nuts.

But when you understand the leverage of dominoes, everything changes. You don't need to push the skyscraper. You just need to knock over the first domino. That one small action creates momentum. It sets off a chain reaction that makes the impossible inevitable. The right first move makes everything else easier… or even unnecessary.

And that first domino? It's your Power Hour. Your Power Hour obliterates the whirlwind. It clears a path and creates power, peace, and productivity. It gives you space to plan your day with intention. It helps you stay consistent with your health. It unlocks energy, discipline, and emotional resilience. And that energy spills over into your work, your relationships, your finances, your family.

Wake up just one hour earlier… and suddenly, the rest of your day becomes smoother. Your goals? Easier. Your stress? Lower. Your results? Bigger.

Waking up early for your Power Hour is the highest-leverage activity of your entire day. Do this one thing right… and everything else starts falling into place.

Slow Down to Speed Up

Have you ever been in the shower and suddenly had a big idea? Or maybe you were driving and had one of those "a-ha" moments? I believe the Universe is always speaking to us.

Call it the little birdie. Call it your gut. Call it the Holy Spirit. Whatever name you give it, you're constantly being guided. That whisper is the Universe giving you clarity. Sometimes it's the answer to a question

EVERY. DAMN. DAY.

you've been wrestling with. Other times, it's a gentle nudge pointing you in the right direction.

The truth is, the Universe has all the answers. Every solution you'll ever need is already out there. But here's the problem… the Universe speaks softly. And most of us can't hear it because our lives are just too loud.

Kids crying. Horns honking. News blaring. People yelling. Dogs barking. Phones buzzing. Emails dinging. Notifications flying in every direction. And right in the middle of all that chaos, the Universe is whispering. But we miss it. Not because the answers aren't there, but because we're too noisy to hear them.

That's why the quiet of the early morning is so sacred. Before the world starts spinning, when everything is still… that's when the whispers come through. When you give yourself just one hour of undistracted peace with no kids, no chores, no to-do lists, you finally create space for the Universe to speak.

And here's the kicker: slowing down is actually the fastest way to speed up. I know… it sounds backward. You might think the way to be more productive is to wake up and immediately start hustling. But think about Olympic sprinters. They don't just show up at the track and take off running. They arrive hours early. They stretch. They breathe. They get their mind, body, and spirit in sync. Then they step up to the line, and when the gun goes off, they explode.

But if they skipped all that and just started running, they'd pull a muscle and limp across the finish line. Sound familiar? That's how most people go through life. They wake up and instantly start sprinting, only to pull their mental and emotional muscles and crawl home exhausted at the end of the day.

That's why the Power Hour… just one solid hour of intentional stillness in the morning, is your warm-up. Your sacred prep time. It's what allows you to run your day at lightning speed instead of limping through it.

Beat the Sun

There's no magic formula for what time you should wake up. Your exact wake-up time is relative to your life, your demands, and your goals. But there is one universal truth:

If you don't give yourself at least one hour every morning of undistracted alone time, you will start the day at a massive disadvantage… and the whirlwind will eat you alive.

That's why I recommend "Beating the Sun."

The rising sun is the universal signal that the day has begun. Our biological clocks are tuned to its rhythm… literally. That's where we get the term circadian rhythms. Our bodies are synced with the Earth's rotation, so as the sun rises, so does our internal energy. It's no coincidence that most people naturally wake up around sunrise.

The average sunrise across the globe happens between 6 a.m. and 7 a.m., depending on the time of year. And that's exactly when the world begins to stir… emails start flying, text messages roll in, calls are made, kids are waking up, news breaks, and the whirlwind begins to spin. That's why your Power Hour should start at least one hour before sunrise. In most cases, that's around 5 a.m. That's how you stay ahead of the chaos… you beat the whirlwind by beating the sun.

When I first started mastering my mornings, I woke up at 5 a.m. That gave me just enough time for my Power Hour before heading to my 6 a.m. cycling class. Life was simpler back then… no wife, no kids, no companies, no chaos.

EVERY. DAMN. DAY.

Fast forward to today… two kids, a company with employees, and about a thousand balls in the air. My kids are up by 5:30 a.m. (they're Morning Heroes too!) which means if I want time for a big goal or project *(like writing this book)* I've got to be up by 3:30 or 4 a.m.

But hear me on this: I'm not saying you need to wake up at 4 a.m. That's just what I need based on my whirlwind starting at 6.

All I'm saying is this… whatever time your chaos begins, you need to be up at least one hour before that. Whether your day starts with kids, dogs, emails, or the gym, you need one sacred hour of uninterrupted, intentional time to set the tone for your day. And more than likely, that's going to require you to wake up while it's still dark outside (before 6 a.m.).

And there's another, deeper reason to wake up before the sun: there's something sacred about being awake while it's still dark. There's a stillness, a peace, a sense of solitude you just can't get once daylight hits. When the sun is up, your brain senses that the world is moving, and it starts to nudge you to move with it. Your mind speeds up. You feel pressure to respond, to act, to engage.

But in the dark, there's no pressure. There's just quiet. And that quiet is where you tune into the whispers of the Universe. Your brain can't enter that active "listening state" when it sees light outside. Light is a signal to start doing. Darkness is your invitation to just be.

The whole point of waking up early is to slow down. To listen, reflect, and get still. But if you wait until the sun's already up, your brain will trick you into speeding right back up. So give yourself that hour in the dark. That's where the magic happens.

JARVIS LEVERSON

Magic in the Margin

I was talking to a friend of mine, and she was telling me about the struggles she was going through. At the time, she was stuck in a joyless job that kept her grinding 8 to 10 hours a day. And on top of that, she had three kids being homeschooled because this was in the thick of COVID when the schools were shut down.

She was frustrated. She'd been in the same role for over seven years. Passed over for promotions, overlooked constantly. She knew deep in her bones that she was overqualified for the position she was in. She felt underappreciated and underpaid. She knew she had more in the tank. She was capable of being at the next level... but she wasn't moving.

So I asked her straight up, "What should you be doing to get to that next level? What's in your control that could move the needle?"

She paused. Then she said, "Well, in a perfect world... I'd have more time to network and build relationships that could possibly open doors for me." And then she said, "That's the part I think is missing... I don't spend enough time doing those things."

So I asked her, "Why not? Why can't you?"

And she looked at me and said, "Jarvis, look at my life. My job alone consumes most of my time and brain space. Every day is chaos. I'm constantly fighting fires, constantly trying to keep my head above water. And then there's my family. My kids are home because of COVID, so I'm homeschooling, managing their schedules, getting them through lessons, keeping everything afloat. I don't have the time, the brain space, or the energy to do anything else."

So I asked her one more question... "What time do your kids wake up?"

She said, "5:30 a.m."

EVERY. DAMN. DAY.

Then I looked her dead in her eyes and said, "If your kids wake up at 5:30 a.m., then you need to be up no later than 4:30 a.m.!"

"Right now, you've got a heavy whirlwind. Your job, your family, everything on your plate, it's all part of that whirlwind. And every day you wake up spinning in it. You're waking up straight into the storm. The only way you're gonna get ahead is if you create some distance between you and the whirlwind. You need to carve out time for yourself before it starts. You need margin. And what you'll find is that there is magic in the margin!"

That margin? That's where peace lives. That's where clarity lives. That's where inspiration shows up. In that quiet hour of the morning, your ideas flow more freely. You get divine downloads. You reconnect with your inner compass. That's when you get spiritual guidance, new strategies, fresh energy. That's when you start moving forward again. Without margin, you're stuck in maintenance mode. You're just treading water trying to survive.

So she said, "Jarvis… you're crazy! But I'll give it a try."

She started waking up at 4:30 a.m. She'd do a quick workout before sitting down with her journal and jotting down her ideas and inspirations. Then she'd hop on LinkedIn and start reaching out to people, rekindling old relationships.

Thirty days in, she called me.

"Jarvis… you'll never guess what happened."

She said, "I did what you said. I started waking up early. I started reaching out to people on LinkedIn before flipping into Mom-mode with the kids. And just in the last 30 days, I've had three different job opportunities fall into my lap that could massively advance my career!"

Thirty days later, she messages me again. "Jarvis, I just officially accepted a new position as Chief Strategy Officer at a very prestigious institution. And it doubles my salary!"

Let me say that again... she had been stuck for seven years. Same role. Overlooked. Overworked. Underpaid. And in less than two months, just by carving out one hour of margin in her morning, she broke free.

She escaped the trap of the whirlwind and stepped into her full potential.

That's the power of the margin.

She found out what I want you to know: there is magic in the margin.

All her progress had just been... waiting for her. Stagnant. Dormant. Sitting in the shadows. The moment she created margin in her morning... just one hour of time, space, and peace before her whirlwind began... she activated momentum and reconnected with the version of herself she was meant to be.

I believe that whatever is missing from your life right now is waiting for you in the margin. You want more time? It's waiting in the margin. You want more peace? It's waiting in the margin. You want more money? It's waiting in the margin. You want to look sexier? It's waiting in the margin. You want a better spiritual connection? It's waiting in the margin. You want more joy and happiness? It's waiting in the margin. Pick any area of your life that you are unsatisfied with right now and I guarantee that if you woke up one hour earlier each day and worked on that area, thirty days from now, that area of your life will be unrecognizable.

From Night Owl to Morning Hero

You may be saying to yourself, "But what if I'm not a morning person?" Guess what? I'm not a morning person either!

EVERY. DAMN. DAY.

I spent the majority of my life as a proud night owl. I went to school for computer engineering, and as an engineer, we were accustomed to staying up all night writing code for our homework assignments. We called them "hack-a-thons." We would get started at 10 p.m. and would often finish up between 3 a.m. and 4 a.m. The engineering library stayed open 24 hours a day to accommodate our lifestyles.

I existed that way for my entire time in college, and it just became a part of my identity. We called ourselves the nocturnals. We actually wore it like a badge of honor. We despised the early risers. It was us versus them. We justified our late-night sleeping habits with science, saying that it was our circadian rhythm. We believed that it was hard-coded into our DNA. We were our most creative, most productive selves late at night.

After I graduated, I continued that lifestyle into my corporate career. Staying up late to do work, banging out emails and hashing out projects until 2 a.m. Little did I know how I was setting myself up for failure for the next day. Eventually, I would cap out in my career and hit a brick wall. Eventually, I burned out, which led to my destruction.

That's when I was introduced to the book The Miracle Morning, and in the very first section of the book, Hal Elrod, the author, completely broke down who I thought I was at the core of my identity. In one sentence, he shattered the crutch that I had leaned on for so many years, justifying my bad habits and behaviors. He said…

"You are who you tell yourself you are."

If you tell yourself that you aren't a morning person, well, that's what your body will manifest for you. But if you want to be something different, start telling yourself something different. He said that the moment you tell yourself that you are a morning person, then your body will obey what you told it. Overnight, you will have a new identity.

Reading that changed my life forever. That was the first time I said to myself, "I am a morning person, and I'm looking forward to waking up at 5 a.m. tomorrow morning." And just like Hal Elrod said, those words planted a seed into my subconscious, and the following morning, my body obeyed the words that were spoken.

Elrod recommends creating a nighttime affirmation. This is a little mantra that you say to yourself right before going to bed. It goes like this: "I am so excited to wake up at [insert time] so that I can [insert activity]." For example, "I'm so excited to wake up at 5 a.m. so that I can pray and meditate," or "I'm so excited to wake up at 4:30 a.m. so I can try that new spin class at the gym." You are affirming what time you are waking up and what you are going to do when you wake up. This essentially programs your subconscious and gives it a set of instructions to follow. It's like setting an alarm clock inside your brain. It's scary how well this works.

The first time I tried it, I said to myself, "I'm so excited to wake up at 5 a.m. so that I can try my new morning routine." Here's the thing… I was lying to myself. I was not excited to wake up at 5 a.m. I was really just going through the motions to prove that Hal was wrong. I didn't believe that I could be turned into a morning person at all, so I was really saying this affirmation sarcastically. In the back of my mind, I was really saying, "Yeah right, this will never work."

As I described earlier in this book, that following day, I woke up at 4:57 a.m., three minutes before my alarm clock. And guess what? I was excited! I wasn't dragging myself out of bed. I actually jumped up with energy. I had successfully reprogrammed my internal alarm clock!

After that first day, I've never used an alarm clock since. My body naturally wakes me up before my alarm clock goes off each day. I went from waking up around 7 to 8 a.m. to waking up before 5 a.m. with no alarm clock in just one day. If you don't think that you can be a morning person, trust me. If a self-proclaimed night owl like me can do it, you can too! And you can literally do it starting tomorrow morning!

The Power of the Subconscious Mind

I want to take a moment to reinforce how powerful the subconscious mind is. Every result you are getting, every behavior that you have, is all a result of the beliefs that you have about yourself and the words that you speak into yourself. If you want to establish a new behavior, it starts with a new belief, and a new belief starts with new words. All you have to do is speak a new truth over yourself and your life, and everything else will become obedient to those words.

You are what you tell yourself. If you want to write a book, say, "I am a writer." If you want to start running, even if you haven't run a mile in your life, right now you can tell yourself, "I am a runner." Everything starts with your words. Your words fuel your belief, and your new belief will fuel your new habits and actions.

The moment I said to myself, "I am no longer a night owl. I am a morning person," it ignited a domino effect that launched a seed of belief into my subconscious that manifested a new version of myself that loved waking up early every single day. Now, I can't sleep in late even if I tried to.

You can decide right here, right now that you are a morning person. C'mon, say it with me.

"I AM A MORNING PERSON AND I CAN'T WAIT TO WAKE UP AT {insert time} FOR MY NEW MORNING ROUTINE."

Congratulations! Now, strap on your cape, hero… it's time to go save the world!

☐ Reflection

- What's one big goal in your life right now that would move faster if you started every day with one full hour of undistracted alone time to work on it (Power Hour)?

- Which old belief ("I'm not a morning person," "I don't have time," "My circadian rhythm") has been keeping you stuck?

- If you were able to shed this old belief and fully transform into a Morning Hero, how would your life benefit?

☐ Take Action

- Declare this out loud: *"I am a Morning Person. I am a Morning Hero. I can't wait to wake up at [insert your time] tomorrow morning for my Power Hour!"*

- *Scan the QR code to join the free Morning Hero community and leave a post with your declaration statement above. By declaring your intentions publicly, you deepen your commitment and tell the universe that you mean business!*

CHAPTER 5
THE COST OF COMFORT

"If you want to go fast, go alone. If you want to go far, go together. But sometimes, you have to start alone to inspire others to follow."

— African Proverb

What About My Family?

I get this question a lot: "How can I do this when my wife or husband doesn't wake up early?"

Here's the truth, it might be a tough pill to swallow, but your spouse or family isn't responsible for your goals, your dreams, your happiness, or your success... you are. It's on you to do what's necessary to live a fulfilled life. And if that means leaving the warmth of your comfortable bed while your family is still asleep so you can rise for your Power Hour, then that's exactly what you need to do.

Will it bother them? Maybe. Could it wake them up? Possibly. But if they're supportive, they'll understand. And worst-case scenario, they're a little annoyed at first. But trust me, they'll be even more annoyed if you settle for low-level living. If you stay in bed, play small, and let your potential go to waste, that's what truly robs your family, not your early alarm clock.

Here's what's more likely: they'll grow to respect you more. Your discipline will speak louder than your words, and it may even inspire them to start rising with you. Sometimes, you have to leave people behind on your growth journey. But more often than not, your decision to grow is the very spark that pushes them to rise too.

Leave Them Behind

My son is four years old and goes to preschool. His school is basically a kid wonderland. They have every toy imaginable, and the staff? I swear they must've been trained by Walt Disney himself! They are some of the happiest, most fun-loving people I've ever met. So it's no surprise that when I show up to pick him up, he's not exactly thrilled to see me.

The minute he spots me, the meltdown begins. Kicking. Screaming. Running in the opposite direction. I try to reason with him, explain why it's time to leave, but it goes in one ear and out the other. He's not trying to hear it. All he wants is to stay and keep playing with his friends.

And the more I try to pull him, the more he resists. I'll grab his arm and say, "Come on, Jetson, let's go," and he'll snatch it back and take off like I'm the villain in his Disney movie. It's our daily after-school struggle, and it's exhausting.

One day, I'd had enough. Instead of begging, pleading, or arguing, I tried something different. I said, "OK, Jet, I'm leaving with or without you," and walked out the door.

At first, he stood there stunned. Frozen. But the moment he saw I was actually leaving, something shifted. The further I walked away, the more distressed he became. Within 30 seconds, he came chasing after me, tears in his eyes, calling out my name. By me leaving and creating distance between me and him, it sparked a desire in him to chase after me. He didn't want to be left behind.

It hit me right then: sometimes, the only way to get people to move is to leave them behind.

While I was in the room with him, trying to explain, persuade, and make logical arguments, he wasn't budging. He didn't care how rational my points were. But once I created distance, once he saw me walking forward without him, it lit a fire. It stirred up a desire in him to move.

That same principle applies to life.

There are people in your life who aren't ready to grow, to change, to level up. And no matter how much you beg, plead, or try to convince them, they won't listen. They won't move.

But when you stop waiting, stop debating, and start walking boldly in the direction of your own growth, that's when they'll take notice. When they see you rising, making moves, and creating separation, that's when the desire might finally spark in their heart to follow.

But not if you stay behind, waiting on them. Not if you accommodate their comfort. Not if you keep being reasonable and mute your vision. You have to play big, and sometimes that means making other people uncomfortable.

You've got to leave them behind… and once they see your progress, they will follow your lead.

Lead by Example

I had been working with John for a few months. He runs his own law firm and came to me completely burnt out. So we designed a Power Hour to help him reclaim his time, peace, and energy.

One day, he said, "Jarvis, I have to be honest. My Power Hour is causing trouble in my marriage. After my wife and I put the kids to bed, that's usually our time. We watch TV, we talk, we unwind. But now that I'm waking up early, I have to go to bed earlier, and I'm sacrificing that time with her." In fact, his wife had straight-up told him to stop waking up early because it was ruining their relationship.

So I asked, "How has the Power Hour benefited you so far? Are you seeing a difference in other areas of your life?"

He didn't even hesitate. "Jarvis, it's made a huge difference. My fitness is better... I finally have time to work out every morning. My business is better because I'm coming up with fresh ideas in the quiet of the morning. And my relationship with my kids? I'm a happier, more patient dad now."

So I told him, "John, stick with it. Your wife will come around." Two weeks later, we checked in again. I asked, "So how are things with your wife?" He lit up and said, "Jarvis, you won't believe this... she's waking up early now too!"

See, his wife saw the shift. She saw how happy he'd become. She saw how much better he was with the kids. She saw how focused and productive he was at work. She saw him getting more fit and more present. And over time... she started to want that for herself.

He didn't have to convince her. He didn't have to coach her. He just had to lead. And sure enough, she followed.

It's Your Fault

Let's say you choose not to get up early because you don't want to disturb your family. You decide their comfort is more important than your goals. The danger in that decision is this: eventually, you'll start blaming them for your lack of success. It's easy to use your family as an excuse. "I never have enough time because of the kids." "There's always some family obligation in the way." But the truth is, it's not their fault. It's your fault.

This book has been in the works for a long time. Every year, I'd tell myself, "This is the year I finally finish it." And every year, life would get busy, and I'd push it to the side again. One afternoon, I picked up my kids from preschool. They were in the backseat, singing and playing together, just full of joy. But inside, I was drowning in guilt. I had been thinking about the book again, how another year had passed and it still wasn't finished. And then something awful happened.

I looked up in the rearview mirror and muttered under my breath, "It's your fault! If it weren't for you, I'd have finished this book by now." I had allowed myself to feel anger, actual resentment, toward my own children. I was staring at two of the happiest kids in the world, and I was mad at them.

That's when it hit me. How dare I blame my kids for me not doing what I needed to do? It wasn't their fault. It was mine. I was projecting my own disappointment onto them, using them as a scapegoat for my lack of follow-through.

Right then and there, I apologized. I told them it wasn't their fault, that it was Daddy's fault his book wasn't finished. And in that moment, I took ownership. I asked myself the hard question: what can I do to create the time I need?

The answer? I committed to waking up at 3:30 a.m. every day. That gave me two undistracted hours before the whirlwind of life began. And it's because of that commitment that you're holding this book in your hands today (or listening to it).

The moment you take radical ownership, that every result in your life is a direct result of your actions, your habits, your priorities, you take your power back. As long as it's "their fault," you're powerless. You become a victim of your circumstances. You stay stuck, angry, resentful, and full of regret, watching your life slip by and blaming everyone else for it. That's a terrible way to live.

And the people you love? They don't deserve that. They deserve the best version of you. They deserve the version of you who's living full out, chasing big goals, and leading by example.

So no, it's not selfish to get up early. It's actually the greatest gift you can give to the people you love.

The Greatest Gift

The greatest gift you can give the people around you is for you to max out your full potential. Let me say that again: the greatest gift is for you to play full out. Every time you shrink yourself, every time you mute your vision or hold back your dreams just to accommodate others, you're not doing them a favor. In fact, you're robbing them. You're robbing them of the gift of you, the fullest, most empowered, and most impactful version of yourself.

Every time you hold back, you're stealing from the people who deserve the best version of you. You're robbing them of the business you could have started, the book you could have written, the income you could have doubled, the confidence you could have gained from feeling good about yourself. You're robbing them of the healthiest, most vibrant you. You're robbing them of the gift of you living a long life because you've prioritized your fitness and health. You're robbing them of the superhero version of you that they deserve.

The greatest gift you can give them is for you to wake up early, tap into your full potential, and show up as the best version of yourself. When you do that, you don't just change your life, you change the lives of everyone around you. You give them more. You give them more money, more gifts, more experiences, more of everything they deserve.

Think about it. If I decided to stay in bed instead of getting up early to write this book, you wouldn't be reading these words right now. But because I chose to play full out, I can give you this gift of insight. I'm not here to tell you what you need to do; I'm here to show you what happens when you choose to step into your potential.

This applies to you too. When you play small, when you take the easy way out, you're denying everyone around you the best version of yourself. Your loved ones deserve you to be your best, your spouse deserves you stepping into your potential, not settling for comfort. Your kids deserve to see you lead by example, chasing your dreams and showing them what's possible when you fully embrace who you're meant to be. Your community, your friends, and every person in your life deserves the fullest, most powerful version of you.

The truth is, the best gift you can give the people you love, the people you lead, and the people you serve is for you to stop playing small. Stop avoiding the hard work. Stop holding back your full potential. The world deserves you showing up as your best self. And that starts with going to bed early… so you can wake up early and get after it!

Non-Negotiable

That word "non-negotiable" has a special place in my heart. One year, one of my friends decided to become a vegan. He wasn't doing it for deeply spiritual reasons or for environmental concerns. He just watched a documentary and thought it'd be cool to try the vegan lifestyle.

That same year, another friend of ours was getting married, and we were organizing the rehearsal dinner leading up to his wedding. The restaurant that we picked for the rehearsal dinner didn't have any vegan options, so I called my vegan friend to discuss the situation. I said, "Hey man, this restaurant doesn't have any vegan options, and it's too late for us to find an alternative. Can you just pause being a vegan for one day so you can enjoy dinner with us?" I continued to make my case, "It's not like you're doing this for religious reasons. Why not just have steak this one night and then go back to being a vegan the next day?"

There was a brief moment of silence. Then he said something that I will never forget. He said, "Jarvis, this is non-negotiable. Don't worry about me. I'll be fine. I'll bring my own meal to the restaurant."

I got off the phone with him that day, and I couldn't stop thinking about the word that he used: "non-negotiable." It was powerful. It was strong. It was serious.

In the aftermath of the terrorist attacks in 2001, the President of the United States famously said, "We do not negotiate with terrorists." Not even to retrieve hostage victims. Not even to save women and children. There are no exceptions to the rule. Under no circumstances do we negotiate against our own morals and principles. The moment that we do, it sets a precedent that we are weak and exposes a crack in the armor that terrorists can take advantage of.

Yet that's what we do on a daily basis. We negotiate with the terrorist that lives in our heads. Our own inner voice is a terrorist. It's not rational, it's not reasonable, and it often doesn't have our best interests in mind. It tells us, "You're tired, go lie down," when we should be going to the gym. It says, "You've had a long day, you deserve pizza," when we know that we're going to regret it later. It says, "There's no reason to call that person. They aren't going to answer anyway," when we know that we should be picking up the phone. Every day, we "negotiate" with our internal terrorist that is trying to steer us off of our committed path.

My friend showed me that he had a level of discipline as strong as the US armed military forces for something as simple as not eating meat and dairy products. He showed up to the rehearsal dinner with a Tupperware bowl filled with his home-prepared vegan meal. Some people thought he was odd, but he stuck to the commitment that he had made to himself. He did not let anyone "negotiate" him away from acting in alignment with his goals.

I had a newfound respect for him after the rehearsal dinner. That day, he proved to me that he was a person of his word. He was a person of strong character. He was a person with integrity. He was a person that stands on his morals. He was someone that didn't bend or break from his principles. He didn't just "flow with the wind." He was trustworthy. He was loyal. He was someone that you could count on. When he said something, he meant it. He showed us that he had an unwavering discipline. And guess what? That same friend is extremely successful today.

I believe that the quality of your life will settle at the level of your non-negotiables. Your non-negotiables are a set of rules and principles that you live by. They clearly state the things you do and the things that you don't do. They define who you are, and you make no exceptions to these rules. A vegan doesn't eat animal products, ever. Even if it's their birthday. Even if they are on vacation. Even if they are out with friends celebrating. It's a clear boundary that they don't cross, and for them, not eating animal products is a non-negotiable.

I believe that you will struggle in every area of your life where you lack a set of non-negotiables. Every area where you make exceptions, make excuses, make compromises, and accommodate other people.

Everywhere that you don't stand firmly on a standard that you have set for yourself, you will see weak, average, and mediocre results.

When you stay true to your principles and honor your non-negotiables, average people will think that you are odd. Mediocre people will think that you are weird. They want you to do, act, and behave just like them so they can feel better about themselves. They want you to fit into the norm, and every time you blend in to the norm by compromising on your discipline, you become one of them. You become average. You become mediocre. You settle for less than what you are capable of.

But you're not one of them. You were called for greatness, and the promise that you were called to fulfill will require a greater level of discipline. You are the exception, and your non-negotiables are what will separate you from everyone else.

And here's the surprising part, these other average folks, at first, will question you. Then they will respect you. Then they will want to follow your lead.

People respect people of strong character. When my vegan friend refused to "act normal" and eat meat during the rehearsal dinner, he showed us that he was a person of high character. At first, we questioned him and called him names. "Dude, that's stupid. You're going to look crazy bringing Tupperware bowls to a fine dining restaurant!"

But after the questioning and name-calling came the respect. I actually looked up to him for standing true to his beliefs. I admired that about him because I wouldn't have done that. I would have been weak. I would have folded to the pressure of the group. I would have accommodated everyone else to make them feel comfortable. And I would have hated myself for it. I admired that he put himself first. He prioritized his goals over making people feel comfortable. I had a newfound respect for him.

EVERY. DAMN. DAY.

And after the respect came the magic. All of a sudden, I wanted to know more about this vegan thing. After that incident, I actually started reading up on plant-based eating and converted to a plant-based lifestyle myself. I did this for about a year before eventually incorporating some meat and animal products back into my diet, but I don't eat nearly as much as I used to. I saw how committed my friend was to this new lifestyle, and it created a curiosity that made me want to try it for myself.

First, they will question you. Then they will respect you. Then they will follow your lead. By making people uncomfortable with your non-negotiables, you are actually doing them a favor because it could eventually lead to them following your lead into their own greatness.

You will have multiple non-negotiables that define who you are, from your eating and exercise habits to your finance and relationship habits. But the one non-negotiable that empowers them all is your Power Hour, at least 60 minutes of undistracted alone time to set your intentions for a 5-star day every morning. Even on your birthday. Even on vacation. Even on holidays. Even on bad days. Even on good days. This isn't something you do every now and then or when you feel like it. This is a lifestyle, and you have to do it every damn day!

☐ Reflection

- Who's watching you? Who sees your habits and might follow your lead?
- What message are they absorbing from seeing you every day?
- What example do you want to set for them?

☐ Take Action

- Declare this out loud: *"I will be a better leader by example. When people see me, they will see someone who Wakes up and WINS EVERY. DAMN. DAY!"*
- *Scan the QR code to join the free Morning Hero community and leave a post with your declaration statement above. By declaring your intentions publicly, you deepen your commitment and tell the universe that you mean business!*

CHAPTER 6
POWER DOWN TO POWER UP

"Early to bed, early to rise, makes a man healthy, wealthy and wise."

— Benjamin Franklin

The Power-Down Hour

Now, let's break down how exactly you can implement that habit into your existence. People ask me all the time how I wake up so early. Well… this may sound obvious, but if you want to wake up earlier, you've got to go to bed earlier. There's just no way around it. You don't want to shortcut your sleep. You still need a full night's rest to perform at your best each day. By no means am I recommending that you cheat your sleep.

It's simple math: if you want to wake up one hour earlier, you need to go to bed one hour earlier. Waking up early is easy if you go to bed on time and get enough sleep. But going to bed on time is easier said than done.

It takes time for your brain to shut down. Even if you physically get in bed early, you might just lie there wide awake because your brain isn't ready to turn off yet. That's why you need a "Power-Down Hour."

Your Power-Down Hour is the final hour before bedtime, and it will determine whether or not you actually get to bed on time. Just like you have a Power Hour to ramp up your day, you need a Power-Down Hour to wind it down.

I recommend setting a Power-Down Alarm, an alarm that goes off one hour before your bedtime to signal that it's time to start shutting things down. For example, if you want to wake up at 5 a.m. and need a full eight hours of sleep, that means you've got to be in bed by 9 p.m. So you'd set a Power-Down Alarm for 8 p.m. That gives you a full hour to ease into rest mode.

The goal of your Power-Down Hour is simple: bore yourself to sleep.

Here are a few quick tips for an effective Power-Down Hour:

Disengage from devices… your goal is to quiet your mind, not stimulate it. Phones, TV, email, and social media light your brain up and keep it awake.

Read a book… reading is naturally soothing and, let's be honest, boring enough to lull your brain into sleep mode.

It will definitely be an adjustment to retrain yourself to go to bed earlier, but the biggest shift isn't retraining your body, it's retraining your mind. Your mind will not want to go to bed earlier, and that's probably because you use your evenings as your "me time." You will have to shift your "me time" from the evenings to the mornings. But trust me… it will be the greatest shift of your entire life.

Toxic "Me Time"

Trust me, I get it. After a long, draining day of work, family, and the endless chaos of the whirlwind, evenings are when you finally get a sliver of peace. I used to live for that moment. I'd come home, sink into the couch, throw on a murder mystery, and dive into some cookie dough ice cream. That was my sacred "me time."

But when I took a closer look at what that "me time" actually consisted of... crappy TV, crappy food, crappy substances, and sometimes even crappy company... I had to ask myself a hard question: was this time actually serving me? The truth? It wasn't.

So I made a powerful decision. I traded my toxic, mind-numbing evenings for productive, life-giving mornings. That one shift changed everything. I still had my "me time," but now it was in the morning, and it was sacred. My new "me time" was filled with prayer, meditation, journaling, goal-setting, planning, and movement. Instead of numbing out, I was powering up. I went from self-sabotage to self-mastery. I stopped ending the day on empty and started beginning it full.

So let me ask you: which version of "me time" will better serve your future? Two hours of Netflix, video games, social media, and processed snacks at night, or an hour in the morning connecting with your higher self, locking in your goals, organizing your day, and energizing your body?

By going to bed early so you can wake up early, you're not losing your "me time," you're just shifting it. And that minor shift in time will create a major shift in your life.

Move Your Phone

If you're like most people, then you probably sleep with your phone charging on the nightstand next to your bed. There's a whole host of reasons why this is bad for you. Let's explore them one by one.

1. It's too easy to snooze!

If you use your phone as your alarm clock and it's sitting right next to your bed, then it's too easy to hit the snooze button when the alarm goes off in the morning. One of the easiest tricks you can do to resist hitting snooze is to move your alarm clock (aka phone) across the room. That way, you can't just reach over and hit snooze. You actually have to get out of bed and walk across the room to deactivate the alarm. And once you are up, you might as well just stay up.

When I first started trying to train myself to wake up at 5 a.m., I actually put my phone charger in the bathroom. Each night, I would set my alarm and then leave the phone in the bathroom to charge up overnight. When the alarm went off in the morning, it would make this loud piercing sound and I had to literally jump out of bed and run to the bathroom to shut off the alarm. So there I was in the bathroom, heart racing, looking at myself in the mirror. There was no way I was going to go back to bed. I decided I might as well just grab my toothbrush and get the day started.

2. It's preventing you from getting to bed on time.

If your phone is sitting right next to you, there's an urge to grab it and start engaging while you are in bed. Engaging on social media, engaging with email, engaging with the news. Every time you engage, you are igniting your brain, which prolongs your ability to fall asleep. Just think of it this way... every scroll and every swipe adds another five minutes to your brain's wakefulness. So by moving your phone across the room (or in the bathroom), you won't have the urge to grab it and start scrolling.

3. It's preventing you from getting deep quality sleep.

Your brain will continue to process the last inputs you give it right before falling asleep. Have you ever noticed that you have weird dreams after watching a scary movie? That's your brain taking the inputs that you just gave it and processing them all night long. The same thing happens when you scroll on your phone right before falling asleep. You're giving your brain the stress of tasks waiting in your inbox, the jealousy of social media, and the anxiety of the news. These are the emotions that you are subconsciously feeling every time you swipe on your phone, and that's what your brain will continue to process all night long. So now, you toss and turn all night from anxiety, or you wake up stressed from that last email you read. This is why you don't sleep well at night. It's because you are feeding your brain negative energy right before bed, which makes it restless.

So what are you supposed to do if you can't scroll in bed? Pick up a book and read.

Read in Bed

The key to going to bed early isn't just about willpower, it's about convincing your brain to let go. You've got to teach it how to shut off. And here's the secret: you've got to get comfortable with boredom. You actually want to bore yourself to sleep. That's how you win.

So here's my recommendation: ditch the phone and pick up a book. Books are beautifully boring in the best way possible. Don't get me wrong, they're full of wisdom and stories, but they don't overstimulate your brain like a glowing screen does. When you're lying there with a book, your eyes start to droop, your mind starts to slow down, and before you know it, you're out cold.

Think of it like this: reading in bed is less about gaining knowledge and more about giving your brain permission to relax. You're signaling, "Hey, we're done for the day. Nothing urgent here. Time to shut it down." That little ritual of boredom is what helps you slip into deep, peaceful sleep.

Eat Light

I noticed that every time I had a really heavy meal, I always felt miserable. I was bloated and I couldn't get comfortable. I didn't realize it, but eating heavy meals right before bed was causing me to have horrible sleep. I would have crazy dreams, and I would wake up all throughout the night. Then one day, I decided to just have a salad for dinner. I noticed a big difference. I didn't feel heavy. I didn't feel bloated. I slept like a baby. And when I woke up in the morning, I sprung out of bed with more energy and zest.

If you are having a hard time getting to sleep and staying asleep, it could be something you ate. Let your last meal of the day be your lightest meal of the day. You'll sleep better and wake up feeling great and with more energy.

My recommendation: eat salad for dinner #Salad4Dinner. When I say "salad," I just mean avoid carbs. Carbs tend to be the heaviest part of our meals: pastas, breads, french fries, rice, mashed potatoes. Stick to just meat and veggies for dinner and you'll notice that your sleep will be deeper and you'll wake up lighter.

Brain Dump

Most sleep issues come from underlying anxiety about something. Your brain is just trying to hold on to too much. It's trying to remember everything that needs to get done, phone calls that need to be made, emails that need to be sent out, the schedule for tomorrow, and chores and errands that need to be taken care of. At any given point in time, there are a hundred things running around in our head and our brain is trying not to forget any of it.

Imagine you have a hundred balloons filled with helium, and you are trying to hold them all down and not let any float away. That's our brain, constantly running around, grabbing the balloons, making sure they don't drift off and get forgotten about. This will cause you anxiety and keep you from sleeping. The easiest way to relieve this stress is to just get everything out of your head and down on paper. That way, your brain can release it, knowing that it won't be forgotten about. This could be as simple as making a "to-do list" of everything that needs to get done tomorrow. If you want to take it a step further, then actually plan your day for the following day. That way, you've already got your tasks and calendar organized for the following day so you can sleep easy at night.

Sleep Meditation

Meditation is one of the greatest tools to help calm an overactive mind. Many people meditate in the morning to get centered for the day. However, meditating at night can be one of the best ways to release the anxiety of the day so you can fall asleep comfortably and stay asleep.

I went through a phase of my life where I woke up every night at 1 a.m., and it was the most frustrating thing in the world. I would wake up and just stare at the ceiling while my mind raced, thinking over all the things I had to get done for the day. I tried everything… counting sheep, watching old TV shows, but nothing worked. Then one night, I decided to put in my headphones and fire up a guided meditation using one of the meditation apps on my phone. I found a calm, soothing voice, and within five minutes, I was snoring like a baby.

When I woke up the next morning, I was amazed at how refreshed I felt. Finally, I had found a way to fall back asleep immediately instead of staying up for hours. After that, I bought a pair of sleep headphones on Amazon. These are super-flat earbuds designed to be worn in bed, so you can sleep on your side without feeling them in your ears. They're perfect for listening to sleep meditations.

I wear them almost every single night. Sometimes I listen to white noise to calm my brain, and other times I use a guided meditation from my meditation app. Either way, it's the perfect way to block out the outside world, quiet your mind, and fall asleep faster, then stay asleep all night long.

The Morning Appointment

Hands down, the number one way to get yourself to start waking up earlier is to schedule something that you have to report to early in the morning. When I was on my Hero's journey, it was hard for me to stay consistent with my 5 a.m. wakeups. So I found a local gym that had 5 a.m. cycling classes. I paid for two months' worth of classes because I knew that if I paid for them, then I wouldn't miss them. I was not going to waste my money. In order to be at the class by 5 a.m., I had to wake up at 4:30 a.m. Guess what? I didn't miss a day. I was up at 4:30 a.m. every morning during that two-month period. The only reason I was able to stick with it was because I paid for the classes and had to report to them every morning to get my money's worth.

This concept of having a "morning appointment" holds you accountable and keeps you consistent with your early mornings. The gym is a great morning appointment. I recommend group classes that have a start time. That way, you have to be at the class by a certain time or you miss it. Group classes are also great because there are other people there, and you start to build a sense of community with the other crazy people who are up super early in the morning. Once you have some relationships built, you start to look forward to seeing that same group of people every day, and you don't want to miss the class because you can't let the people down. It's an added layer of accountability. Not only are you accountable to your wallet, but you are also accountable to the people in the class.

It's because of this concept that I created the Morning Hero Accountability Groups. It's a morning appointment that helps keep you accountable to your early mornings. When you download the Win The Day app, you can click on "Tribes" and join an accountability group that meets every morning via Zoom to set their intentions for the day (you'll learn about this practice later in the book). This becomes your morning appointment to keep you accountable not only to your early wake-ups but also to your practice of setting clear intentions for a super productive day. Download the app, join a tribe, and become a Morning Hero.

Final Thoughts

Waking up early is a cheat code. It's the secret weapon used by the world's highest performers to unlock more time, more clarity, more energy, and more results.

It's not easy. But neither is staying stuck. Neither is living a life you're not proud of. Neither is looking back with regret, wondering what you could've built if you had just created a little more time to focus on what matters.

The truth is, the way you start your day is the way you live your life. If you want to take control of your life, it starts by taking control of your mornings.

You don't need to overhaul your entire existence overnight. You just need to wake up one hour earlier. That's it. One sacred hour to start winning the day before the whirlwind even has a chance to pull you in.

Because once you've won the morning, you've already created the space, the peace, and the power to win the rest of the day.

But waking up early is just the beginning.

The real magic happens in what you do with that extra time. This brings us to the next piece of the WIN-ning formul… the "I"… where we learn how to set intentions with purpose and precision. Because waking up early gives you time… but setting intentions gives you power.

Let's dive in.

☐ Reflection

- What stories do you tell yourself to justify late nights ("I need to unwind," "I deserve it after a long day." What have they really cost you?
- What would happen if you shifted your "me time" from the evening to the morning? What bad habits would stop and what good habits would start?
- What areas of your life would benefit if you were able to create more "margin" in the morning?

☐ Take Action

- Set an alarm on your phone to go off one hour before your desired bedtime and label it "Power-Down Hour."
- When the alarm goes off tonight, start winding your night down. Turn off screens and pick up a book to read! Bore yourself to sleep so you can wake up fresh and energized for your power hour!
- Scan the QR code below to watch a free training on designing your perfect power-down hour.

WAKE UP EARLY
INTENTIONS
N

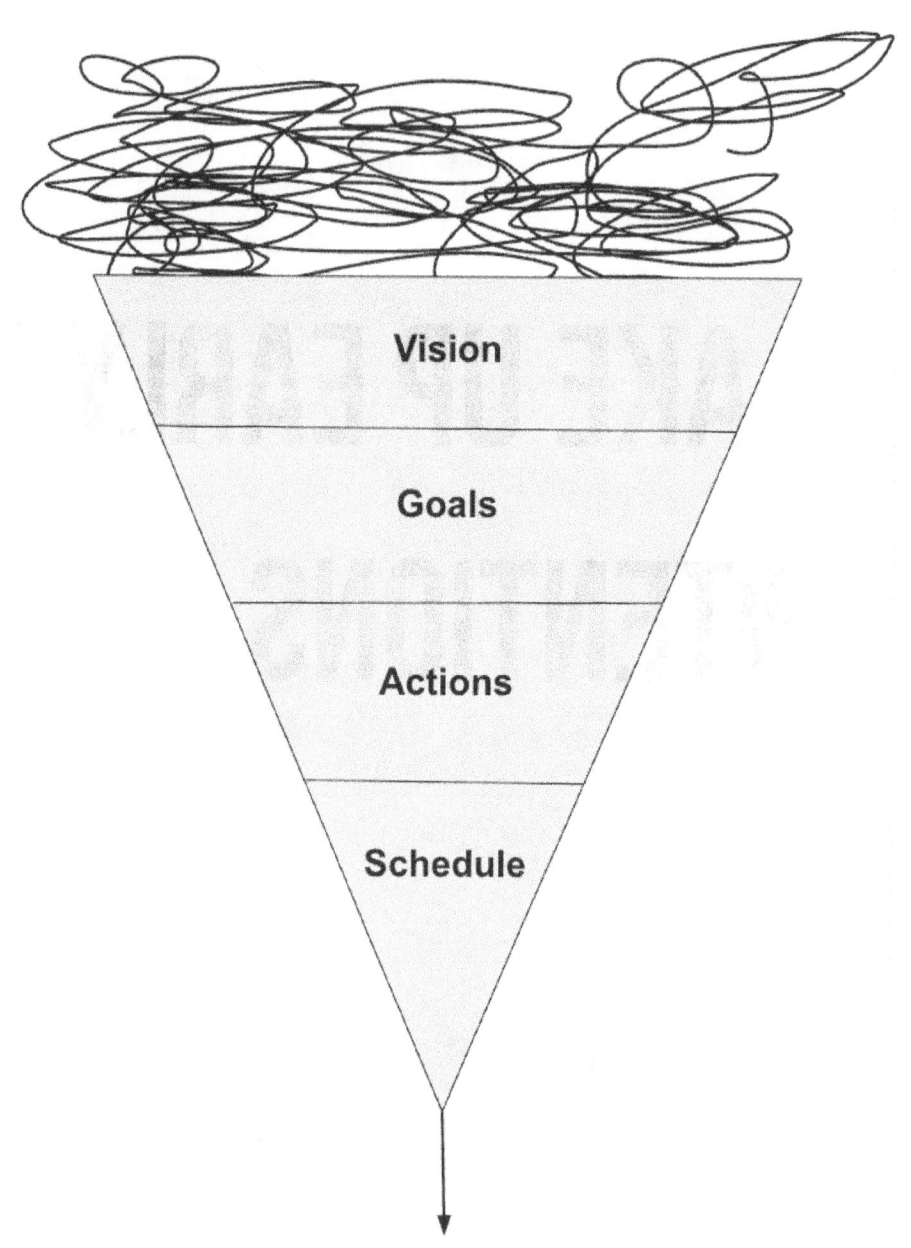

The Focus Funnel

When you wake up in the morning, it often feels like you've been dropped into the middle of a storm. Emails, texts, notifications, to-dos, obligations… all of it coming at you at once in a swirling, chaotic whirlwind. That's why so many people end their day exhausted, wondering where the time went, but with very little to show for it. Here's the problem. They never took a moment of pause to decide how they actually wanted their day to unfold. They never set clear Intentions for their day.

That's why the second step of the WINNING formula after you wake up early for your power hour is to set intentions for your day. We aren't waking up early just to scroll on our phones! You will spend the first 30 minutes of your power hour setting clear intentions for what a successful day will look like. There are four levels of intentions and each level gets you more and more dialed in for a focused and meaningful day. It's kinda like a funnel… a **Focus Funnel**.

A funnel takes a high volume of substance at the top and directs it down into a clear, steady stream at the bottom. In the same way, going through these four levels of intentions will take the overwhelming flood of chaos in your life and concentrate it into a powerful, organized flow of action.

The first level is your **Vision**, the big picture of who you want to become and the life you're building. The next level is your **Goals**, the milestones that move you closer to that vision. Narrowing further, we reach your **Actions**, the tangible steps you need to accomplish to hit those goals. Finally, at the bottom of the funnel, everything flows into your **Schedule**, the precise time slots where you will take those actions.

Each level filters the chaos, stripping away distractions and keeps you locked in on your goals. By the time you reach the bottom of the Focus Funnel, what was once overwhelming noise has been transformed into a simple, high-impact stream of activity.

In this section, we will walk through each level of Intention, and at the end, I'll show you a simple Morning Practice that will allow you to set these four levels of intention in just 15 minutes. It's how you will walk into you every day with clarity, confidence, and control.

Now, let's dive into the first level of Intention… creating your BIG Vision!

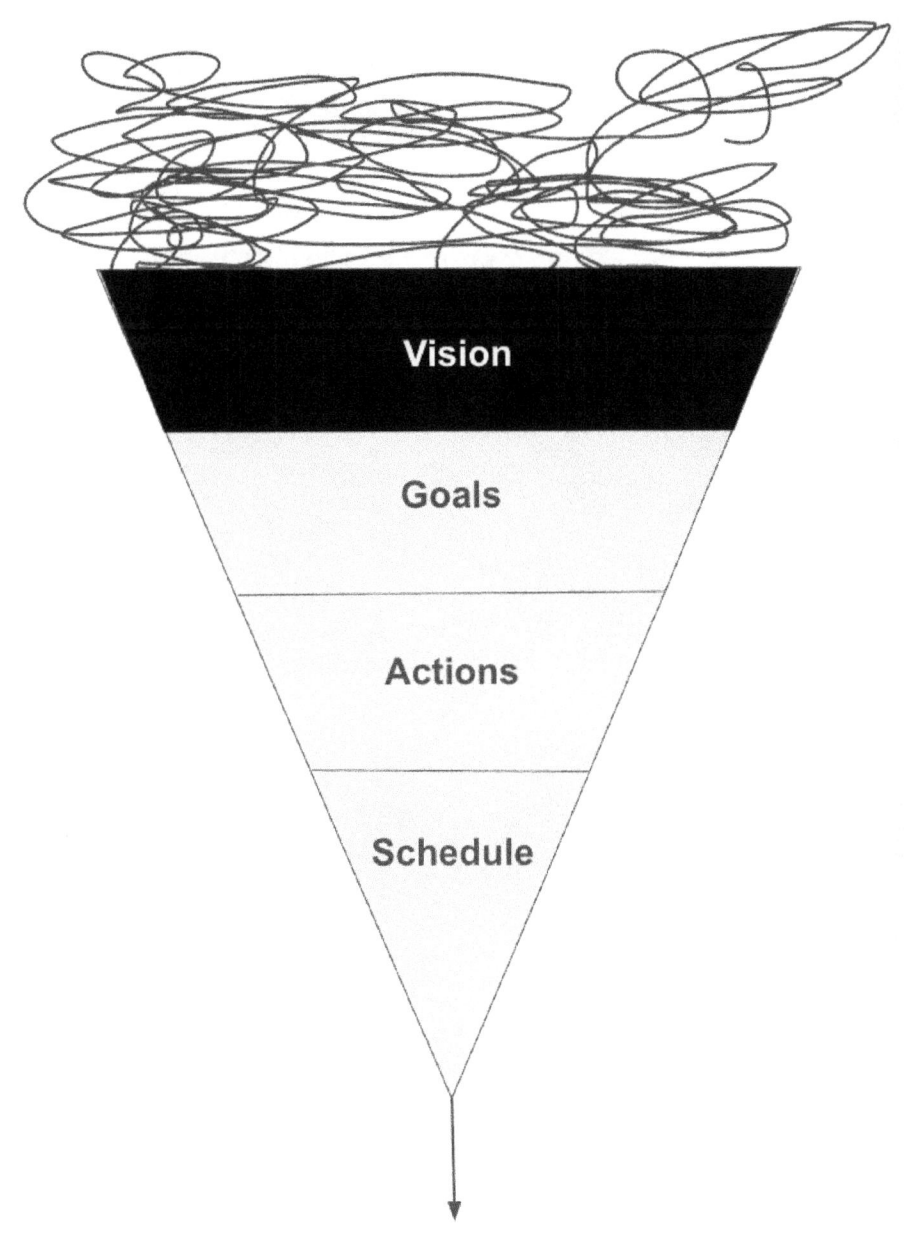

CHAPTER 7
VISION

"Begin with the end in mind."

—Stephen R. Covey

Setting Your Sail

Being intentional just means having a very clear idea of what you want and taking the necessary actions to get it. It's kinda like sailing a boat. A sailboat harnesses the power of the wind to move through the water, but the wind alone doesn't determine where the boat ends up. The captain does.

Once the captain decides on a destination, they "set the sail," angling it just right so the wind pushes the boat in the desired direction. That's what it means to set your intentions. You first choose where you want to go, then you align your actions to head straight for it.

And here's the wild part: Even if the wind is blowing against you, you can still get there. That's right… a sailboat can sail against the wind. It's called tacking. By adjusting the angle of the sail and zigzagging back and forth, the boat continues to make forward progress even in the face of resistance. As long as the boat has a sail and a captain who knows where they're going, it can reach any destination no matter which way the wind is blowing.

This is the perfect metaphor for life.

Most people never "set their sail" to get to a destination. They just drift, tossed around by the winds of life. When the wind blows left, they go left. When it shifts right, they drift right. No direction. No plan. No intention. They're just surviving the sea.

But no seasoned sailor would set out into open water without a map, a compass, a GPS, and a destination in mind. That's the difference between a drifter and someone who is intentional. A drifter becomes a victim of the whirlwind. Life happens to them. Their boat sails in circles, or worse, crashes into the rocks. And if they do end up in a good place, it's by accident, not by any intentional effort of their own.

Life on Accident

Can good things happen without setting your sail? Surprisingly, yes. You can end up with some pretty amazing outcomes without being intentional. But here's the catch… it wasn't on purpose. You got there on accident. And that's one of the greatest tricks of the Whirlwind.

Sometimes, the wind just happens to blow in the direction of a beautiful island, and boom! You drift right into paradise without lifting a finger. You didn't steer. You didn't plan. You just happened to be going with the current. Life felt good. You got the job. The promotion. The girl. The house. The wins were stacking up. You thought you were crushing it. But what you didn't realize was the winds of life were simply blowing in your favor.

So naturally, you assume it's all because of your effort. Your work. Your grind. You start believing you are the reason for the success, even though, truthfully, you were just riding the current of a good wind. But here's the thing about the wind… it's unpredictable. In a split second, it can change direction. Violently. Suddenly. And when it does, you'll feel

EVERY. DAMN. DAY.

helpless, because up until that moment, you weren't actually steering the ship. You were just drifting. The favorable wind was doing the work for you. And now that it's reversed, you have no tools, no direction, and no clue how to get back on course.

You never learned how to actually drive the boat. So now, you're stuck, spinning in circles, drifting wherever the wind blows, completely at the mercy of the storm.

That's exactly what happened to me.

For most of my life, things were going great. In high school, I was a star athlete and an academic All-American. I didn't have to try hard. Success came easy. I was quarterback of the football team, All-Conference in track and wrestling, on the honor roll, the math team, and the debate team, all while holding down a part-time job. After high school, I went on to study computer engineering at the University of Illinois on a scholarship. I made the dean's list. I had multiple job offers from Fortune 500 companies. I eventually got into software sales, where I crushed it as a top-producing rep for over 15 years. I drove a Mercedes. Lived in a downtown condo with skyline views. Rocked high-end suits. My place was the go-to party spot. Life was good.

But here's the truth: I wasn't steering the ship. I wasn't intentionally creating that success. I didn't have goals. I just woke up every day and did stuff. I was accidentally successful. Even though it felt like I was driving my good fortune, I was really just riding the tide of having a strong mother who pushed me to go to a good school. While I was at that school, I studied with some people who were in a technical sales training program. While in that program, I was introduced to a recruiter who worked for the company that hired me out of college. While at that company, I had a good mentor who showed me the ropes. I wasn't consciously setting goals and mapping out game plans; I was just coasting on the breeze of a good wind that was initially kicked off by my mother.

Then I hit 30… and the wind shifted.

I started hanging out with the wrong people. My weekends became about partying and self-indulgence. Within three years, I went from high-performing and high-potential to broke, lost, and burned out. I lost everything… my money, my job, my friends. I had to move back home to Chicago and sleep in my aunt's basement. And I sat there, wondering, what the hell happened?

I'd had it all… a luxury apartment, a beautiful partner, a career I was proud of. And now, I was starting over from scratch. Looking back, I now understand exactly what happened. The wind changed direction. And I had no idea how to navigate. I didn't know how to steer the ship.

All that success? It wasn't due to my own effort. It was life happening to me, not because of me. I was winning on accident. And once the wind shifted… as it eventually does for everyone… I had no sail. No map. No clear destination. I didn't know what it meant to live intentionally. I had no goals, no vision, no plan. I didn't know how to live on purpose.

Then one day, sitting on that couch, I stumbled across a video of a man named Jim Rohn. Jim is one of the greatest life philosophers of all time.

Jim said something that shook me: "Everything that's happening to you in your life is your fault."

OUCH.

He said you get what you ask for in life. But the problem is, most people never ask for anything. They just take whatever life gives them. Sometimes, life gives you good things. Other times, it smacks you upside the head.

Most people never learn to aim. They never learn to set a target. They never learn how to steer. They don't take time to get clear on what they really want. They don't break their goals down into daily actions. They don't design a life. They just drift through one.

But once you learn to set your direction every day it doesn't matter what the wind does anymore. You take the power back. You stop drifting and you start driving.

It's like strapping a motor to your boat. You can cut through the storm and go full speed ahead, straight toward your destination, no matter the conditions.

That's what it means to live life on purpose. That was the moment I got intentional. That was the day I stopped drifting and started designing. That's when my life began to change.

Ten-Year Review

Here's an exercise I love: I call it the Ten-Year Review.

Project yourself ten years into the future. You're sitting at a beautiful dinner table, surrounded by your closest friends. Everyone's joyful and they're toasting you. You've accomplished something incredible, and they are so proud of you.

You grab the fanciest bottle of champagne on the menu. You stand up, raise your glass, and begin to tell the story of the last ten years.

Now, pause. What are you saying?

What happened over the past decade that brought you so much joy and pride? What did you achieve? What does your health look like? Your family life? Your finances? Your impact?

I like to close my eyes and spend ten full minutes vividly dreaming about it. I think through every aspect... career, health, family, fun, contribution. Then I open my eyes and write it out. Pen to paper. Old school.

It usually takes about twenty minutes. And sometimes, I revisit and rewrite it, making it even more vivid, more emotional. The more detailed it is and the more emotion it has, the more passionately I'll pursue it. If it doesn't make me tear up, I know I haven't gone deep enough.

Many people just dive right into setting near-term goals without getting clear on their long-term vision first. Here's the problem with that approach: If you set goals from where you are now, without first anchoring into where you want to be, you'll likely set goals that reflect your current limitations instead of your future possibilities. And that creates a life that's out of congruence.

Congruence

"Congruence" is the state where everything you're doing right now is in complete alignment with your passions, your purpose, and your grand vision for life. It's when you're in flow. When you're operating in your superpower, doing the very thing you were put on this earth to do. Nothing feels forced. Everything feels effortless.

I remember when I first got serious about spreading the message of being a Morning Hero. At the time, I was doing lots of speaking, but people would always ask, "Hey, Jarvis, I really love the idea of winning the morning, but I can't stick with it. Do you offer coaching?" That's when I went all in and started building out a full Morning Hero coaching offering with courses, training, and an accountability community all designed to help people transform into Morning Heroes.

That first year was a huge success. We got some amazing testimonials about the impact the program was having on people's lives. One

EVERY. DAMN. DAY.

woman 5x'd her income in just one year after becoming a Morning Hero. Another woman lost thirty-two pounds within three months of joining. But the most memorable testimonial came when I was taking my son for a walk and a woman came running up to me on the street. She said, "Are you the Morning Hero?" I was a bit skeptical at first. I had no idea who this woman was or why she was running toward me. After I told her who I was, she gave me a hug and said, "Thank you for what you did for my husband." She told me her husband had been in a really dark place. He was unemployed, unhappy, and had lost the will to live. One day, he discovered my content on Instagram (@the.morninghero). After he started following me, he signed up for one of my courses and began his Hero's Journey. She said he started waking up early every day and going to the gym again. He mapped out his goals and went back to school to start his own business. One year after becoming a Morning Hero, he had a job he loved, was making more money than ever, and had become a great role model for their children again. She said, "Thank you, Jarvis, for not only saving our marriage… you also saved his life." Hearing stories like that really solidified my purpose: to help people transform into the superhero version of themselves.

By year two, I got even more ambitious. I set a goal to double the size of the coaching company. I built the Morning Hero Framework and started training others to become certified Morning Hero Coaches. We grew to four coaches, a team of five support staff, and a packed calendar. Life was good, until it wasn't.

By year three, we plateaued. Growth stalled. The team started unraveling. Clients weren't being served at the highest level. And worst of all, I wasn't enjoying it anymore.

So I went back to a trusted tool: the Year in Review. I visualized my dream life. I saw myself traveling the world with my family, speaking on massive stages, inspiring thousands to become Morning Heroes. When I opened my eyes, it hit me. I had drifted off course. I was building goals based on where I was, not where I wanted to go.

I had seen quick success with coaching, so I defaulted to scaling a coaching company. But that was never my true vision. My dream wasn't to run a business with eight hours of Zoom calls a day. My dream was to speak on stages, write books, and move audiences to action. I had slipped out of congruence, and that's when everything started to feel hard.

Here's what I've learned: when you make goals based only on your current situation, without starting with your end vision, you'll get stuck in short-term thinking. You'll chase opportunities that feel right in the moment but pull you further from your long-term dreams.

Once I realized that, I made a radical shift. I scrapped the coaching model and pivoted to focus on writing and speaking. That's when everything clicked. I was finally in alignment again. I felt flow. I felt purpose. I was back in my superpower.

So before setting your goals, start by getting crystal clear on your long-term vision. That ensures that what you're doing today is aligned with where you want to be one year, five years, even ten years from now.

That's how you live a life of congruence. That's how you step into flow. That's how you build a life of effortless success.

☐ Reflection

- What do you want to accomplish in Life?
- What brings you happiness?
- What do you want to be remembered for?
- What do you feel like you were put on this Earth to do?

☐ Take Action: Create Your Big Vision

- Write your "10-year Review."

  - Project yourself 10 years (or more) into the future and act as if you are reflecting back on the most successful... the most memorable... and the most fulfilling 10 years of your life! You have lived up to your highest potential in every area of your life. Your Finances... Your Fitness... Your Family Life... Your Friends... Your Free Time.... Everything has flourished beyond your wildest dreams.
  - Now, write the story of how it all happened. Go into very deep, emotional detail of what happened, how it happened, and who it impacted.

- Scan the QR code below to watch a video of me reading my 10 year review. WARNING... It's pretty emotional. Have some tissues handy!

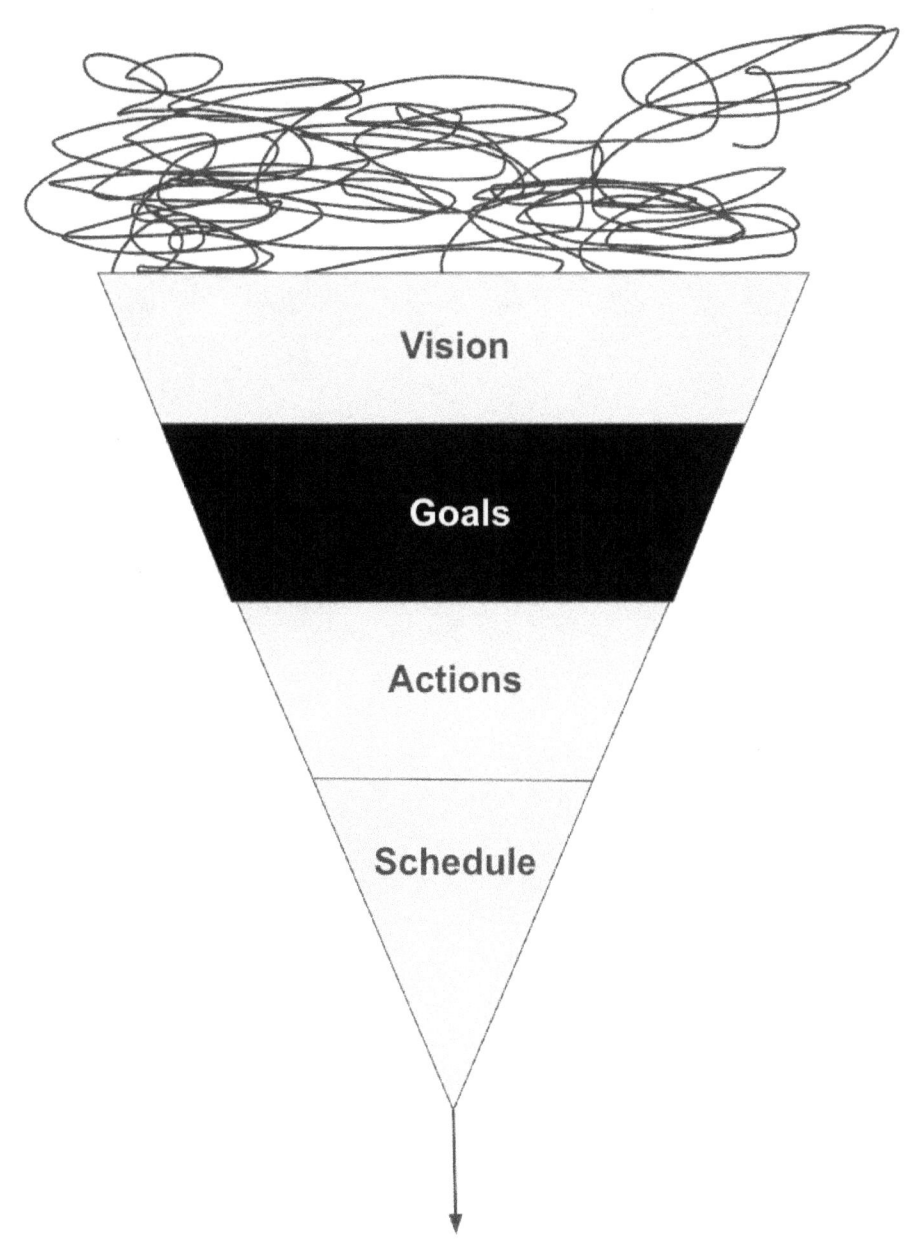

CHAPTER 8
GOALS

"A good goal is like a strenuous exercise — it makes you stretch."

– Mary Kay Ash

The Three-Legged Stool

I believe there are three fundamental areas that determine your success and happiness in life: health, wealth, and relationships. Health represents your physical vitality and emotional well-being. Wealth includes your finances, your career, and the pursuit of meaningful work. And relationships encompass your family, your friendships, your community, and your connection to the people you love.

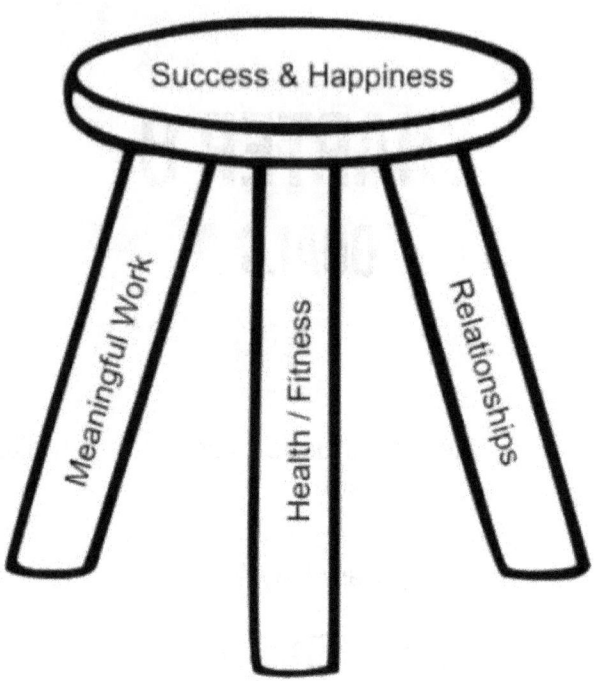

Think of these three areas as the legs of a stool.

When you're making good money or doing work that lights your soul on fire, when you feel strong and confident in your body, and when you're surrounded by love, connection, and people who matter to you… that's true success and happiness That's the kind of life that feels grounded, rich, and fulfilling.

But just like a real stool, if even one of those legs is weak or missing, the whole thing becomes unstable. You might have money pouring in but if you're overweight, out of shape, and your family can't stand being around you, then sure, maybe you're "successful" by society's standards… but you won't feel happy. You won't feel whole. You won't be fulfilled.

EVERY. DAMN. DAY.

Your income won't comfort you when your kids don't talk to you. Your luxury car won't matter when no one calls you on your birthday. The trophies and accolades won't mean a thing when you're eating dinner alone in silence.

Now, flip it.

Let's say you're in peak shape. You wake up early, hit the gym, count your macros, meal prep, meditate, and flex in the mirror daily. That's great. But if you're stuck in a dead-end job that drains your spirit, or worse, a job that doesn't pay you what you're worth… guess what? You're not going to feel successful. You'll have abs, but you'll also have anxiety. You'll look like a beast on the outside while feeling broken on the inside. Because your financial life isn't aligned with your full potential. Your work isn't honoring your gifts.

A stool needs all three legs to stand.

Sure, you might be able to balance on one or two for a little while. You might even convince yourself you're okay. But eventually, gravity takes over. Sooner or later, imbalance leads to collapse.

And when it does? You fall.

Just like your life will start to unravel when one of those core areas… health, wealth, or relationships is ignored or neglected for too long.

So be honest with yourself… would you sit on a stool with only two legs? Of course not. It's just a matter of time before it gives out from under you.

Your life works the exact same way.

If you want long-term stability, you have to strengthen all three legs of the stool. You have to prioritize your health. You have to pursue wealth through work that is meaningful and aligned with your purpose. And you have to invest deeply in your relationships because that's what makes life worth living.

That's what creates a WINNING life!

Health

Your level of health will directly determine the size of the goals you're able to pursue and actually achieve. You can't live up to your highest and fullest potential if you're tired, sluggish, and lethargic. You've got to be physically capable of running full speed in the race of life. And not just running it... you're trying to win. Life is going to throw challenges at you. You'll have to leap over obstacles, push through adversity, and solve complex problems on the fly. The stronger you are, physically and mentally, the more equipped you'll be. The more fit you are, the more energy you'll have, the clearer you'll think, and the more presence and power you'll bring into every room you walk into.

Being in great shape is one of the clearest reflections of your discipline. It takes discipline to exercise consistently. It takes discipline to say no to sugar and junk food, even when it's calling your name. It takes discipline to wake up early to go to the gym instead of hitting snooze. And that discipline will transfer into everything you do.

If you can say no to a piece of cake at a birthday party when everyone else is indulging, then you're also the type of person who can make the hard calls to grow your business even when it's uncomfortable. If you can push through a two-mile run, you can push through a tough conversation with your partner. The habits you build with your health don't just stay in the gym. They spill over into your business, your relationships, your parenting, your finances, your mindset. Your entire life gets sharper.

EVERY. DAMN. DAY.

But there's another reason why your health matters, and this one's bigger than you: because your body is a billboard. It's a visible display of your discipline, your energy, and your self-leadership. It's a visual representation of your ability to hit your goals. And just like a billboard, people will make a snap judgment about you within seconds.

Think about it. When you're driving past a billboard at sixty miles an hour, you only have a few seconds to make a decision. "Do I trust this?" "Do I want this?" "Should I take action?" People do the same thing with you. When you walk into a room, they instantly decide: Can I trust this person? Should I listen to what they have to say? Do I want what they have?

That's why living a healthy lifestyle isn't just about you. It's about who's watching you. When you look like you're crushing your goals, you inspire others to crush theirs too. You silently lead by example.

I remember walking into a cycling class one day. As I came in, I noticed a heavyset guy on the instructor's bike. I'd been to this class before, and I knew who the instructor usually was and this guy clearly wasn't him. He was drenched in sweat, breathing hard, and looked like he was struggling to turn the pedals. I figured he had just picked the wrong bike. No big deal.

I got my shoes on, hopped on a bike, and started warming up. A few minutes passed, and I noticed the guy was still on the instructor's seat. Start time was approaching, and I kept thinking, somebody better tell this guy he's on the wrong bike.

Just as I was about to walk over and say something, he jumped off the bike, dimmed the lights, grabbed the mic, and shouted, "Alright guys, let's go! Hop on your bikes and pedal to the beat!"

Turns out, he was the substitute instructor. And I instantly checked out. Why?

Because in that moment, I thought, how the hell is he going to lead me to my greatness if he's not even leading himself to his own greatness?

I grabbed my things and walked out. I didn't give him a chance. He could've been the best cycling instructor on the planet, but I didn't care. I had already made a decision based on how he looked. It wasn't fair. But it was real. His physical appearance sent a message about his discipline. And I didn't see someone who was walking the talk.

Here's the hard truth: people are watching you. And whether you like it or not, they're asking themselves, does this person look like they're living in their full potential? If the answer is yes, they'll lean in. They'll want to follow you. They'll want to listen to you. They'll want what you have. If the answer is no, they'll tune out before you even open your mouth.

That's why your health is not just about you. It's about your leadership. It's about your influence. It's about inspiring others to step into their greatness by showing them what it looks like to fully embody your own.

So live it. Own it. Be the billboard that shouts, "I am a HERO and you can be one too!"

Because you never know who's watching… and waiting to follow your lead.

☐ **Reflection**

- On a scale of 1 to 10, how would you rate yourself in your **Health**?
- What would need to change for you to be a **10/10**?

Wealth

Let's be honest, money matters. The more money you make, the more you can do. Not just for yourself, but for the people you love. There is nothing wrong with wanting to earn more. In fact, it's one of the most powerful ways to increase your impact. Some might see the pursuit of wealth as greedy or self-serving, but I believe it's quite the opposite. The more money you have, the more resources you can direct toward people, projects, and ideas that leave this world better than you found it.

You can invest in businesses that solve real problems. You can donate to causes that matter. You can create the lifestyle your family deserves. You can send your kids to better schools. You can take your parents on that dream vacation. You can bless others with your abundance. Because money is not evil, it's a tool. And tools aren't good or bad. They simply amplify the hand that wields them. The more wealth you possess, the greater your ability to be a force for good.

Let me be clear: it is your birthright to be rich. Rich in money, rich in experience, and rich in giving. You were not born to struggle through a paycheck-to-paycheck life. You were born to thrive. To overflow. To impact others through your strength, your resources, and your leadership.

So don't be shy about it.

Each morning, write down your wealth goal. Be bold. Be specific. Don't whisper your desires, declare them. Tell the Universe what you want and ask for it unapologetically. Your clarity creates your reality.

Now, with that said, I also want to clarify something that's extremely important, especially for the rest of this book.

Whenever I use the word wealth, I'm not just referring to money.

In this book, wealth means work, work that is aligned with your purpose. Work that makes you feel alive. Work that stretches you, grows you, and reminds you that you matter. And every single person has work, whether it's connected to a paycheck or not.

A stay-at-home parent has work. A student has work. A retiree has work. A schoolteacher, a caregiver, a volunteer, an artist, everyone has work. Because work, in its truest form, is how you serve the mission you were put here to fulfill.

You may not be in an income-producing role right now. Maybe you're raising incredible kids, running your household, or pouring into a passion project that hasn't generated revenue yet. That's still work. That's still purpose. And it matters just as much, if not more, than any job that pays you a salary.

Even if you won the lottery tomorrow and never had to earn another dollar again, you'd still need a reason to wake up. You'd still need a mission. Something to give your time, your energy, and your heart to. That's your work. That's what we're talking about when we say "wealth."

So throughout this book, when I refer to wealth, I want you to hear meaningful work. I want you to think of your mission. Your contribution. Your purpose.

Because that, not money alone, is what gives you the fire to rise early, to push through the whirlwind, and to win the day.

☐ **Reflection**

- On a scale of 1 to 10, how would you rate yourself in your **Wealth/Work**?
- What would need to change for you to be a **10/10**?

EVERY. DAMN. DAY.

Relationships

This is the final piece of the success and happiness equation. And ironically, it's the one that usually gets forgotten.

I remember when I first started working in corporate America. The company I worked for had a gym on campus, and every day, a group of us would meet after work to play basketball. It became our religion, we never missed a day. I was in great shape back then, so running full-court for two hours straight was no problem. Most of the guys were in their twenties and thirties, but there was one man who stood out, Mark.

Mark was in his fifties, but he could still run circles around all of us. The man was a beast, one of the best players on the court, hands down. We'd show up early just to see who was there because once teams were picked, you were locked in for the next two hours. Getting on a good team mattered. And let me tell you, if Mark was on your team, you were going to have a good day. If he was on the other team, brace yourself.

Mark could do it all, pull up from three, take it to the hole, defend, rebound, and run the floor like he was twenty-five. And when he took his shirt off, it was like the statue of David had stepped onto the court. Chiseled. Lean. Zero body fat. We all admired Mark, not just because of his game, but because of how he carried himself. Poised. Articulate. Handsome. Accomplished. He was a senior VP at the company, had been there for over twenty years, and was sitting on enough stock to be a multimillionaire. He drove a cherry-red Corvette that was always spotless, like someone followed him around waxing it after every drive.

Over time, Mark and I became close. We'd grab lunch, talk life, career, and sports. He became a mentor to me. One year, he took a month-long trip around the world. He had the money, the tenure, and the freedom to do things like that. When he got back, we met for lunch, and he told me about it all, five-star dinners in France, gondola rides in Italy, beer gardens in Germany.

Then he told me about this tiny café he stumbled across while hiking in the Swiss Alps. He said it was perched on the edge of a mountain with the most breathtaking view he'd ever seen. He sat there sipping coffee while the sky lit up with shades of violet, fuchsia, gold, and orange, like God was painting a masterpiece right in front of him.

And that's when it hit him.

He looked around at all that beauty, felt the crisp air, tasted the perfect espresso, and was overwhelmed with sadness.

He said to me, "Jarvis, I have all of this, but no one to share it with."

Despite all the money, all the accolades, all the freedom, he had no wife. No kids. No real relationships outside of work and our basketball crew. He told me, "You're the only person I talk to regularly."

He sat on that mountaintop and cried. Even though he had success, he didn't have happiness.

And here's the truth. At the end of your life, no one measures you by your success. You measure your life by your fulfillment. And you can't have real fulfillment without meaningful relationships. It doesn't matter how far you climb, how many titles you collect, or how much money you make, if you're alone at the top, it's a lonely place to stand.

Success means nothing if you don't have people to laugh with, cry with, sit beside, and celebrate the journey with you. Don't climb so hard that you forget the people you're climbing for. Don't win the game and lose the ones who were cheering for you.

Every day, you must be just as intentional about your relationships as you are with your health and wealth.

> ☐ **Reflection**
>
> - On a scale of 1 to 10, how would you rate yourself in your **Relationships**?
> - What would need to change for you to be a **10/10**?

Define Your Goals

Now that we've explored the three core areas of happiness and fulfillment, it's time to set some goals for each one. This is where the real work begins, not just dreaming, but defining. And there's one golden rule you need to know when it comes to setting goals: the more specific, the better.

As a general best practice, every goal should be quantifiable and time-bound, meaning there's a clear way to measure progress and a clear deadline for achieving it. Because clarity creates focus. And urgency fuels action.

How do you know if your goal is quantifiable? Simple. It has a number. And just as important, it has a timeline.

By saying, "I want to grow my business," that is a nice intention. But it's vague. It gives your brain no target, no finish line, no scoreboard, and no sense of urgency. A real goal sounds like, "I want to grow my business to $500K in revenue by December 31st." That's clear. That's measurable. That's actionable. Now your brain knows exactly what it's aiming for, and by when.

Same thing with health. Instead of saying, "I want to lose weight," say, "I want to lose 20 pounds by the end of the quarter." Now your habits have a deadline. And that deadline creates pressure and motivation. You've given your goal a pulse.

Without a finish line, you'll procrastinate. You'll drift. You'll let "someday" turn into "never." But once you put a date on it, it becomes real, urgent, and inevitable.

And yes, I understand not every goal in life can be measured with numbers or deadlines. Some areas are more about feeling than figures. Take relationships, for example. You might say, "I want more love in my marriage." That's a beautiful desire. But how do you quantify love?

You don't. And that's okay.

Some parts of life are meant to be felt, not calculated. There's no scoreboard for intimacy. No stopwatch for connection. But that doesn't mean you can't still set goals around those areas. It just means you'll track them differently. Maybe it's committing to a weekly date night. Maybe it's a 30-day challenge to do one thoughtful gesture every day. Maybe it's setting a goal to plan a weekend getaway with your partner this month. Even in the immeasurable, you can still give yourself a direction and a timeframe.

But when it comes to things like health, wealth, productivity, or discipline, if you can add a number and a date to the goal, do it. Because once you can measure it, you'll know if you're still on track or if you're slipping. And most importantly, you'll know exactly what to do to course-correct.

EVERY. DAMN. DAY.

Course Correction

If an airplane takes off from San Francisco en route to New York, but it's even just one degree off its intended flight path, it won't land in New York. Instead, it'll end up in Philadelphia, nearly one hundred miles off course. That might sound extreme, but it's a powerful metaphor for how life works. At the beginning of the journey, a single degree of misalignment may seem small. It's barely noticeable. But as time goes on, that tiny miscalculation compounds, and the distance from your intended destination widens. Before you know it, you've ended up somewhere entirely different from where you meant to go.

This is what happens to so many people. You don't realize you're off track until you look up one day and wonder how you drifted so far from the life you wanted. You wanted a thriving business, but now you're just trying to keep the lights on. You wanted a fit, energetic body, but now you're embarrassed to take your shirt off at the beach. You wanted a deep, connected relationship, but now you feel like strangers under the same roof. You didn't crash. You just drifted. Slowly. Silently. One small misstep at a time.

Airplanes never fly in a perfectly straight line. They're constantly being knocked off course by wind, turbulence, and unexpected weather. Sounds a lot like the whirlwind, right? That's life. You will get knocked off course. That's not a flaw in the system, it's part of the journey. The key isn't avoiding turbulence. The key is building a system that allows you to keep course-correcting along the way.

Every commercial airplane is equipped with a tool called a gyroscope. This device takes over ten thousand measurements per second to determine the plane's precise position and direction. When the wind pushes it off track, the gyroscope immediately sends a signal to the flight computer, which then makes a tiny adjustment to steer the aircraft back toward its target. It's happening constantly, invisible, automatic, and without drama. But none of that is possible without a clearly defined destination. The plane knows exactly where it's going, and it has a system in place to measure whether or not it's on track. That's what allows it to make consistent, real-time corrections. That's what allows it to still arrive at its intended destination.

Your life is no different. You will face resistance. You'll get distracted. You'll lose focus. You'll get overwhelmed, sidetracked, and thrown off by circumstances outside your control. That's inevitable. But if you've set a clear destination, and if you have a system to track your progress, you can always bring yourself back into alignment.

The problem is most people never define the destination. They don't set clear goals. They don't measure progress. They're flying blind, just drifting, hoping that they'll somehow end up somewhere worthwhile. But drifting doesn't lead to destiny. It leads to detours. And that's how you wake up five, ten, or twenty years later, wondering, "How did I get here?"

That's not going to be your story. Now that we know the theory behind crafting strong goals, let's go ahead and build the goals and mission statements that you will write every day.

Goal Examples

Now, it's your turn. Let's walk through crafting one powerful, specific, and time-bound goal for each of the three pillars of a successful life:

1. Health

This is about energy, longevity, and how you show up in your body. Ask yourself:

- What do I want my body to look like?
- What is my ideal weight?
- Is there a habit I want to stop or start for my long-term health?

Examples:

- I will get down to 12% body fat by July 1st.
- I will run a marathon in under four hours this November.
- I will stop drinking alcohol for the next 90 days.
- I will work out 5 days a week for the next 12 weeks.

2. Wealth / Work

Remember... wealth doesn't just mean money. In this book, *wealth* refers to your **work**... your calling, your mission, your purpose. Whether you're an entrepreneur, a school teacher, a stay-at-home parent, or a volunteer... your work is how you show up and serve the world.

Ask yourself:

- What impact do I want to make through my work?
- What measurable results do I want to achieve?
- What outcome would light my soul on fire?

Examples:

- I will double my income this year by launching a new offer.
- I will close 25 real estate transactions by December 31st.
- I will build a movement of 100,000 Morning Heroes in our online community.
- I will gain 100 new clients by the end of Q3.

3. Relationships

This is the soul of your life. Your people. The ones you do it all for. Your spouse, your children, your friends, your community. And most importantly, your relationship with *yourself*.

Ask yourself:

- Who do I want to be in my closest relationships?
- What kind of connection do I want to build?
- What actions can I take to be more intentional and present?

Examples:

- I will go on 52 date nights with my spouse this year (one every week.)
- I will be named "Father of the Year" by my own children (through my actions, not an award).
- I will call my mom once a week for the rest of the year.
- I will build a brotherhood of five high-performing men to mastermind with monthly.

☐ **Take Action**

- Take a moment right now and write down one specific, measurable, and time-bound goal for each category:

    1. Health:
    2. Wealth/Work:
    3. Relationships:

- Scan the QR code for a free journal template that you can use to write your goals EVERY. DAMN. DAY!

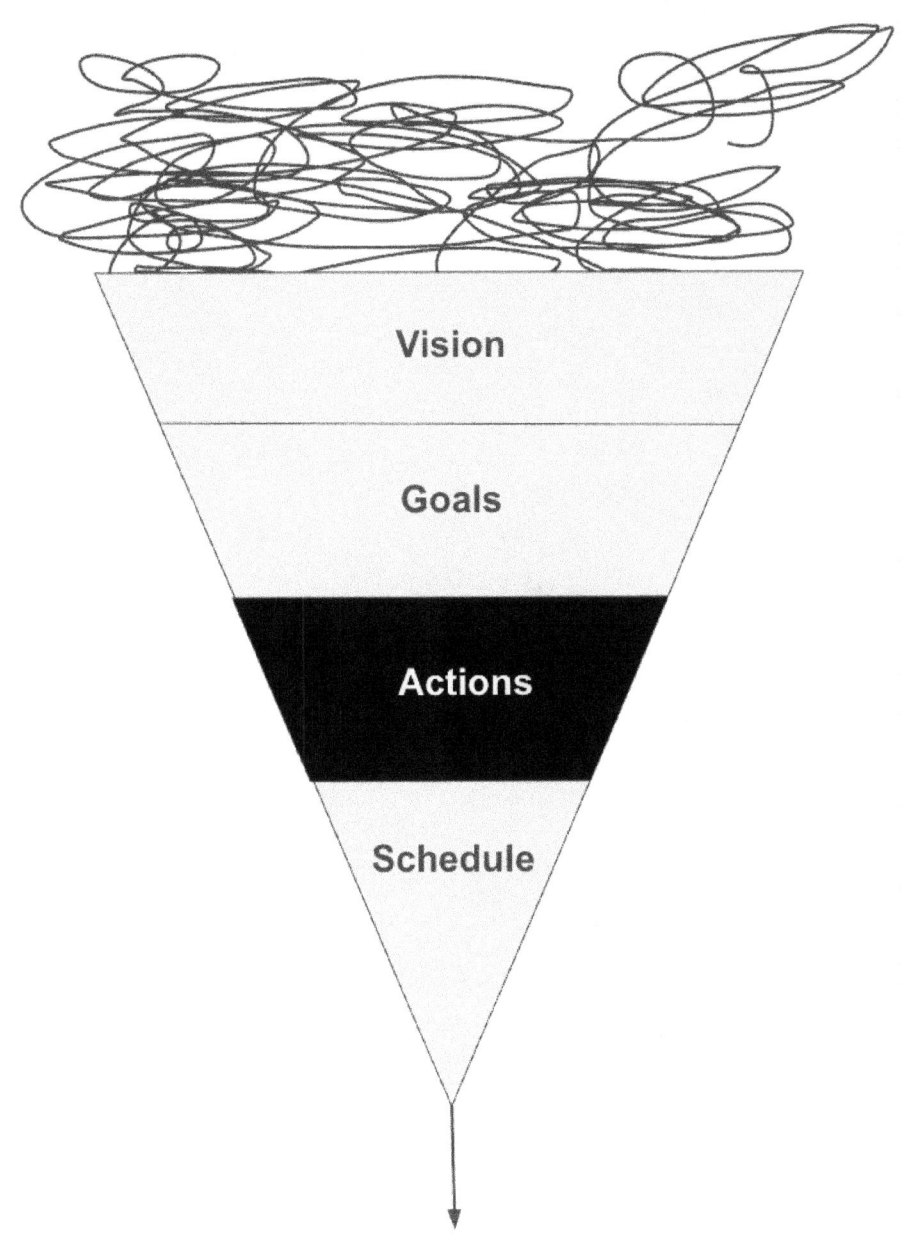

CHAPTER 9
LEVEL 3 INTENTIONS: ACTIONS

"Faith without action is dead."

— The Bible (James 2:26)

Where the Rubber Meets the Road

My mom had all these sayings I never fully understood as a kid. One of her favorites was, "This is where the rubber meets the road."

I'd look around, confused. "What rubber? What road? We're in the living room!"

What she meant was the point where the tire actually connects with the pavement. That contact point is where things get real. The tire can spin as fast as it wants, but if it's not touching the road, it's not going anywhere.

She also used to say, "You're just spinning your wheels." That meant you were using up a lot of energy but making no progress. See, it doesn't matter how fast the wheels are going. If the rubber isn't hitting the road, it's all wasted motion. The wheels are just spinning in place. But once that rubber hits pavement, that's when the car takes off.

Up until now, all the work you've done, clarifying your vision, creating your goals, that's just spinning the wheels. That's potential energy. But your car isn't actually moving yet. We've got to convert that potential into kinetic energy. It's time to let those wheels hit the ground.

It's time to take action on those beautiful goals you created. That's the only way your race car will actually zoom forward and cross the finish line of life.

So the big question is, what actions should you be taking every day to create a life of success and happiness? Enter… the HERO'S Habits.

HERO'S Habits

If success and happiness truly rest on a three-legged stool… health, wealth or meaningful work, and relationships, then the next logical step is to reverse engineer each of those pillars. In other words, if we know where we want to end up, we can work backward to identify the daily habits and actions that will get us there. This idea of reverse engineering is a concept widely used in the world of technology and innovation. Companies will take apart an existing product piece by piece just to understand how it works. Once they identify the key components, they can recreate it using cheaper parts to bring the price down. This approach is how China built a manufacturing empire. They studied what worked and then replicated it at scale.

So I started applying that same engineering mindset to life. I dissected these three areas and worked backward to determine the core habits that would lead to the highest return. If you want better results in these areas, you don't need to guess or rely on motivation. You need a system. You need habits that you can repeat every single day.

Health

Let's start with health. When it comes down to it, health is built on two foundational pillars: movement and nutrition. But not just any kind of movement. It has to be intentional movement that elevates your heart rate. That's the key. Of course, there are other factors that play a role in your health such as sleep, hydration, supplements, and hormones, but if we're keeping it simple and actionable, the two biggest levers you can pull daily are getting your heart rate up and eating clean. Daily exercise that makes you sweat. Clean, nourishing food that fuels your energy. Those two habits alone can change your entire physiology over time. So those are the two habits of better health.

- **H**eart Rate (daily heart-pumping exercise)
- **E**at Right (a clean, healthy diet)

Wealth

Now, let's move to wealth and work. Jim Rohn once said, "Your income will rarely exceed your level of personal development." And he was right. **The more you learn, the more you earn**. Your income is a direct reflection of your ability to solve problems. And the bigger the problems... the more money you make. ... That's why reading is so powerful. Reading unlocks new thinking, new mindsets and new skills that help you solve bigger problems for people or for the company that you work for... resulting in you increasing your income potential... aka, wealth.

But reading alone isn't enough. You also have to take massive action. Gary Keller explains in his book The ONE Thing that every big goal can be boiled down to one single, most impactful action that moves the needle furthest.

When I worked in sales, there were a hundred different things I could have done to generate leads... email campaigns, networking events, advertising, referrals. But one strategy outperformed them all: cold calling. It wasn't sexy, but it worked. So I doubled down. I stopped wasting time on the hundred different things I could do each day and just focused on taking that ONE BIG ACTION of making cold calls. That single habit made me the top sales rep in my division.

The lesson? Each day, focus on taking the ONE BIG ACTION that directly drives your goals forward. It doesn't matter what your goal is... there's always ONE BIG ACTION that trumps all the others for that goal. The problem is that most people don't want to do that action because it's usually the hardest or scariest one. The most successful people, and the richest, don't overwhelm themselves with all the little actions. They have a deep focus on taking the ONE BIG ACTION that really moves the needle.

So those are the two daily habits for growing your wealth: read every day to expand your capacity, and take ONE BIG ACTION.

- **R**ead
- **ON**E BIG ACTION

Relationships

This is the area most often neglected, but it's also the one that defines the quality of your life. At the end of the day, you get what you give. If you want more love, more joy, more connection in your life, you must become the source of it. You must give what you want to receive. If you walk into every room with the intention of lifting someone up, you'll never lack love or community. That's not just feel-good advice. It's a universal principle. It's the law of attraction at work. The more love and positivity you pour into others, the more it pours back into you. Every day, ask yourself: Who can I encourage? Who can I check in on? Who can I praise or acknowledge? The smallest gesture can have the biggest ripple. When you become the source of joy, the world responds in kind. So "spreading Joy" is the daily habit to nurture fulfilling relationships.

- **S**pread Joy

After reverse engineering all three areas of life… health, wealth, and relationships… five daily habits emerged. These habits are simple, powerful, and proven. First, get your heart rate up through daily movement. Second, eat clean and nourish your body. Third, read daily to expand your mind. Fourth, take one bold, needle-moving action toward your biggest goal. And fifth, spread joy by reaching out, encouraging others, and becoming the energy you want to attract.

- **H**eart Rate
- **E**at Right
- **R**ead
- **O**NE BIG ACTION
- **S**pread Joy

The first letter of each of these five habits spells the word "**H.E.R.O.S.**" That's why I call them the HERO'S Habits. These are the five daily actions that lead to a big, full, purpose-driven HERO-ic life. Accomplish each one, and you've just had a 5-star day!

The 5-Star Day

The most popular and most effective way to measure the quality of anything is the 5-star rating system. Whether it's a hotel, a product, or a restaurant, five stars is the gold standard. It's simple, it's intuitive, and it's everywhere for a reason: It works.

When my wife and I got married, we made a vow that extended beyond our wedding day. We promised each other that no matter how busy life got, we would never stop dating. Every single week, without fail, we carve out time for date night. It's not just a nice-to-have; it's a religion! It keeps our relationship vibrant, fun, and connected.

Now that we have two kids, date night has become more than just important… it's non-negotiable. It's not a luxury. It's a necessity. In the whirlwind of parenting, work, responsibilities, and exhaustion, we need time that's just for us. Time to talk. To laugh. To flirt. To remember that we're not just co-parents or business partners… we're soulmates. Because the truth is, if you don't intentionally invest in your relationship, your marriage can slowly erode into nothing more than a roommate agreement for raising kids. And that's not the life we signed up for.

So every week, we take our date night seriously. We choose the restaurant with care. We send each other ideas and compare menus. But we don't just pick a place at random. We check the reviews. Because this isn't just dinner. It's sacred time, and we want to make it count. The tool we trust the most? Yelp.

Yelp, like Amazon, Google, and Walmart, uses a 5-star rating system to evaluate the quality of experiences. If a restaurant has 4.8 stars, it's not just a guess. They're doing something right. The feedback loop is powerful: High ratings reinforce what's working, and low ratings signal something needs to change. It's an elegant system, providing both encouragement and correction in one simple metric.

That's the magic of a good scoring system. It shows you where you're winning, and it gives you instant feedback when you're not. It lets you know when to keep doing what you're doing, and when to course-correct. It's accountability and affirmation wrapped into one.

So that got me thinking… why not use that same system to rate the most important thing of all… *your life?*

That's how the **5-Star Day** was born.

EVERY. DAMN. DAY.

Here's how it works: Every day, you have five opportunities to earn a star... one for each of the **HERO'S Habits**. Each habit is tied to one of the three pillars of a 5-Star life: Health, Wealth/Work, and Relationships.

You earn one star when you:

1. Get your H**eart Rate** up through exercise.
2. **Eat Right** by fueling your body with clean, intentional nutrition.
3. **Read**, learn, or listen to something that develops your mind.
4. Take **ONE Big Action** that moves the needle on your business or work goal.
5. **Spread Joy** by lifting someone up with a message, a moment, or an act of service.

Each habit is worth one star. Do all five in a day? That's a **5-Star Day**. Do it day after day? That's a 5-Star Life!

It takes that universal concept of a 5-star review and applies it to your daily performance. And when you start scoring your days this way, something powerful happens. First, it gives you a tangible sense of winning. You're not just drifting through the day hoping it went well. You *know* whether it did. Your score for the day tells you exactly if you won or not, which creates motivation and a desire to keep showing up. It also gives you instant awareness when something's off. If your score slips, it doesn't go unnoticed. You catch it early, and you can make adjustments before bad habits take root or burnout sets in.

But perhaps the most important reason for scoring your day is that it creates a sense of completion.

Completion

In order to officially win the day, you first have to define what a win even looks like. That might sound obvious, but it's where most people get it wrong. They wake up and dive headfirst into a never-ending to-do list, checking off tasks as fast as they can. But no matter how much they accomplish, it never feels like enough. The unfinished items keep looming in the background, whispering, "You're still behind."

That's the trap. When your day has no clear finish line, you never truly arrive. You end the day feeling incomplete, like you've left a bunch of open loops spinning in your head. And those open loops don't just disappear when the workday ends. They follow you into the evening, into dinner, into bedtime. Your body might stop, but your mind keeps racing.

This is why so many high performers suffer from stress, anxiety, and burnout. It's not that they didn't work hard enough. It's that they never felt done. There was no closure. No signal that said, "You did what mattered today. You can rest now."

But when you define a clear, intentional finish line for your day, everything changes. That one shift, deciding in advance what a win looks like, gives you something powerful: completion.

Completion is what creates peace. It's what allows you to exhale, power down, and go to bed with a sense of accomplishment instead of guilt. It's the mental checkmark that tells your brain, "We're good. We did what we came to do today."

Without that sense of closure, your mind will crave it. And when it doesn't get it, it'll reach for substitutes, something, anything, to escape the discomfort of incompleteness. That's why so many people end their days in front of a screen, binge-watching shows, scrolling endlessly, drinking wine, or reaching for snacks they don't need.

They don't feel like they won, so they try to numb the loss. And this pattern of numbing from incomplete to-do lists is slowly killing them.

EVERY. DAMN. DAY.

Death By 1,000 To-Do's

How many items are on your "to-do list" for today? Twenty? Fifty? Realistically, is it feasible for you to do everything that's on your list for today? Probably not.

When you come up with your list, you write out everything that you want to do, but you probably don't take into account that each item on that list will take a certain amount of time to complete. And there are only 24 hours in the day. So realistically, it's not possible to do all 50 items on your list because you are limited by time.

So what happens? You only get eight items done on your list. Even if they are the 8 most important things on the list, you still only do 8 out of 50. The result: You won't feel accomplished. You will feel defeated and unproductive because you still have a lot on your list. Your brain won't give you credit for the eight items that got accomplished. It will focus on the 42 that didn't get accomplished and say, "Damn, today was a bad day. I only did eight things on my list." You will always feel overloaded, overwhelmed, and stressed out. This is self-defeating and demotivating.

As a result, you might search for a "quick fix" of joy to bring your spirits back up. This usually takes shape as some greasy, fattening food, alcohol, or other mind-numbing substances, or mindless bingeing on TV or social media. These mental "escapes" are a direct result of coping with an overloaded list and unrealistic expectations of what you could or couldn't accomplish in a given day.

This is what turned me from a high producer to plateauing and eventually going down hill until I ended up nearly homeless, living on my aunt's couch. I never truly felt like my days were productive because every day, so much would go undone. The only thing that I looked forward to was a vodka soda at the end of the day. That gradually went from one vodka soda to three or four. It went from me at home by myself to me being out with friends all night. That nightly "mental escape" routine grew out of control until my life started to dismantle.

Subconsciously, you feel defeated when you look at your "to-do list," and you don't feel like you're making progress. This will kick off a knee-jerk reaction to over-indulge in self-soothing habits that lead to self-destruction. A harmless glass of wine every night, a little bit of marijuana to close out the day, a harmless cheeseburger in front of the TV… all of these give you temporary satisfaction, so you feel a little better when you feel like you don't have control. These things keep you stuck in place, or worse, moving backward. And in some extreme cases, on a downward slope to demise.

When I was on my downward slope, I met a guy who owned a successful fitness boutique. He owned a high-end townhome in the middle of downtown and was doing very well for himself. Like me, the pressures of his day-to-day drove him down a path of self-sabotage and destruction. While I was on my sabbatical in Chicago, I got news that he had passed away from a drug overdose. The bad habits that he developed as a coping mechanism to deal with the pressures of his "to-do list" literally killed him.

I would argue that many of our bad habits are subconscious coping strategies to deal with the underlying stresses of our lives. The overwhelming pressures of things to do or things going undone. At best, these bad habits keep us unhappy and unfulfilled. At worst, they will kill us.

But that won't be your life. Starting right here… right now, you will start your day by defining the the five actions that will bring closure to this day (the HERO'S Habits) and then setting out on a path to "WIN THE DAY!"

WIN the Day

Instead of jotting down a scattered to-do list with a hundred random tasks you'll never finish, set an intention for the five actions that actually move the needle. The five actions that will lead to **your** success and happiness.

Ask yourself these five questions every morning:

- **H – Heart Rate**: How will I break a sweat today?
- **E – Eat Right**: What healthy meals will I eat today??
- **R – Read**: What will I read (or listen to) to grow today?
- **O – ONE THING**: What's the single most important action that will grow my business or mission?
- **S – Spread Joy**: How will I put a smile on someone's face today?

This is your blueprint for a **5-star day**.

Once you complete these five simple actions, you can rest easy knowing you **WON** the day. No stress. No overwhelm. No guilt. No need for that wine. No need for that weed. Your reward is something far better... a sense of **completion**. A deep sense of **accomplishment**.

You'll walk taller, smile wider, and carry a contagious energy into every room you enter. You'll be showing up like a **HERO**... for your health, your wealth, and your relationships. And every night, you'll go to bed proud... feeling **successful** and **happy**.

☐ **Reflection**

- Do you ever feel drowned by your to-do list?
- How do you know if you "Won the day" or not?
- If you don't feel like you won the day, what's your knee-jerk reaction to make yourself feel better?

☐ **Take Action**

- From this day forward, you will start defining your "WIN" for each day.
- Reflect on each of these questions:

    - How will you raise your Heart Rate with exercise?
    - How will you eat right today?
    - What will you Read for your personal growth? (This book is the obvious answer!)
    - What's ONE BIG THING that you can do to push your work or career forward?
    - How will you Spread Joy by putting a smile on someone's face?

- Write your answers in your journal and at the end of the night, check off how many you completed. The goal is to have a 5-star day!

EVERY. DAMN. DAY.

- Scan the QR code to download the free WIN THE DAY app. This app will help you set your 5-star intentions and gamify your life so you can Wake up and WIN… EVERY. DAMN. DAY!

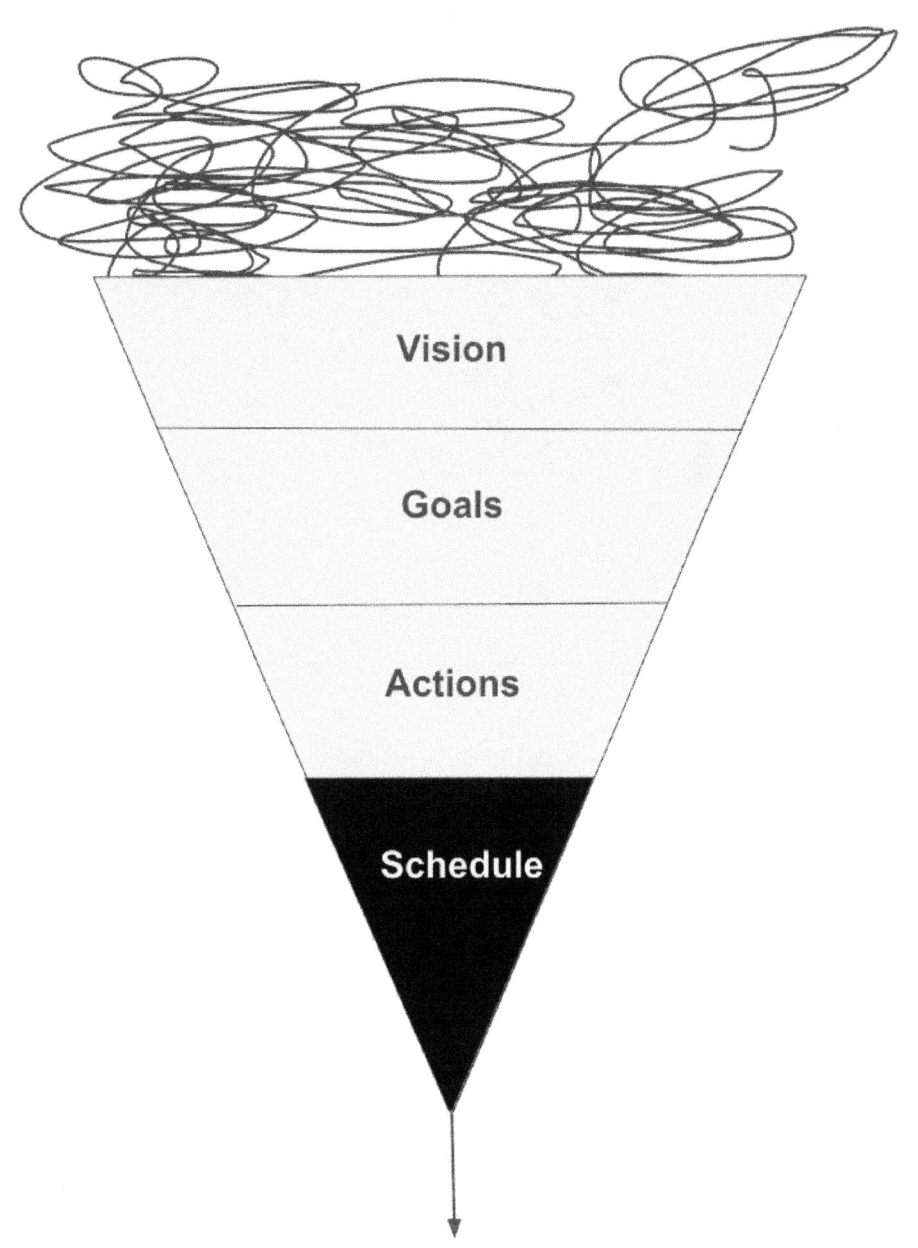

CHAPTER 10
LEVEL 4 INTENTIONS: SCHEDULE

"Every minute you spend in planning saves 10 minutes in execution."

— Brian Tracy

The Scranton Study

In 1997, The University of Scranton conducted a fascinating study on productivity. The researchers asked participants to write down everything they wanted to accomplish that day, just a standard to-do list. At the end of the day, they had to score themselves on how many of those tasks they actually completed. The results were eye-opening. On average, participants only completed about 40% of their lists. Let that sink in. That means more than half of the things people set out to do in a day remained undone.

Sound familiar? If you glance back at your own list from yesterday, I'd bet it tells a similar story. Maybe you started the day with good intentions, motivated and ready to crush it. But then the whirlwind came crashing in. Fires to put out. Messages to respond to. Unexpected distractions. And suddenly, the day was over before you even got to the things that mattered most.

Now, here's where the study gets really interesting. The researchers repeated the experiment with a twist. They asked the same participants to make another to-do list. But this time, instead of simply jotting down tasks, they had to schedule each one, assigning an exact time on the calendar for when they'd do it. "Call Susan" became "Call Susan at 9 a.m." "Exercise" turned into "Go for a run at 7 a.m." The people didn't change. The tasks didn't change. The only variable they added was time.

What they discovered was mind-blowing! Execution rates jumped from 40% to 90%! That's right. Just by assigning a time slot, people more than doubled their follow-through. Why? Because writing down a task is a hope. Your calendar is where your commitments are. Think about it. If something is on your calendar, you won't miss it. Important appointments, work meetings, events that you have to attend. If it's on your calendar, it is locked in as a commitment. However, everything on your to-do list is just a wish. It's like saying, "It will be nice if I get these things done today if I have enough time in between all of my calendar commitments." Everything on your calendar will get attended to. Everything on your list is just icing on the cake. When you schedule something on your calendar, it tells your brain, "This matters. And this is when it's happening." And when you do that, it gets locked into your subconscious, which is the one running the show.

I saw this principle come alive in my own life. Around the time that I read the Scranton study, I had been trying to do a better job of staying connected with my mom. She's my heart and soul. And yet even with the best of intentions, I found myself going days, sometimes weeks, without picking up the phone. Every morning, I'd tell myself, "I need to call her today." And every night, I'd go to bed realizing I hadn't. The day slipped away again, lost to the whirlwind.

Then I remembered the Scranton study. So I gave it a shot. I opened my calendar, found a 30-minute gap between two client calls, and scheduled it: "Call Mom, 1:30 p.m." Simple. Clear. Set in stone. The next day, as I walked out of my meeting and got in the car, I wasn't thinking about it at all. My brain was spinning, thinking about all of the follow-up actions from the client meeting. But then, like magic, a little voice whispered in my ear, "Jarvis, aren't you supposed to be calling your mom right now?"

I stopped. I smiled. I picked up the phone and spent that entire drive reconnecting with the woman who means the world to me. That call wouldn't have happened if I hadn't scheduled it. That's the power of assigning time to your intentions. It's like handing the baton to your subconscious. And your subconscious? Oh, it remembers. It will whisper, nudge, and gently pull you back on track, even when the whirlwind tries to blow you off course. This is because your subconscious obsesses over anything that's predetermined.

Predetermination

Predetermination is one of the most underrated superpowers we have access to. It's the practice of deciding in advance exactly how something is going to happen. When you lock in the decision ahead of time, your subconscious takes over, and at that point, your conscious brain can completely forget about it. Your subconscious will carry the memory for you, and right on cue, it will nudge you when the moment arrives.

Think of your subconscious like the world's most loyal personal assistant. It's with you 24/7, silently sitting beside you with a notepad, paying attention to everything you commit to. While your conscious mind is getting bombarded with distractions, conversations, emails, and emotions, your subconscious is calmly taking notes in the background, waiting for the right moment to whisper, "Hey, remember that thing you said you were going to do?"

That's exactly what happened the day I scheduled a call with my mom. When 1:30 rolled around, I didn't consciously remember it. I wasn't scanning my to-do list or wracking my brain for what came next. I was just moving through my day like normal. But as soon as I got in the car, that inner voice, my subconscious copilot, spoke up. It was as if it had been riding shotgun all along. "Hey Jarvis, it's 1:30. Weren't you supposed to call your mom?"

I smiled and reached for my phone.

That's the beauty of predetermination. It's not about micromanaging your day or becoming some robotic version of yourself. It's about offloading mental clutter. Once you've scheduled your commitments, you no longer have to carry them. Your calendar becomes the command center. Your subconscious becomes the reminder system. You just follow the plan you already created.

It's a remarkably peaceful way to live. No anxiety. No decision fatigue. Just trust in the process. When your day is built on clear intentions that are locked in ahead of time on your calendar, you stop reacting and start flowing. Your brain isn't scrambling to remember everything. You don't waste energy switching gears. You just execute the next move, knowing that your most important priorities are already accounted for. And if, for a moment, you forget, don't worry. That voice inside will be right there, nudging you back on course.

But there's an even more powerful explanation for why predetermination works so well, and it's highlighted by some profound research from INC. Magazine.

The Inc Magazine Study

In 2020, Inc. Magazine conducted a study on worker productivity. They followed 1,000 professionals through the course of a standard eight-hour workday to answer one simple question: How much actual work gets done in a typical day?

What they discovered was both surprising and sobering. Out of those eight hours, the average person only completed two hours and fifty-three minutes of real, meaningful work. Less than three hours of true productivity. Now, before you shrug that off, it helps to understand how they defined the work being measured. The researchers broke it into two distinct categories: high-impact activities and low-impact activities. High-impact tasks were those that directly moved the needle. These were the actions that aligned with a person's primary goals and responsibilities... in other words, the things that mattered. Low-impact activities included things like reading newsletters, scrolling social media, online shopping, messaging friends, doing chores, or running errands. These were the distractions that pulled people away from meaningful progress.

The results were eye-opening. Every single participant stayed busy all day long, but most of that busyness was spent on things that didn't actually matter. It gets even more interesting. When asked how much productive work they thought they had done, most people estimated around six hours. But in reality, they had done less than half that. This reveals a deeply rooted disconnect. They had fallen into the same trap that most people do confusing being busy with being productive. The truth is, staying in motion is not the same as making progress. And that illusion of progress is exactly what keeps people spinning their wheels, stuck in a cycle of high effort but low results.

When the researchers dug deeper into why people waste so much time in their day on low-level activities, they noticed one thing that they all had in common. Their day was filled with blank space.

Blank Space

Most of the participants in the study used a to-do list and a calendar to map out what they needed to get done for the day. Their calendars were filled with the usual appointments... client meetings, team huddles, Zoom calls, and check-ins. But outside of those clearly defined appointments, their schedules were wide open. Blank space. Gaps in time where nothing was planned.

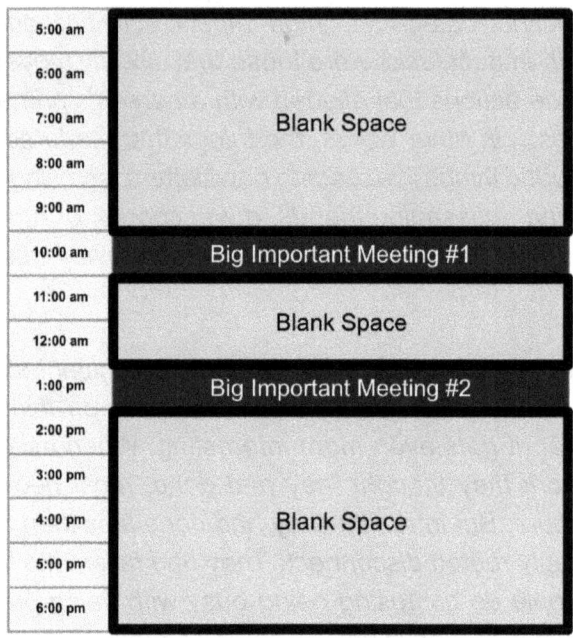

And that's where the day fell apart.

What do you think happens in the blank space of someone's day? I'll give you a hint… it starts with "Whirl" and ends with "Wind." That's right. The whirlwind happens! The chaos. The noise. The endless stream of emails, text messages, news alerts, social media scrolls, and that sudden, unexplainable urge to reorganize your desk for no reason at all. That's the whirlwind, and it loves blank space. It feeds on unclaimed time. And the moment your calendar has a gap, the whirlwind swoops in and fills it with everything *but* the important stuff.

If you don't have a clear plan for what you're doing in any given time slot, the whirlwind will take over. Every time. It's not a question of *if*... it's a guarantee. And once it grabs you, it doesn't let go. You get to the end of the day wondering where the time went. Wondering how you were busy for eight hours but didn't have time to do the #1 thing on your list.

It's not just you. We all suffer from this. It's because we have Prehistoric Brains.

The Prehistoric Brain

To understand why we waste time or avoid doing the most important things on our list, we have to go all the way back... to our prehistoric roots.

Back then, survival was the name of the game. Most of our energy went toward three things:

- Running **from** predators
- Running **after** food
- Running **after** mates

All three required sudden, explosive bursts of energy. So over time, our brains evolved with one primary goal: conserve as much energy as possible. That way, we'd always have enough gas in the tank if a tiger started chasing us or if dinner bolted across the field.

This energy-saving system worked brilliantly for thousands of years. It helped us survive, thrive, and eventually dominate as a species.

But here's the problem... we don't live like that anymore. There are no tigers. We're not chasing buffalo across the plains. But our brain is still wired to conserve energy at all costs. That's why when your calendar has empty space, when nothing specific is planned, your brain defaults to the easy stuff. Scrolling. Snacking. Distracting. Procrastinating.

Because your prehistoric brain is whispering, "Let's not waste energy on something hard right now, we might need that later."

So no, it's not your fault that you procrastinate. You were literally born this way. But now that you know this, you can do something about it. You don't have to stay a victim of your caveman wiring. Each morning, you must make an aggressive assault on any blank space in your calendar. Schedule your entire day so that there is zero blank space. This is what we call the Zero Calendar.

EVERY. DAMN. DAY.

5:00 AM	Power Hour
6:00 AM	★ Go To Gym
7:00 AM	Get Ready For Work
8:00 AM	Commute / Transition
9:00 AM	★ My One Big Action - Send Sales Proposals
11:00 AM	Emails & Admin
12:00 PM	Lunch - Chicken, Broccoli and Brown Rice
1:00 PM	Meetings and Appointments
3:00 PM	Work on Presentation
4:00 PM	Admin Work
5:00 PM	★ Pick up Kids and take them to the park
6:00 PM	★ Cook a Healthy Dinner for the family
7:00 PM	Netflix Time
8:00 PM	★ Power Down Hour - Read a book
9:00 PM	Sleep

The Zero Calendar

The Zero Calendar is going to be your secret weapon to living a powerful and productive life. You will no longer waste time... you will no longer procrastinate. You will move through your day with precision and poise, executing everything that matters without even thinking about it. Let me walk you through the process that you will go through each morning step by step.

Step 1: Confirm Your Appointments

First things first, look at your calendar. Your day is already likely to have some appointments, meetings, or other commitments. Look them over, confirm that they are correct, and then mentally commit to them.

But don't stop there. As you're confirming your appointments, add buffer times around them. Whether it's a commute to an in-person meeting or a few minutes to prepare mentally for a call, you want to ensure you're not rushing between tasks. Add in a buffer so you're never scrambling. Buffer time is your gift to yourself. It allows for smooth transitions, and that means less stress and more control.

Step 2: Fill in the Blank Spaces

Now that you've confirmed your appointments and scheduled your buffer times, it's time to fill in all the blank spaces on your calendar. You know the habits that fuel your success. The ones that give you the energy, focus, and drive to keep going day in and day out. These are your Hero Habits, and now it's time to lock them into your calendar.

First, schedule in your exercise time. Your heart rate commitment is the foundation for high energy and peak performance, so treat it like any important meeting. Block out a time that works for you and make sure it's non-negotiable. This is a must-do, not a nice-to-do.

Next, get clear on your eating schedule. Block out time for each of your meals, but don't just schedule the time. Be specific. Write down exactly what you're going to eat in that time block. The goal is to eliminate decision fatigue. You've already planned it, so when that time comes, all you have to do is show up and enjoy your meal.

After that, schedule your growth activity. This could be your reading, training, or any other activity that adds value to your personal or professional growth. For me, I like to combine my exercise and growth activity by listening to audiobooks while I work out. This way, I get a two-for-one: physical activity and mental stimulation all in one. But whatever works best for you, be sure to lock that into your calendar.

Step 3: Block Time for Your One Big Thing

Now, we're moving on to the most important commitment of your day: your One Big Thing. This is the task that will move the needle the most toward your goals. It's the thing that, when completed, will make you feel the most accomplished. It could be something related to your business, a big project, or something personal. Whatever it is, make sure to block out at least two hours for it.

This is not just a quick task… it's a significant commitment. It's the work that requires your undivided attention and energy. Don't skimp on this block of time. The goal is to create enough space to dive deep into your most important work and do it without distraction.

Step 4: Time for Spreading Joy and Downtime

Your calendar needs to reflect the importance of rest and rejuvenation too. As much as you need to schedule your work, you also need to prioritize time for spreading joy and your downtime.

Block out time to enjoy your family, to relax, and to recharge. If dinner with your family is important to you, put it on the calendar. Block out time to play with your kids, watch a movie, or simply unwind. Your calendar should be a reflection of a balanced, fulfilling life.

Step 5: The Final Step

Once you've added your appointments, your Hero Habits, your One Big Thing, and your downtime, look at your day. It should be full… from the moment you wake up until you go to bed. The goal here is to create a day that flows seamlessly, with every single commitment scheduled and accounted for. When you have this structure in place, you're no longer wasting time deciding what to do next, and you're certainly not left wondering where your time went.

This is your Zero Calendar, your roadmap to a productive, balanced, and purposeful day. By filling your calendar with the things that matter most… your work, your health, your family. You're setting yourself up for a day that reflects your highest priorities. This is your blueprint for living a 5-star life!

☐ **Reflection**

- Where did blank space swallow your day yesterday? Be specific.
- What % of your time do you spend on high-impact vs. low-impact activities?

☐ **Take Action**

- Let's do your zero calendar right now!

    1. **Confirm + Buffer** Open tomorrow's calendar. Confirm all appointments. Add buffers before/after each.
    2. **Block Your "One Big Thing"** Schedule a **60 to 120-minute** deep-work block for the task that moves your Work or Career goal forward. Title it with a verb + outcome (e.g., "Draft 2 pages of Chapter 3" or "Make 25 calls" etc).
    3. **Schedule the remaining HERO Habits**
        - Heart Rate (exercise): block the exact time and what activity you will do.
        - Eat Right: block meals + **actually write what you are eating** in the event notes.
        - Read/Grow: If you listen with Audible, you can combine with other activities like working out or commuting.
        - Spread Joy: block time to text/call someone intentionally.
    4. **Zero the Gaps** Fill the remaining blank space with purposeful labels (prep, commute, admin sweep, family dinner, unwind). No unnamed hours.

** The 5-Star Planner has a built-in Zero Calendar so you can plan your perfect day every day. If you want a free copy, just scan the QR code below:

CHAPTER 11
THE MORNING PRACTICE

"Either you run the day, or the day runs you!"

— Jim Rohn

Putting It All Together

Let's put it all together into what I call "The Morning Practice." This is how we take all the pieces of the V.G.A.S. framework and put them into one powerful, explosive routine that you can do in as little as 15 minutes each morning.

And it's fitting that it spells VGAS because what happens when you pour gas on a flame? It *explodes*! That's exactly what will happen every single morning when you "GAS up" your day. When you pour GAS on the fire of your goals, you'll explode with power. You'll explode with productivity. You'll fly through your day like a task-chopping ninja, executing with precision, and becoming the superhero version of yourself.

So let's break this down, step by step, and show you exactly how to make your mornings the most powerful time of your day in as little as 15 minutes.

Step 1: Connect to Your Vision (5 to 10 mins)

The very first step of the Morning Practice is to connect to your vision. Before you leap into the rush of the day, before emails, phone calls, and responsibilities start competing for your attention, you need to anchor yourself in something higher. This step isn't about doing more. It's about doing less. It's about slowing down. Because paradoxically, the fastest way to speed up is to first slow down. If you want clarity, if you want focus, if you want the kind of guidance that keeps you moving toward your biggest goals, you must first stop and listen.

Think of this as an active pause. For most people, mornings begin in chaos... alarms buzzing, phones lighting up, kids needing attention, the mental chatter already racing ahead into the whirlwind of the day. But clarity does not come from chaos. Wisdom does not come from noise. The universe does not shout; it whispers. And if your life is too loud, you'll miss it. That's why this step is so important: it's about creating enough silence in your morning to hear those whispers. Some call it meditation. Others call it prayer. I call it listening. Because that's really what it is. It's a deliberate moment of quiet where you are open to receiving the answers that are already trying to find you.

When you connect to your vision, you're tuning your mind and heart like a radio dial. The answers are already being broadcast, through your intuition, through the Holy Spirit, through that little birdie on your shoulder, but unless you dial into the right frequency, the message comes through as static. Active listening is how you clear the static. I recommend you give yourself at least five to ten minutes of stillness. Set a timer if you need to. Close your eyes. Put on some meditation music, ambient soundscapes, or binaural beats to help drown out external distractions. And then, simply listen. Not with the intent to think, not with the pressure to force anything, but with an openness to receive.

In this silence, you are seeking. You are waiting for a word, a phrase, a spark of wisdom. Sometimes it comes as a download, an idea that rushes in fully formed. Other times, it's just a small nudge, a gentle direction, a subtle impression that feels like it's pointing you forward. Don't overanalyze it. Don't question it. Just notice it. Write it down if you need to. This is your guidance for the day. This is the universe aligning your steps with your vision.

When you consistently practice this morning connection, you'll notice something remarkable: your days start to feel guided. You'll feel less like you're running blind through the whirlwind and more like you're walking in step with a bigger plan. You'll begin to recognize patterns, synchronicities, and opportunities that you might have missed otherwise. By beginning every morning with a pause, you give yourself permission to move through the day with purpose, not just speed. And purpose always outpaces hustle in the long run.

Step 2: Write Your Goals (2 mins)

Earlier in this book, you did the work of defining your goals. But here's the truth: writing them down once is not enough. That's why 90% of people who set New Year's resolutions fall back into their old ways within just two weeks. The problem isn't that they lack ambition. The problem is that they forget. They let their goals fade into the background noise of life, and when the goals fade, so does the motivation to pursue them.

That's why in the Morning Practice, you will write your goals every single day. This simple act accomplishes two powerful things. First, it keeps your goals top of mind. When you begin the day by writing down what you're after, you start to see the world through a different filter. Your mind is tuned, your awareness sharpened. Suddenly, opportunities that align with your goals jump out at you. Decisions become easier because you already know what matters most. Daily reminders create daily alignment.

The second reason you write your goals every day is what I call behavioral alignment. Here's how the brain works: You have two operating systems. Your conscious brain is the visionary. It's the part that dreams, sets intentions, and imagines the future you want to create. But your conscious brain isn't in the driver's seat. Your subconscious brain is the one that controls your behaviors, and your behaviors are what ultimately shape your results. The challenge is that your subconscious is lazy. It defaults to comfort, shortcuts, and cravings. It would rather reach for the donut than the dumbbell. That's why so many people say they want to lose weight but end up binging on pizza. It's not a lack of willpower. It's misalignment between the conscious and the subconscious.

The key, then, is to bring your subconscious into alignment with your conscious intentions. And the way you do that is through repetition. Every time you write your goals, you're giving your subconscious its marching orders. You're programming it with the vision you want it to serve. Over time, the gap between what you say you want and what you actually do starts to close. You begin to notice your behaviors naturally shifting to support your goals rather than sabotage them. Writing your goals every morning is not just a ritual… it's a rewiring process. It's how you train your subconscious to carry out the life your conscious brain designed.

So don't underestimate this step. It may feel redundant. It may even feel unnecessary. But this simple discipline creates alignment, and alignment creates results. The act of writing your goals daily is the bridge between wishing for a better life and actually living it.

Step 3: Define Your 5-Star Actions (2 mins)

Once you've sat in silence to get some clarity on your vision, and then written your goals, it's time to set your intentions for the day. This is where you plan your 5-star actions, the specific tasks that will move you toward your goals. We've already covered your HERO'S Habits, which are the five habits that will shape your success: *heart rate, eating right, growth, one big action, and spreading joy.*

Go through each one and set an intention for the day:

1. **Heart Rate** – How will you move your body today? How will you raise your heart rate and break a sweat? This is non-negotiable. This activates your HERO inside of you so you show up with power all day long.
2. **Eat Right** – How will you stick to your eating discipline? What will you fuel your body with to ensure maximum energy and focus? Set an intention to nourish your body with clean, high-quality food.
3. **Read**– What will you read or listen to today to keep your mind growing? This could be a book, a podcast, or anything that enriches your knowledge and helps you grow in your personal or professional life.
4. **One Big Action** – What's the one big action you can take today that will move you the closest to your wealth goal? This is your *one thing*, and it should be your top priority.
5. **Spread Joy** – Who can you send a thoughtful message to today? Who can you put a smile on their face? Spreading joy isn't just about helping others. It's about lifting your own energy in the process.

Set an intention for each of these areas. This is your 5-star day. The only thing left to do is plan out exactly how you're going to get it all done. That takes us to the final step of the practice.

Step 4: "Zero Out" Your Calendar (5 mins)

The final step of the Morning Practice is where everything comes together. Once you've connected to your vision, written your goals, and set your 5-star intentions, it's time to translate all of that clarity into an actual game plan. This is where you **zero out your day.**

Zeroing out means you don't leave a single hour to chance. Instead of drifting through the day, reacting to whatever shows up, you take full control by assigning a purpose to every block of time. From the moment you wake up until the moment your head hits the pillow, every hour has a name, a job, a reason for existing. This includes your HERO'S Habits, your most important work tasks, your meetings, your family commitments... even your downtime. If it matters, it belongs on the calendar.

When you zero calendar, you are essentially telling your time where to go instead of wondering where it went. You eliminate the gaps where procrastination and distraction usually creep in. You build a roadmap that ensures the things that matter most don't get crowded out by the noise of the whirlwind. And because your HERO'S Habits are built into that roadmap, you've already stacked the deck in your favor for having a 5-star day.

Think about how powerful that is. Imagine waking up each morning and knowing exactly what you'll be doing, when you'll be doing it, and why it matters. No wasted energy trying to figure out what's next. No falling into rabbit holes because you didn't have a plan. Just clarity, confidence, and momentum carrying you forward hour by hour. By the time you finish this step, you've already won half the battle. The rest of the day is simply following through on the plan you've laid out.

And here's the best part: when you consistently zero out your days, 5-star days stop being the exception and start becoming the norm. You won't just hope for a good day... you'll design it. You won't leave your success to chance... you'll schedule it. And with enough 5-star days stacked together, you create a 5-star life.

The 5-Star Life

Imagine this: you wake up to peace and quiet. No email notifications, no kids screaming, no whirlwind waiting to hijack your day. Just silence. Stillness. You sit down, and before the world has a chance to pull at you, you plan your day with intention. You schedule your exercise, your healthy meals, your one most important task… the one thing that will move your life forward today. You even carve out space to do something thoughtful for a friend because you're not just building a productive life, you're building a meaningful one. Since you have the extra time, you go break a good sweat to ignite your energy for the day, and you feel amazing.

You move through the day with ease and flow. No more procrastinating. No more spinning in circles, bouncing between half-finished tasks. No more collapsing into bed at night, wondering where your time went or what you actually accomplished. Because you planned it. You owned it. And now, when your head hits the pillow, it hits with peace because you crushed everything that matters most.

This is the power of your morning practice. When you take control of your day, when you map out every hour from wake-up to wind-down, you stop drifting through life. You stop living on accident. And you start executing with surgical precision. You start choosing how your energy gets used, where your focus goes, and what gets your time. And that's when the magic happens.

This isn't just about productivity. It's not just about getting more done. It's about becoming someone different. Someone intentional. Someone powerful. Someone fulfilled. This is about becoming the version of you who always shows up, who leads their day instead of reacting to it, who follows through, who builds a life of purpose on purpose.

Your Morning Practice is how you gain your superpowers for the day. It's how you strap on your cape so you can go save the world.

Strap on Your Cape

This isn't just a morning routine... it's a ritual of transformation. It's your powerful pause before the chaos, the stillness before the storm. It's how you slow down in order to speed up. And it happens in complete silence. No phone. No email. No notifications buzzing for your attention. No kids tugging at your leg. No whirlwind chasing you down. That's the reason you wake up early. Not because it's trendy or tough, but because you need that space. You create that space. You protect that space like your life depends on it. Because in many ways, it does.

Earlier in this book, I talked about how Clark Kent steps into a phone booth to transform into Superman. The booth itself doesn't give him powers; it simply gives him the privacy and peace to go through his transformation. In that phone booth, he straps on his cape. It's the cape that actually gives him his superpowers.

Your morning practice is your cape.

Every time you sit down in the quiet, every time you write out your goals, every time you set your intentions for a 5-star day, every time you zero out your calendar, you're undergoing your own HERO transformation. You enter as the distracted, overwhelmed version of yourself, but you emerge locked in, fired up, and fully activated. You become the superhuman version of you. The one who follows through. The one who executes. The one who leads with clarity and conviction.

This isn't just how you win the day. This is how you save it.

You save it for your goals. You save it for your family. You save it for your company. You save it for your community.

This is how heroes are made, not in the spotlight, not in the noise, but in the shadows of early morning silence, inside their phone booth.

EVERY. DAMN. DAY.

So wake up early. Sit in silence and set your HERO'S intentions. Strap on your cape. Win the morning. Win the day.

Every. Damn. Day.

☐ **Reflection:**

- Which of the HERO'S Habits is most natural for you right now? Which one do you tend to neglect?
- What's one thing you could add to your Morning Practice tomorrow that would instantly make your day more intentional?

☐ **Take Action**

- **Download the Win The Day App** – It will guide you through your morning practice every single morning so you can WIN every day!
- **Grab the 5 Star Planner** – If you prefer putting pen to paper, these tools will help you map out your day with total clarity and structure.

** Scan the code to get both of these free resources.

WAKE UP EARLY

INTENTIONS

NO DAYS OFF

CHAPTER 12
THE POWER OF CONSISTENCY

"Long-term consistency beats short-term intensity"

— Bruce Lee

Be Gritty

We have now come to the heart and soul of this entire book. This is truly where the rubber meets the road. I know I've said that before, but this time, I *mean* it! If taking action is how you start moving the car forward, then *No Days Off* is how you accelerate across the finish line. Because let's be honest: Anyone can start fast and still lose the race. The people who win are the ones who can keep accelerating when the excitement wears off. They don't just start. They keep going. Your consistency is the secret. It's the difference between burning out halfway and crossing the line with your hands held high in victory.

Consistency is the number one determining factor in a person's success. Not skill. Not knowledge. Not intelligence or raw talent. In her book *Grit*, Angela Duckworth shares a decade of research studying what truly separates the successful from everyone else. The answer? Grit. Not a shiny degree. Not natural ability. Grit. She defines it as the unshakable fortitude to do hard things, even when you don't feel like it. Even when it's uncomfortable, inconvenient, or unrewarding in the moment.

To me, grit is just another word for consistency. The people who experience outrageous success, they're not superheroes. They're just consistent. They get up early even when they're tired. They complete their ONE BIG ACTION for the day even when the results are invisible. They choose the healthy meal even when no one's watching. They show up to the gym when every excuse is screaming at them to skip. They bring joy, energy, and presence to others even on days they feel off. Their power comes from discipline. Their edge comes from follow-through. And their results are a direct byproduct of that consistency. They're not better... they just show up more often.

And that's the great equalizer. You don't need to be the smartest or the strongest. You just need to be the most *consistent*.

There's no greater display of this concept than examining the growth of a little 'ol penny.

The Penny

Let's take a moment to examine the true power of consistency. Imagine I gave you a single penny and told you to double it every day for 30 days. That's it. No fancy math, no elaborate formula. Just one simple action. Take that penny and double it. Day after day. On the first day, you've got one penny. The next you have two pennies. Then four. Then eight. Sixteen. Thirty-two. It sounds small and insignificant, almost laughable. But you keep at it. You double it every single day for 30 days straight. Now, here's the big question: How much do you think you'd have on Day 30?

EVERY. DAMN. DAY.

- A. $50
- B. $500
- C. $5,000
- D. $50,000
- E. $500,000
- F. $5,000,000

I've walked through this exact scenario with audiences at countless speaking events. And let me tell you, the answers are all over the place. Most people throw out numbers anywhere from $100 to maybe $100,000. Logical guesses. But every time, I get to deliver the jaw-dropping truth that stops people in their tracks.

If you doubled a penny for 30 straight days, on the final day, you would have $5,368,709. That's right… **over five million dollars!** That tiny, insignificant penny becomes a massive fortune. And not because of luck or timing. Because of one thing: consistent, relentless action over time. That is the compounding power of showing up. The power of doing the small thing, day after day, even when it doesn't look like it's making a difference. Until one day, it changes everything.

But let's take this tough experiment to the next level. Let's say I told you it was okay to skip a few days. No need to be perfect. Instead of doubling the penny every single day, you only need to double it every *other* day. That doesn't sound too bad, right? I know you're not greedy… you don't need $5 million. So go ahead. Give yourself a break. It's OK to take you foot off the gas a bit.

Naturally, most people assume that doing half the work would mean getting about half the results. I usually hear guesses somewhere between $10,000 and maybe $2.5 million. But the actual result?

Just $327.

You read that right! Skipping days drops your outcome from over $5,000,000… to a measly $327. That's the cost of inconsistency. That's the hidden tax of "every now and then."

And it's the greatest lesson life will ever teach you.

Most people operate on an "every now and then" rhythm. They wake up early every now and then. They eat clean every now and then. They go to the gym every now and then. They stick to routines every now and then. And then they wonder why their results are average at best. They wonder why they feel stuck. Frustrated. Unfulfilled. But here's the truth they're missing: $5-million-level results don't come from what you do *every now and then*. They come from what you do *every single day!*

The people who win big in life are not always the smartest, the most talented, or the most connected. They're simply the ones who made a decision to stop dabbling, and start dominating! Not sometimes. Not when they feel like it. But *Every. Damn. Day!*

I learned this lesson the hard way on the night of the *almost* Perfect Game.

The Perfect Game

I remember one year I joined a bowling league. Now, let's be clear, I wasn't anything special. I was an average bowler at best, holding steady around a 160 average. But then, there was this one night. A magical night. I was locked in. Every throw felt perfect. Strike after strike. Frame after frame. I could feel the momentum building with every ball I released. At first, I didn't think much of it. But then people from the other lanes started to notice. They glanced over, saw the scoreboard filling up with X after X after X, and suddenly, the entire bowling alley was watching me.

By the time I got to the final frame, a full crowd had gathered. Phones out. Cheers echoing down the lane. I was one throw away from doing the unthinkable, scoring a perfect 300!

People were literally holding their breath. One throw stood between me and bowling immortality. One final chance to etch my name in the record books and go down as a local legend.

I stepped up, took a deep breath, and let it rip.

The ball kissed the pocket clean, but one pin, just one stubborn pin, stood tall. I missed the perfect game by a single pin. My final score was a 299.

Still, the crowd erupted. People were jumping up and down. They lifted me into the air like I'd just won the Super Bowl. I'm not exaggerating… they literally picked me up and carried me around the alley! It was surreal. One of the best days of my life. (I mean, my wedding day still holds the crown, but this was a close second!)

But here's what's wild. Out of the 100 bowlers in that league, I finished the season ranked 60th.

How is that possible?

Because despite that one near-perfect night, my average was still just 160. My consistency, or lack thereof, caught up with me. One magical night couldn't erase the mediocre weeks that came before it. One brilliant moment didn't make me a champion. It made me a highlight. A blip.

That experience taught me something I'll never forget. One exceptional day doesn't mean much if it's surrounded by inconsistency. One A+ day can't rewrite a C-average life. You might have moments of greatness, but unless you show up like that again and again and again, it won't change your trajectory.

That's because the Universe is watching you, and it has your goals on layaway.

Goals on Layaway

Back in the day, department stores had this system called "layaway." This was before credit cards were popular. If you wanted to purchase an item but you didn't have all the money to pay for it, you could reserve it and the store would hold it for you until you could pay for it. They had a little room in the back of the store called the "layaway room." The item would be sitting there, waiting, and you could make gradual payments over time until you paid down the balance of the item, and then you get to take it home.

EVERY. DAMN. DAY.

I still remember going to the store with my mother, wanting to get the newest Nintendo gaming system. My mother agreed, but I had to pay for it myself. At the time, I was cutting lawns for my neighbors to make extra money. Nowadays, you can get a fancy lawnmower with a self-driving motor that pushes with very little effort, but that didn't exist when I was a kid. We had a big, heavy lawnmower that was bigger than me. It felt like I was trying to push a car across the grass. I would spend all weekend dragging this big hunk of metal and steel all around the neighborhood in 90-degree heat until I had made enough money to make a payment on my Nintendo system. We would go to Toys-R-Us and I would run to the layaway room and put the cash on the counter. The kind lady would take the money, tell me the new balance, and we would walk out of the store empty-handed.

The next weekend, we would do the same cycle. Hustle and grind, pay down the balance, and walk out empty-handed. This went on for months, until finally, we walked in there and we made the final payment. I still remember the feeling when that kind lady walked into the back of that room and came out with a brand-new shiny Nintendo gaming system in her hand. When she handed it to me, it was the greatest feeling in the world. All of the hard work wasn't in vain. All of the scrapes and bruises, all of the times that I had missed out on doing fun things with my friends, all of the times that I walked out of the store empty-handed. I was finally holding in my hands my reward for all of the sacrifices that I had made!

You see, I think the Universe has all of your goals waiting for you on layaway. You won't immediately get everything that you ask for. There is a balance to be paid. And your "discipline" is the currency that you use to pay down your balance. "Discipline" is the act of doing hard things even when you don't feel like it. Waking up early is a discipline. Setting your intentions is a discipline. Exercising and eating healthy are disciplines. These things don't show an immediate return, so it's hard to stick to them, but every day that you do them you are paying down your balance.

Every day that you get up and do your morning practice, it's like you're paying down the balance. It's like you're walking into the store and making a deposit. Each day you're walking away empty-handed. Each day you're not seeing the result. Until one day, you hit your tipping point, and that's the day where all of a sudden, it seems like a windfall of favor is coming out of nowhere. All of the goals that you've been writing every morning are finally starting to materialize. Everything is just flowing in your life.

You've hit your tipping point because you've been consistently paying down the balance. You've consistently paid your dues every day. You showed up even on days you didn't feel like it. And the Universe rewards the people who stick to their disciplines EVERY. DAMN. DAY. Everything you want is waiting for you in layaway. The Universe is just waiting to see how bad you want it.

☐ Reflection

- Where in your life are you operating on an "every now and then" rhythm instead of EVERY. DAMN. DAY consistency?
- What one daily habit would compound the fastest if you simply stopped skipping days?

☐ Take Action

- Declare this out loud: *"I am not satisfied with $300 level results in my life. I was built for greatness! From this day forward, I will Wake up and WIN, EVERY. DAMN. DAY!"*
- *Scan the QR code to join the Morning Hero community and post the declaration statement above. This will solidify your intentions with the Universe and let the world know how serious you are!*

CHAPTER 13
PROGRAM YOUR AUTOPILOT

"We are what we repeatedly do. Excellence, then, is not an act, but a habit"

— Aristotle

Your Toddler Brain

If you want to get yourself to do something consistently, you have to program it into your autopilot. When something becomes part of your natural autopilot programming, you do it without even realizing it. You probably don't even remember brushing your teeth this morning. You just got up, walked into the bathroom, and performed the same robotic routine you've done thousands of times. That's because you don't have to consciously think about it anymore; it's built into your subconscious.

If you want to turn any behavior into an automatic routine, you have to program it into your subconscious so it happens naturally. But here's the tricky part: your subconscious brain is like a toddler.

That's right. The part of your mind that drives 90 percent of your behavior is basically a 3-year-old on a sugar high. It wants what it wants, and it wants it now! It doesn't care about your goals. It doesn't care about your vision board. It wants pizza. It wants to scroll Instagram. It wants a nap.

And you can't reason with a toddler. You can't sit your 3-year-old down and say, "Listen, sweetie, if you don't get in the car right now, we'll be late for school, and that will affect your long-term education trajectory." They don't care. They'll still throw a tantrum in the parking lot.

And here's the kicker: that toddler is running your life. Because your subconscious, the toddler, is the one driving your autopilot behaviors. Until you train it, it will always choose what's easy over what's necessary.

Training the Toddler

At the time that I'm writing this book, my daughter Jordan is 3 years old. Not only is she the most beautiful little princess on the planet (again, check my Instagram for verification @the.morninghero), she is also the most irrational being on the planet!

- "Daddy, I want ice cream on my pancakes topped with some pasta!"
- "Daddy, I don't want to brush my teeth, I just brushed them yesterday!"
- "Daddy… why can't I write my name on the couch??"
- "Daddy, I don't love you anymore… *(5 minutes later)*… Daddy, I love you!"

No amount of reasoning and negotiating works with her. If I want her to do something, I can't just explain all the benefits and give her the pros and cons. That strategy may work on an adult, but not her. The only thing that works with her is bribery!

I'll offer Jordan a gummy bear if she stops running in circles, takes her pants off her head and puts them on her legs, puts on her shoes, and goes and stands by the door so we can leave for school. It's surprising how well this works. Immediately, she falls in line and starts obeying. She calms down, she locks in, she focuses on the task, and she executes. All with the hopes of getting one little red gummy bear! That little reward is the only way that I'm able to get her to follow through and do what I want her to do.

You have a little Jordan in your brain and it's responsible for all of your actions and behaviors. Giving it rational arguments of why it needs to behave a certain way or take a certain action won't work. If it were that easy, it wouldn't be so hard to lose weight. You would just tell yourself, "I'm not eating pizza or burgers or cookies ever again because they make me fat and unhealthy and I could actually die from heart disease." That's a very rational and convincing argument; however, that still doesn't stop you from indulging in these guilty pleasures! You see? Rational arguments don't work against your toddler brain.

So how do you train your inner toddler? Just like with Jordan, you have to bribe it. You need to present it with a reward so that it can lock in, focus, and execute the desired task. That's exactly how my friend Aaron was finally able to build a habit that he was trying to lock in for years but never could. And it was all because of an app called Duolingo.

Duolingo

I had known Aaron back when I lived in San Diego. We hadn't talked in a while, so when his name popped up on my phone one afternoon, I figured it would just be a casual catch-up between old friends. I wasn't expecting much more than a friendly check-in. But the moment he started talking, I could tell something was different. His voice carried an energy, a spark I hadn't heard from him before.

"Jarvis," he said, practically shouting through the phone, "I just hit 365 days of learning Spanish!"

I congratulated him. A full year of language learning is impressive, sure, but at first I didn't fully grasp the depth of what he had just accomplished. It wasn't until he started telling me the backstory that I understood the weight behind his words.

"You don't get it, man," he said. "I've struggled with this for years."

Aaron, who's originally from South Africa, is married to a Mexican woman. They have two young kids together and are raising them to stay connected to their roots. At home, his wife speaks to the children exclusively in Spanish. The kids go to a Spanish immersion school where nearly all instruction is in Spanish. And to add to this, his mother-in-law, who speaks no English, lives with them full-time and helps care for the kids.

His household is full of Spanish all day long and Aaron couldn't speak a word of it.

He told me how painful it was to sit at the dinner table and watch his entire family laughing, bonding, and sharing stories while he sat there, lost and silent. He couldn't engage. He felt like a guest in his own home.

He had tried before. Multiple times. He'd enrolled in courses. Downloaded language apps. Tried Rosetta Stone. Bought books. You name it, he'd done it. But nothing stuck. Life would get busy. He'd lose steam. Something would always come up. He'd do a couple of weeks and then it would all fall apart.

So when he told me he had just completed 365 consecutive days, an entire year of Spanish lessons, I was stunned.

"I can finally talk to my kids in Spanish," he said. His voice cracked. "And the other day, I had a full conversation with my mother-in-law. For the first time."

I actually got emotional because I knew what that meant to him. I had to ask what changed. What made this time different?

His answer: an app called Duolingo.

Duolingo is a mobile app that teaches languages. But what made it different from everything else he had tried wasn't the lessons; it was the way it turned the process into a game. With every completed lesson, he earned points. After a few days in a row, he built a streak. The more days he stacked together, the stronger the streak became. He became obsessed with not breaking the streak.

Even on days he was exhausted. On days he was traveling. On days when he had every excuse to skip. He still opened the app and knocked out a lesson. Not because he was motivated. Not because he was disciplined. But because he didn't want to lose the game.

Somewhere along the way, learning Spanish stopped being a chore. It wasn't about discipline or willpower anymore. It had become a daily competition with himself. It wasn't about learning a language; it was about winning the game.

And the beautiful part? By playing the game, he was accomplishing the real goal of learning Spanish.

That is the power of gamification. When something becomes a game, consistency becomes automatic. And once consistency becomes automatic, results become inevitable.

The Science of Gamification

I couldn't stop thinking about Aaron's transformation. How a simple app took a man who had failed over and over again and helped him finally follow through for an entire year. It worked because the app turned the habit of learning Spanish into a game.

It reminded me of when I used to play video games as a kid. I would spend hours glued to the screen. My fingers would cramp, my eyes would go dry, but I couldn't stop. I'd lie in bed at night thinking about the next level. I'd wake up already strategizing how I'd beat the next boss. I didn't need to be told to play. I didn't need reminders. No one had to motivate me. I was addicted.

And there's a very specific reason for that. Games are engineered to be addictive. Every time you beat a level, collect a reward, unlock a hidden item, or earn an achievement, your brain gets a hit of dopamine. That's the brain's pleasure and motivation chemical. It's what fuels desire. It's what keeps you going. It's the reason you instinctively check your phone when you hear a notification buzz. It's the reason you crave a cookie or light up when someone gives you a compliment. Dopamine is the driving force behind habits, both good and bad.

The gaming industry understands this better than anyone. That's why they design games to trigger dopamine again and again. They hook you. They keep you engaged. You're always chasing that next win. And it works. The gaming industry generates over 180 billion dollars a year. People spend billions of hours in front of screens, completely immersed in virtual worlds, driven by nothing more than points, levels, streaks, and stars.

But here's the thing. Most games don't offer any real-world return. They drain your time, your energy, and your focus and give nothing tangible in return. You get fake rewards for fake progress.

But what if we flipped the script?

What if we took the same psychological triggers that make video games so compelling and applied them to our own goals? What if we used the same mechanics that kept Aaron glued to his Spanish lessons not just for a few weeks, but for an entire year, and built them into our daily habits?

What if we gamified all of the habits that build a winning life?

Take Score

The Daily Debrief is a simple but powerful check-in you do with yourself every day, either in the morning or in the evening. Its purpose is to reflect on your day, stack your wins, give yourself kudos for what went well, and course-correct on what didn't. This is the same approach I use when training my children. I affirm the behaviors I want to reinforce and gently redirect the ones that don't serve them. Over time, this shapes habits, reinforces good behaviors, and replaces the bad ones.

Here's how it works. First, you will tally up your HERO'S score for the day (or the previous day if you're doing this in the morning).

- Did you raise my **H**eart rate with exercise?
- Did you **E**at right?
- Did you **R**ead?
- Did you take **O**ne big action towards your wealth goal?
- Did you **S**pread joy?

After you tally your score, you will ask yourself three simple questions:

1. What did I do well today? This is where you celebrate your wins. Think of it as giving your subconscious a gummy bear. You're saying, *"Hey, you crushed these things today. Way to go."* This recognition releases dopamine, that feel-good chemical, so your brain rewards itself and wants to repeat the behavior.

The problem for many high achievers is that we're constantly looking forward, focusing on what we lack, highlighting where we fall short, and pointing out what needs fixing. That's great for progress, but it often leaves us stuck in a loop of stress and tension, never pausing to recognize what's going right. If we don't consciously acknowledge our wins, we spiral downward. Daily debriefs break that cycle. They stack your wins and give you that personal high five: *"That was amazing. Keep doing that."*

2. What didn't I do well? Now, it's time to face the areas where you fell short. Maybe the whirlwind of the day got in the way. Maybe you slipped up or didn't perform at your best. That's okay. Acknowledging the missteps is not about self-punishment... it's about awareness.

3. What could I have done differently? This is the course-correction step. Think of it as the gyroscope on an airplane. When turbulence pushes the plane off course, the gyroscope signals the system to gently adjust and get back on track. By asking yourself what could have been done differently, you create a simple action plan so you don't repeat the same mistakes tomorrow.

This process, celebrating wins, acknowledging losses, and course-correcting, is exactly how you train a toddler. Give the gummy bear when they do something right, gently redirect when they don't. Over time, your subconscious starts craving the dopamine, the kudos, the attaboy. It wants to see the score go up, it learns from the gentle corrections, and slowly, those behaviors become autopilot.

After enough practice, you stop having to force yourself to do the things you want to do. You automatically wake up early, go to the gym, eat healthy. These behaviors become baked into your subconscious, part of your identity. The Daily Debrief isn't just reflection... it's habit reinforcement, behavior shaping, and self-coaching rolled into one. Over time, it trains your mind to seek what's good and course-correct when you fall off track, setting you up for consistent wins every single day.

EVERY. DAMN. DAY.

And if we want to kick it up a notch, all we have to do is sprinkle in a little accountability, which is what we'll touch on next.

☐ **Reflect**

- Where did your toddler brain win today? Name two moments you chose easy over necessary. What did each choice cost you in health, wealth, or peace?
- Which single habit would change your trajectory the most if it lived on autopilot? Why does it matter right now?
- If you stacked a 30-day streak on that habit, how would life at home or work look different? Who else would feel the benefit?

☐ **Take Action: Score Your Day**

- Take score on your day from yesterday. How many stars did you get?
    - Heart Rate
    - Eat Right
    - Read
    - One Big Thing
    - Spread Joy
- What did you do well?
- What didn't you do well?
- What will you do differently tomorrow?

** Get the WIN The Day app to set your daily intentions and score your progress each day! Keep a high score and watch your name climb the leaderboard!

CHAPTER 14
ACCOUNTABILITY IS EVERYTHING

"Left to ourselves, we rationalize. With accountability, we rise"

— Michael Hyatt

Report Your Score

Doing your Daily Debrief is a good first step to building consistency. It will give your toddler brain a little bit of candy each day to bribe it to do the things that it normally wouldn't do. But there will be times when even a 5-star day won't be enough to keep you motivated. There are times where the gummy bear doesn't work on my daughter. That's when we will have to tap into the strongest force of motivation… accountability.

In his book *Willpower Doesn't Work*, Dr. Benjamin Hardy lays it out plainly:

Willpower is a muscle, and like all muscles, it gets fatigued. Willpower alone is not enough to build lasting habit change because it will eventually fail you.

It might get you started. It might give you a good day, or even a good week. But eventually, motivation runs dry. And that's when most people fall off. So what's the solution?

External Accountability.

There are two kinds of accountability: internal and external. You'll hear people say, *"I just need to hold myself accountable."* But internal accountability doesn't work. True accountability means there's a consequence, and when you're "holding yourself accountable," it's way too easy to let yourself off the hook and say:

"Screw it. I'll just do it tomorrow."

Because guess what? Nothing bad happens if you don't follow through. There's no real consequence.

But **external** accountability? That's a whole different game. That's when someone else is watching. That's when your pride is on the line. That's when failing means **letting someone down, embarrassing yourself**, or **looking bad** in front of the people you respect. And pride is one of the most primal, powerful human emotions. Pride will push you to do things you never thought possible, just so you don't have to eat the shame of falling short in front of others.

That's why **external accountability is the only real accountability**. Because it creates a consequence. And when there's a consequence, you'll stretch far beyond your limits to avoid the pain of disappointing someone or losing face.

I remember one time I had told my aunt that I wanted to take my son swimming. She immediately said, "I've been wanting to go swimming too! Let's go together." We agreed that we would go on that upcoming Monday. Then Monday came and it was a whirlwind of a day!

EVERY. DAMN. DAY.

Clients were in crisis. I was running on fumes. I was exhausted and irritated. Swimming was the last thing I wanted to do. So I carefully crafted my excuse to tell my aunt... "Hey, I'm not feeling well. Work was brutal. Let's do it later this week." In my mind, I was already on the couch watching Netflix with a big bowl of Kraft mac and cheese.

And then my phone rang. It was her. She answered the phone and said, "Hey baby, I can't wait to go swimming! I'm all packed. Are you on your way to pick me up?"

My mouth opened to deliver my beautifully rehearsed excuse.... And this is what comes out...

"I'm on my way."

What?! *"I'm on my way??"* Even I was surprised.

But that's the power of *external accountability*. It gets you to show up *even when you don't feel like it*. And thank God I did. That day turned out to be magical! We took my son and he had the time of his life! My aunt ended up teaching him how to swim, and he had the biggest smile on his face!

We laughed. We played. We made a core memory. If it were up to me, we would never have gone. I would have been cemented on the couch, wasting space and killing brain cells. My willpower would have failed me. But instead, I ended up following through because someone else was counting on me.

That's the power of external accountability.

Knowing that other people are watching will get you to show up time and time again. You will let yourself down over and over, but you will stretch yourself far beyond your limits for other people.

Accountability Groups

I have a friend named Jeff Fenster. He's the CEO of Everbowl and WeBuild and one of the most high-functioning, successful people I know. He's built multiple eight- and nine-figure companies, leads massive teams, and juggles more in a week than most people do in a month.

And yet... even *he* struggled with staying consistent on his health goals.

Until he found his tribe.

Jeff told me he hadn't missed a workout in over a year. An *entire* year, working out every single day. Even when he had the flu, he'd go out for a walk just to close his exercise ring on his Apple Watch.

I was stunned. I asked him, "What drives that level of dedication?"

He told me about a group of close friends he teamed up with. They were all in a daily challenge using their Apple Watches to track calories burned. Their goal? Burn at least 500 active calories every day.

At the end of each day, every person in the group had to report their calorie burn in a group text thread. If any one of them missed the mark, they would be kicked out of the group (ouch!)

Now, here's what blew my mind...

After a year, not one person had missed a single day. Not. One!

Because their pride was on the line. It was about the commitment they made to each other. It was about not letting the tribe down.

That thread became his driving force. Everyone in that group found a way to hit their number... even if they were traveling, sick, or swamped with work.

That's the power of accountability. It doesn't matter how successful, disciplined, or high-performing you are… if Jeff Fenster, a CEO running multiple companies, needs a tribe to stay consistent, then what makes you think you don't?

We're not meant to do this alone. If you want to truly level up your life, you need to **find your tribe.** The kind of people who will hold you to a higher standard than you hold yourself.

But I get it… it can be hard to find other people on the same page as you. Not everyone is crazy enough to wake up early and aggressively get after it every day. It takes a special type of person to be on this level, so you might have a hard time building your own tribe. In that case, you can just join an existing Accountability Group.

Find Your Tribe

A research study was done by the Association of Talent and Development. There are five levels of execution when it comes to accomplishing a goal. At each level, there is a different likelihood of success:

- Level 1 (10%) - You have a goal or an idea
- Level 2 (25%) - You consciously decide that you will do it
- Level 3 (40%) - You create timeline for achieving the goal
- Level 4 (50%) - You create an action plan.
- Level 5 (65%) - You commit to someone that you will do it
- Level 6 (95%) - You meet with that person (or persons) on a regular basis to report your progress

This is staggering! When you go as far as creating an accountability appointment to report your progress for your goals, it's 95% certain that you will follow through until you hit the goal!

After discovering this, I decided to kick the 5-star scoring system up a notch and create an accountability group for myself.

I asked four friends to join me on a call every 5 a.m. to set our intentions for the day. We also had to report our scores from the previous day's intentions.

I had a scoreboard that tracked each person's score and leaderboard that ranked each person based on their score. It almost turned it into a friendly competition!

Often, people would join the call and say, *"Jarvis, the only reason I followed through on that task is that I want to see my score go up on the leaderboard!"*

That year turned out to be the most explosive year in each person's life! One woman was a real estate agent and she 5x'd her sales from the previous year! Another woman was able to double the revenue in her tax firm while losing 35 lb! One of the guys got six-pack abs while making the most money he's ever made in his sales role at his company.

And me? That was the year I got in the best shape of my life, got married, and started the Morning Hero, which has since impacted the lives of thousands of people around the world.

Every person in that group had the best year of their life because of daily accountability.

Having your own goals is good…

Knowing what actions to take is even better…

Scoring those actions on a daily basis is Elite……. but having an accountability tribe that you check in with on a regular basis? That's the secret sauce that will almost guarantee you follow through and show up EVERY. DAMN. DAY!

The Tipping Point - 30-Day Challenge

The reason it is so hard to stay consistent is the microwave thinking.

Back in the day, it was an all-day process to cook a meal. The animal had to be hunted. The grains had to be harvested. The meat had to be gutted, cleaned, and then slow cooked over a fire. The vegetables had to be picked and boiled. By the time everyone sat around the fire for dinner, they had earned that meal.

But now we have been conditioned by the microwave to have a completely cooked meal in two minutes flat. We have turned an experience that used to take two days into two minutes.

And now we apply those same instant expectations to everything. If we eat a salad, we expect to see 3 lb. drop off the scale. If we hit the gym once, we expect to see six-pack abs in the mirror. If we make one phone call, we expect to land one new client.

We have tricked ourselves into believing that every action should deliver an immediate result. But life does not work like that. You will go a period without seeing any results… until you reach the tipping point.

Earlier in this book, I shared the story of the penny. That magical little coin that, when doubled every day for 30 straight days, grows to over $5 million.

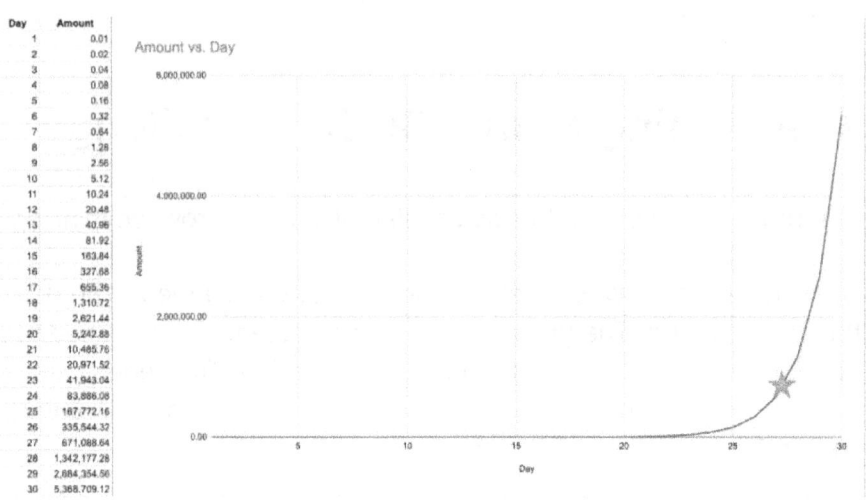

The Tipping Point Illustrated

Now, if you were to chart that penny's growth, to plot it day by day on a graph, something fascinating happens. The curve stays flat for a long time. Like painfully flat. Like *this cannot possibly be working* flat.

For 10 days straight, it barely moves. Even by day 20, it still has not cracked $10,000. But then, something wild happens. Around day 27… boom. That little curve shoots up like a rocket breaking through the Earth's atmosphere. It looks like magic. But it is not magic. It is **compounding momentum**. And it took 26 full days of quiet, invisible work before that one day of breakthrough.

You are the penny. Your morning routine is the penny. Every act of consistency is a deposit into your future millions. Even if it feels like you are just tossing pebbles into the ocean. But here is what separates the few who *make it* from the many who do not: The ones who win are the ones who stay consistent long enough to reach their tipping point.

EVERY. DAMN. DAY.

This proves it takes at least 30 days of showing up with consistency before your brain starts making it automatic. Before you start seeing results.

So here is your challenge: **Build a 30-day hot streak.** That is when the tipping point will kick in.

1. Wake up one hour earlier
2. Do a Daily Debrief and take score on the previous day
3. Set your HERO'S intentions for the day ahead
4. **Do it for 30 days straight!**

And I will say this with confidence. Your life will be unrecognizable 30 days from now if you commit to the process.

Remember… a tiny little penny can grow to over $5 million in just 30 days with every. damn. day consistency.

Imagine what *you* could do.

Go download the *WIN The Day* app and start building your streak today. I want to hear from you 30 days from now when your life has erupted.

Send me an email at jarvis@themorninghero.com and tell me how everything has changed.

☐ **Reflect**

- When was the last time you said "I'll do it tomorrow?"
- Which single goal keeps stalling even though you "know what to do." Why has self-accountability not been enough?
- Imagine if you had deeper accountability for the next 30 days. What will be different at home or at work? Who else benefits from the new you?

☐ **Take Action**

- Scan the QR code to join the Morning Hero 30 day challenge.
- After signing up, click "Join a Tribe."
- Report your 5-star score each day and watch your name climb the leaderboard!

PART III
THE CHEAT CODES

EVERY. DAMN. DAY.

Contra

One Christmas morning when I was a kid, I tore through my presents like a madman. Among the gifts, my mom (bless her heart) got me three new video games: Super Mario Brothers, The Legend of Zelda, and Contra. I must have stayed up for 37 days straight trying my hardest to beat each one. Super Mario and Zelda were challenging but manageable. I could work my way through the levels and eventually come out victorious. But Contra? Contra was a different beast entirely. That game was nearly impossible to beat.

This was 1987. There was no internet. No YouTube tutorials. No TikTok gamers revealing level-by-level hacks. If you wanted to figure out how to beat a game, you had to put in the hours. Or, if you were lucky like me, you could convince your mom to take you to the local Barnes and Noble. That's right, back then bookstores had entire shelves dedicated to video game strategy guides. I remember sitting cross-legged on the floor of that store, flipping through page after page, hungry for any tip or trick that would help me take down Contra once and for all.

That's when I stumbled across something magical, something that would change my gaming life forever. A secret. A hack. A hidden sequence buried deep in the guide titled "The Ultimate Cheat Code." It was a precise combination of button pushes that had to be entered at the exact right moment just as the game was starting. If you nailed the sequence, it would unlock the ultimate power-up, giving you all the weapons and unlimited lives. You could die a hundred times, and it didn't matter, you'd keep respawning and playing until you eventually won.

I still remember that cheat code like it was etched in my DNA: "Up, up, down, down, left, right, left, right, B, A, B, A, select, start." Once activated, it basically guaranteed victory. That little sequence of buttons gave average kids like me a chance to defeat what once felt unbeatable.

And that's what I want to give you right now. The cheat codes. The secret combination that unlocks the ultimate power-up, not for a video game but for your real life. I want to give you the exact steps, the precise inputs, that will almost guarantee you have a 5-star day every single day.

CHAPTER 15
HEART RATE

"Leave all the afternoon for exercise and recreation, which are as necessary as reading. I will rather say more necessary because health is worth more than learning."

— Thomas Jefferson

Cheat Code #1 - Activation

Every morning, you'll wake up an hour earlier than usual and enter your Power Hour. This is your sacred hour of solitude, your time to beat the sun and the world to the punch. In the first 15 to 30 minutes, you'll sit quietly with your journal for your morning practice. This is your time to check in with yourself, to set your intentions, to center your mind before the chaos of the day comes rushing in. You'll align your thoughts, your energy, and your goals. And once you've done that, once your mind is clear and your purpose is locked in, then it's time to activate!

Right after you sit alone with your journal for your morning practice, I recommend going straight into your exercise routine. This will be your first big win for the day. Imagine getting your first star for the day before anybody else has even rolled out of bed. While they're still sleeping, you're already winning! That sense of victory carries over and gives you momentum to crush everything else on your plate. Your morning workout is how you officially press the play button on your day.

You may believe that your physical fitness routine is purely for your body, but I think the greater benefits come from what it does for your mind. When you do something physically exhausting, it's hard. You're sweating. You're huffing and puffing. Then you look at yourself in the mirror and you see a warrior, a victor, a champion! You see someone who just crushed something difficult. You see someone who doesn't take the easy road. Someone who leans into hard things. Someone who doesn't make excuses, who has discipline, and who has fortitude. You see someone who makes great decisions. You see a hero! You stood up to the test of that hard thing, and because you conquered that, nothing else will get in your way for the rest of the day. Everything else becomes easier when you activate in the morning. It's like you've awakened the beast inside of you, and that beast carries confidence into everything you do.

But here's the thing… your beast doesn't just wake up on its own. It doesn't rise with your alarm clock. Your beast lies dormant. Every night when you go to bed, it goes into hibernation. When you open your eyes in the morning, that beast is still sleeping. It takes a spark, something intense, to wake it up. And that spark is sweat. That spark is discomfort. That spark is doing something hard, something you can be proud of. When you activate your beast, you're sending a message to the world that says, "I'm ready for you, and there is nothing you can do to throw me off my game today!"

It's like Bruce Banner turning into the Incredible Hulk. When he transforms, he's indestructible. He's invincible. He's unstoppable. Nothing can stand in his way, not even a building. But before he turned into the Hulk, he was just little old Bruce. On his own, he's weak. He couldn't hurt a mosquito if he tried.

EVERY. DAMN. DAY.

You have that same choice every morning. You can go through the day as Bruce, the one who makes excuses, the one who runs from hard problems, the one who's always tired, the one who's lazy, the one who eats junk and procrastinates and wastes time. Or you can activate your beast. You can activate your Hulk! You can turn into a goal-crushing machine.

Start the day with a good, strenuous sweat. That's how you activate your superhero self so you can show up powerfully for the rest of the day.

There are several reasons why you should activate early in the morning. Let's go through a few of those now.

Reason 1: It Activates Your Metabolism

You might be tricked into thinking it doesn't matter what time you exercise. If you do the same exercise routine, it should result in the same number of calories burned no matter what time of day you do it. That's not the case. If you look at the total net-effect of calories burned, it's a combination of calories burned during the routine plus calories burned after the routine.

Studies show that when you work out in the morning, it ignites your metabolism, and your body turns into a calorie-burning furnace that lasts for a long period of time after the workout is completed. That means that while you're sitting at your desk working, your body is actually burning more calories than otherwise because you've activated your metabolism.

As an example, if you sit at your desk for an hour, you'll probably burn on average about 100 calories. However, if you sit at your desk for an hour after a good strenuous workout, you'll burn around 180 calories. You are doing the exact same activity, just sitting at your desk, but the number of calories you are burning has almost doubled all because you've activated your metabolism! Can you believe that? You can actually burn more calories while sitting on your butt just from moving your workout from the evening to the morning!

Reason 2: It Activates Your Discipline

There's this concept of the interconnectedness of decisions, which means that one good decision leads to another. Conversely, one bad decision leads to another. Do you ever have those days where you have some pizza, and then all of a sudden, you say to yourself, "Well, eff it! I might as well have some cookies now." And then you say, "Well, eff it! I already had pizza and cookies, I might as well have some ice cream." And then you say, "Well, eff it! I've been eating like shit. I don't feel like working out. I'll just go to the gym tomorrow." Then you say, "Well, eff it! Since I'm not going to the gym, I might as well go out for a drink tonight." If you look at the final decision to go out for drinks, you may believe that that decision was made in isolation. But that's not the case. It was a chain effect of bad decisions, starting with having the pizza earlier in the day.

There is no decision made in isolation. Every decision is connected to all previous decisions. Everything that led up to that moment plays a role. The fact that you woke up and had a big plate of pancakes for breakfast will kick off a domino effect of decisions that lead to you having a burger for lunch, then pizza for dinner, and then because you are so tired and lethargic, you'll end up scrolling social media on your couch till midnight. That one decision led to every other poor choice that you made all day long.

On the flip side, if you wake up and start the day with a good, heart-wrenching sweat by doing a cycle class at 6 a.m., then you say to yourself, "I had a great workout. I don't want to mess that up. I'll just have a fruit smoothie for breakfast." Then you go to lunch and say, "I feel great from my workout and smoothie this morning. I'll just have a chicken caesar salad." Then you go out for dinner and still have a burger, but you get the side salad instead of the fries. Then you get home and your brain isn't wired on sugar, so you actually go to bed early and on time without watching trashy TV or social media. In this case, your going to bed on time was actually kicked off by the very first

EVERY. DAMN. DAY.

decision you made that morning. Every decision is impacted by the decisions before it, so when you start the day with one great decision, like a good workout, it locks in your discipline to make good decisions all day long.

I'm a huge foodie, and every time my family travels, I love eating my way through the city. I'm almost guaranteed to gain at least one pound per day of vacation. So if we were gone for five days, on average, I would gain at least 5 lb., sometimes more. I came to just accept this, and I would try my hardest to lose 5 lb. prior to traveling because I knew, without a shadow of a doubt, that I was going to gain it all back once I got there.

One year, I decided to stick to my same morning practice of getting up early every day and starting the first hour with myself before diving into family time. I had done some research and found a cycle studio five minutes away from our hotel, so I bought a one week pass for their 5 a.m. classes. Since the class was at 5 a.m., I knew that I would be back to the hotel before my family woke up, so it wouldn't impede on our vacation time together.

Everything went exactly as planned. Each morning, I woke up and I went to my 5 a.m. spin class. The class ended at 6 a.m., and since my family was still asleep, I had time to stop by a coffee shop to meditate and journal my intentions while watching the sunrise. I would then get a latte for my wife and go back to the room around 7 a.m., just as everyone was waking up!

To my kids, I was Super Dad because I came running in the room, tossing them up in the air and rolling around on the bed. To my wife, I was Super Husband because I came in with bright spirits and a latte for her (coffee and foot rubs are her love language!) It was five of the most fun-filled days of adventure and indulging. When we got back home, I stepped on the scale to see the damage, and you would never believe what the scale said.

Instead of me gaining 5 lb. like I usually do, I actually lost 3 lb.! How was this possible? How could I splurge for five straight days and actually lose weight?

The difference was that morning spin class. It "activated" my discipline and good decision-making. So instead of having pancakes and syrup for breakfast, I would eat an acai bowl. And since I had a pretty healthy breakfast, instead of eating fried fish tacos for lunch, I'd have a poke bowl with fresh fish. I made healthy decisions all day long, even without trying, all because of that very first good decision: starting the day breaking a good sweat. It ignites a discipline and creates a snowball effect of good decisions that flows through your day without you even recognizing it.

Reason 3: It Activates Your Spirit

When you work out, it's one of the easiest things you can do to raise your frequency. What do I mean by that? Let's get a little "woo-woo" for a bit. We are all energetic beings. We all operate at a certain frequency. We are just vibrating atoms, living in a vibrating universe. Everything has a frequency… our thoughts, our spirits, our emotions, our bodies. And you attract the things that are vibrating at the same frequency. It's just like how a radio can tune into a certain radio station. It has a transmitter that transmits at a certain frequency, and any radio that is receiving at that same frequency can pick up what's being transmitted at that same frequency.

Whatever frequency you are vibrating at will attract the things that are also vibrating at the same frequency. For example, if you are late for work, and in the back of your mind, all you can think of is, "Please, no red lights! Please, no red lights!" Guess what you will attract?

Every single red light on your path. It's not by coincidence that somehow every red light was timed perfectly to stop you on that particular day. You attracted them with the frequency that you were emitting.

EVERY. DAMN. DAY.

Every time you dwell on something, that thing will manifest for you. So if you're operating at a low frequency, such as being stressed, anxious, or mad, then you'll attract negative circumstances into your existence. It's kind of a self-fulfilling prophecy.

Have you ever been around someone who complains all the time? It seems like there's always something bad happening to them. They say that when it rains, it pours, but for them, it's a full typhoon! In their eyes, they are complaining because bad things always happen, but it's the other way around. Bad things keep happening to them because they are complaining! You see, they are emitting a negative frequency, which continues to attract more negative circumstances, negative people, and negative outcomes.

The first thing you should do every morning is raise your vibration. When you start to operate at a higher frequency, you'll attract people, places, and things that operate at that higher frequency. It's hard to put this in layman terms, but this is absolutely true. Things don't just happen to you. You are the cause in the matter. If something happens, it's because YOU attracted it. The good and the bad. This is a tough pill to swallow, but everything that happens to you is your fault!

Studies show that exercise is the best way to raise your vibration. After a good workout, you release dopamine and serotonin and ignite your pleasure sensors in your brain. It's the same effect that drug addicts get when they take a hit. You feel good. Your emotions are balanced. Your hormones are intact. It's like a natural High. Immediately, you see the world differently. Things that were problems before don't seem that bad anymore. Now you see things through a different lens. Now you're in a better mindset, which will allow you to see things in a more positive light, thus attracting more positivity in your direction.

You are creating everything in your life. Both the good and the bad, and if you want to create better results, it first starts with you creating a better, more positive mindset. It starts with you raising your vibration with early-morning exercise. The moment you think more positively, you'll attract more positive results, and early morning exercise "activates" your positive vibration.

Cheat Code #2 - Train Like an Athlete

I used to meet with an accountability group on Saturday mornings at 5 a.m. for a bootcamp style workout. We had a trainer named Josh who led the sessions. Josh had a fire in his belly. He was loud and passionate. The kind of coach who could push you beyond your normal limits. He would yell motivational sayings at us mid-rep, calling us higher, calling us out. And every session ended the same way: with a final round where we had to put it all on the line.

During that last set, Josh would look us dead in the eye and shout, "Are you average… or are you an athlete?" Then louder, over the thumping music and the burn in our muscles, "Average or athlete! Average or athlete!" And we would scream back, "ATHLETE!"

Here's the thing… we weren't athletes in the traditional sense. We were all working professionals. Real estate agents, accountants, computer programmers, wealth advisors, and loan officers. We were far from competing in a sporting match, so "athletes" is the last thing you would think if you saw our group.

But if you think about it, what is an athlete? It's someone with extreme discipline… someone practiced, prepared, and skilled in their craft. Someone who has dedicated their life to being exceptionally great at what they do. Someone who practices their craft daily and is obsessed with WINNING!

In that definition of the word… **you** are an athlete too!

You may not play football on Sundays or run track for medals, but every single day, you're strapping on your gear to compete in the most important arena there is: **the game of life**. And you're not just here to participate… you're here to **win**.

So if you're going to live like an athlete, you need to **train** like one too. I don't mean that you have to spend hours upon hours at the gym or run 20 miles at a time. But you have to do more than just take a leisurely stroll around the block. Sure, technically, that's "exercise," but that's not **training**. You won't break a sweat. It's not challenging. It won't push you physically or mentally.

Training like an athlete means you're doing something strenuous. It means you're pushing your limits. It means your heart is pounding, your lungs are burning, your muscles are screaming. You're not just working out… you're going to war with your comfort zone. It's something that you resist. You don't want to do it, but you do it anyway.

That kind of training doesn't just sculpt your body… it *forges your mind*. It shuts down that soft voice that whispers, *"Let's just take it easy today."* That voice is the enemy. That voice is the reason you've stayed stuck, plateaued, or coasted for so long.

Every time you show up and push yourself beyond what's easy, you're silencing the quitter inside. You're proving to yourself that *you do hard things*! You're building mental armor. Grit. Discipline. Confidence. Focus. That's what athletic training does. It rewires your nervous system to stop flinching when things get uncomfortable.

Because if you can dominate yourself in the gym… you'll dominate everything outside of it. Your business. Your parenting. Your relationships. Your emotional control. That's why this isn't just physical. It's psychological. It's spiritual.

- So join Crossfit
- Take a spin class
- Try a boxing workout

- Sign up for a marathon (or half-marathon)
- Join a bootcamp
- Do something… anything that gets your heart rate up and pumping!

Because when you train hard like an athlete, you're building the most important muscle of all: **character**.

You're not just someone who exercises… you're an **athlete in the game of life**. So start training like one!

Cheat Code #3 - Break a Sweat

There's a moment, right after you finish a workout, when you look in the mirror, drenched, dripping, chest heaving, muscles on fire… and you smile. Not because it was easy, but because it was hard, and you did it anyway. That moment matters. That sweat on your forehead is a symbol of victory.

Sweat is proof that you did something difficult. It's evidence that you pushed past your comfort zone. And that, right there, is why I believe you should break a sweat every single morning. Not just to move your body, but to activate your mind, your discipline, and your hero, your identity.

When you start your day doing something hard, something that gets your heart pounding and your shirt wet, you've already won, and whatever comes next in your day won't compare. That email won't shake you. That client call won't throw you. That tantrum from your kid won't faze you. You've already done something harder. You've already faced resistance and moved straight through it. And that creates a ripple effect of confidence that follows you all day long.

EVERY. DAMN. DAY.

I don't believe in just going for a leisurely walk. That's good for clearing your mind or bonding with other people, but that won't fully activate you. If you want to start your day in power, you need to break a sweat. You need to give your body a challenge. This isn't about chasing six-pack abs. This is about declaring war on that little voice in your head that's always trying to take the easy road.

Breaking a sweat is also one of the most powerful tools for releasing stress and tension. It's not just a physical response... it's an emotional release. Your body stores stress. Every meeting. Every argument. Every bill. Every obligation. It all builds up like pressure in a valve. And if you don't find a release, that pressure explodes. You end up snapping at your kids, or emotional eating, or laying in bed all night wide awake with anxiety.

But when you sweat, when you really go hard and force your body to move, you release that pressure. You exhale the tension. You unlock something primal. You vent it out. Sweat becomes your therapy. It's your detox. Your nervous system reset. Every drop of sweat is carrying a little bit of stress out of your body and onto the floor. That's why you always feel better after a hard workout. It's not just endorphins. It's emotional purification.

And the best part? It's simple. You don't need a gym membership or fancy equipment. All you need is your body and a willingness to push it. Go for a run. Hit some burpees. Take a spin class. Turn up a YouTube workout in your living room. Just do something that gets your heart rate up and your body working hard.

Because when you start the day by doing something that makes you sweat, everything else gets easier. The resistance is lower. Your mind is clearer. Your body is lighter. Your spirit is stronger.

And most importantly, you start the day already proud of yourself.

JARVIS LEVERSON

Cheat Code #4 - Group Fitness

Something magical happens when you sweat alongside other people. You start showing up not just for the workout, but for the people.

I remember when I first got into cycling. I joined a spin studio near my house that had 5 a.m. classes. It was intense. Loud music. Flashing lights. A room full of half-asleep warriors fighting their way to greatness before the sun even came up.

And it wasn't cheap. It cost me $200 a month. Yeah. Two hundred dollars! That price tag wasn't just a membership fee, it became a form of wallet accountability. I wasn't about to throw away that kind of money by hitting snooze. So I showed up because I had skin in the game.

But the real power didn't come from the bikes or the beats. The real power came from the people. Kenny. Wendy. The familiar faces I saw every morning. Over time, those people became my tribe. And after a while, it wasn't just about me anymore. I wasn't just working out to raise my heart rate, I was showing up because I enjoyed seeing Kenny and Wendy each morning.

That's the secret weapon of group fitness: relational accountability. Because when your actions involve someone else, when your absence is felt, you start thinking differently. You push a little harder. You show up a little more consistently. You don't just do it for yourself, you do it for your tribe.

So if you struggle with staying consistent with your workouts, if you've been starting and stopping a fitness habit every few weeks, if your treadmill is collecting more dust than miles, I want to challenge you to try this cheat code: join a group fitness class. It could be spin, CrossFit, yoga, bootcamp, OrangeTheory, or even pickleball. I don't care what it is, just find your crew.

Because the best way to stay consistent with your heart rate habit isn't just to exercise, it's to exercise with people who expect you to show up. It goes from something you dread doing to something you actually look forward to!

Cheat Code #5 - Running

After doing spin class for a while, I realized something: as much as I loved the energy, the beats, and the sweat, there were some real limitations. It was expensive. It wasn't convenient, and it wasn't always consistent. Whenever I traveled, it was hit or miss trying to find the same vibe or quality. Some studios were incredible. Others were pretty drab.

Then, one year, a friend challenged me to run a half-marathon. Now, you gotta understand, I wasn't a runner. I was a football player. I'm built like a bowling ball. Running? Nah. That was for those lean, long-legged folks in neon shorts who float when they run. Not me.

But I accepted the challenge. And get this… I was starting from scratch. I could only run a few blocks at a time before having to stop and catch my breath. So I just started with walking. That's it. I walked. Then, over time, I added a jog. Then I ran a mile. Then two. Eventually, I was logging four to five miles a day.

And guess what? I got into the best shape of my life. Not from fancy gym equipment. Not from elite coaching. Not from expensive memberships or top-tier instructors. Just from one thing: consistency.

With spin, I wasn't consistent because there was too much friction. I had to find a studio, then I had to make sure they had classes that fit my schedule, then some instructors were good and others weren't. If I was traveling, I'd have to buy a week-long pass even though I'd only be in town for a few days.

However, running? I could do anywhere, anytime. It allowed me to be consistent because there is absolutely no friction to do it.

That's why I recommend running as your go-to method for raising your heart rate. No gym required. No instructor. No equipment. Just two feet and a surface. That's it.

Traveling for work? Go for a run. On vacation with the family? Go for a run. Only have thirty minutes in between meetings? Go for a run. You can do it anywhere, anytime.

There's no scheduling or coordination. No app to download. No waitlist to join. No gear to pack. You just lace up and go. From the moment you decide to go for a run to the moment your feet hit the pavement can be as little as two minutes. It's the most friction-free form of exercise there is.

That's why it's a cheat code. Because anything that removes friction increases consistency. And when it comes to your health, results don't come from one intense workout; they come from a hundred small, consistent ones stacked on top of each other.

But here's something most people overlook: running isn't just a workout for your body, it's also a workout for your mind. It's meditation in motion. Think about it. Meditation is simply intentional time where you shut out the outside world to go inside, quiet the noise, and search for clarity and inspiration. That's exactly what happens on a run. The rhythm of your feet becomes the metronome that slows your mind. The chaos of the day fades. Thoughts untangle themselves. Ideas appear out of nowhere. I've left my house stressed, overloaded, and mentally jammed up, only to return with the answer to a problem, a new perspective, or a stroke of genius that seemed to come out of thin air. My runs have given me some of my clearest ideas and boldest breakthroughs.

Another reason I love running is that it meets you exactly where you are. In his book Can't Hurt Me, David Goggins tells the story of how he weighed over three hundred pounds when he decided he wanted to join the Navy SEALs. He had to lose weight fast. But at the time, he couldn't even run to the mailbox at the end of the street. So he walked, similar to how I started. Walking turned into a slow trot to the mailbox. Then a jog. Eventually, he could run there without stopping. Then he ran a mile, walked a mile. Then two miles. And eventually, he was running without stopping.

Today, he runs two-hundred-fifty-mile races and is known around the world as the toughest man alive. But it didn't start with a two-hundred-fifty-mile race. It started with walking to the mailbox.

That's the beauty of running. It meets you at your current level. You don't have to be a runner. Start with walking. Then alternate, run a block, walk a block. Keep going until you can run a mile without stopping. That's exactly how I did it.

No matter where you start, just start. Whether it's walking your street or training for a marathon, running will push your body, clear your mind, and unlock the kind of clarity and inspiration you can only find when you step away from the noise and into your own head. It will train your discipline, strengthen your heart, and give you a peace you didn't even know you were missing.

Cheat Code #6 - Sign Up for a Race

The moment you sign up for a race, whether it's a 5K, 10K, half-marathon, or even a fun run, you've created an immovable deadline. A hard stop. A day you can't reschedule, postpone, or negotiate with. And that is a cheat code for hitting your heart rate goals and staying consistent with your training.

Before I signed up for that half-marathon, I had tried running, but I could never be consistent. Sure, I'd jog here and there. If I felt like it, I ran. If I didn't feel like it, well, Netflix won. But once that race was on the calendar, everything changed. The stakes were suddenly real. I had skin in the game. I'd paid for the entry, told people I was doing it, and knew that on race day, I'd have to show up, ready or not.

That race became my north star. I had a training plan taped to my fridge and followed it religiously. Rain or shine, busy day or not, I got my runs in. Missing a workout was no longer an option because I knew that every skipped mile would show up on race day in the form of burning lungs and lead legs. Signing up for that race gave my workouts a purpose. It wasn't just exercise anymore; it was training. And training is different. Training means you show up even when you don't feel like it because you're preparing for something bigger.

The accountability didn't stop with the race itself. I was training with a friend who was also signed up, and he became my built-in competition. He'd call me and say, "I just knocked out five miles today." Instantly, I'd feel the urge to lace up my shoes and hit the pavement. I didn't want to be the guy gasping for air while he cruised past me on race day. That friendly rivalry kept me sharp.

After that race was over, I started signing up for races all the time. It gave me something to train for year-round. There was always another deadline, another finish line in sight. The consistency came naturally because there was always something on the horizon that demanded my best.

We humans thrive under pressure. We need deadlines. Without them, we tend to drift. We procrastinate. We let excuses creep in. But when you've got a clock ticking toward a specific day, you'll train differently. You'll eat better. You'll go to bed earlier. You'll work out with the focus and discipline of an athlete.

So if you want a surefire way to keep your heart rate goal on track and keep yourself consistent, don't just plan to work out. Put a race on the calendar. Pay the entry fee. Tell your friends. Get a group to join you. Let the deadline work its magic. Because when the pressure is on, you'll rise to meet it and cross that finish line stronger than you ever thought possible.

Cheat Code #7 - Burpees4Breakfast

I did CrossFit for about two years, and I can honestly say it's one of the most intense, grueling, and transformative styles of training I've ever experienced. CrossFit will humble you. It'll make your lungs scream and your muscles cry. But it'll also make you proud of yourself in a way few things can.

After a typical CrossFit workout, you're not just sweating, you're soaked. You're not just tired, you're wrecked. You're laid out on the floor, gasping, dizzy, borderline nauseous, and smiling. Because you know you gave it everything you had. There's something beautiful about being completely emptied like that. It's a purification of sorts, mind, body, and soul.

One of the biggest lessons CrossFit taught me was that you don't need to spend hours in the gym to get an incredible workout. You can get in, go hard, and get out. Many of the workouts are under twenty minutes, but those minutes hit different. They're full-body. They're functional. They use your body weight in dynamic, explosive ways. And they leave no muscle group untouched.

One of the hardest workouts I ever did was just ten minutes long. It was called a burpee Tabata. We did ten rounds of burpees: thirty seconds on, thirty seconds off. That was it. Ten rounds of thirty-second burpee sprints with thirty seconds of rest in between. And by the time we hit that last round, my heart was pounding out of my chest, my lungs were on fire, and every cell in my body was begging me to quit. But I finished. And when I did, I felt unbreakable.

After just ten minutes, I walked out of that gym feeling like I had conquered the world. My body was fried. My shirt was drenched. But my mind was laser-focused and my spirit was elevated. That day, I had one of the best workouts of my life, and then that momentum carried into the day and I had an amazingly productive day. And the best part? It was only ten minutes. That experience made me ask a powerful question: what would happen if I did that every morning?

So I committed to it. I started a thirty-day challenge I called Burpees4Breakfast. Each morning, I'd wake up and do just ten minutes of burpees. No gym. No fancy equipment. No excuses. Just me, my body, and the floor.

And the results?

Of all the fitness routines I've done… running, spinning, boot camps, weightlifting… nothing gave me the type of visible, functional results that burpees for breakfast did. After thirty days, I didn't just feel fit, I looked fit. I didn't quite have a six-pack, but I had a strong four-and-a-half pack, more definition than I'd ever had in my adult life! From just ten minutes a day. That blew my mind.

I realized I didn't need two hours in the gym. I didn't need equipment or machines or a personal trainer. All I needed was consistency and the willingness to do something hard every morning. That's when I started challenging others to join me. In our 5 a.m. Morning Hero accountability group, I opened up a challenge for the tribe: thirty days of burpees for breakfast.

One of the women in our group accepted that challenge, and it changed her life! She stuck with it not just for thirty days, but for an entire year! Every morning for 365 straight days, she did ten minutes of burpees.

And if you saw her now, you'd think she was a fitness model. Legit shredded abs. Defined arms. Full-on transformation. And she still says, "All I do is burpees for breakfast."

The reason burpees are so powerful isn't just because of the movement, it's because of the accessibility. Ten minutes. No equipment. No gym. No excuses. I've done burpees in hotel rooms. I've done them in my living room. I've done them in my office in between Zoom calls. You can do them anywhere, and they will always deliver a full-body, sweat-drenched, heart-pounding workout.

If you ever catch yourself saying, "I don't have time to work out," this is your answer. Ten minutes. That's it. No matter how busy your day is, you can carve out ten minutes to move, sweat, and build strength.

Burpees for breakfast are my go-to heart rate habit when time is tight. They're efficient. They're portable. They're powerful. And most of all, they remind me that victory doesn't take hours. It just takes commitment.

Conclusion

Conclusion

So there you have it. Sven powerful cheat codes to help you dominate your day by raising your heart rate and establishing your power each day:

1. **Activate** – Wake up your beast early in the morning.
2. **Train Like an Athlete** – Push beyond comfort and build character.
3. **Break a Sweat** – Release stress and start the day already proud of yourself.
4. **Group Fitness** – Surround yourself with a tribe that pulls you higher.

5. **Running** – The friction-free workout you can do anytime, anywhere.
6. **Sign Up for a Race** – Create an unmovable deadline that keeps you sharp.
7. **Burpees4Breakfast** – Just 10 minutes a day to the best shape of your life.

When you put these strategies into motion, exercise stops being optional. It stops being "something you try to fit in." It becomes automatic. It becomes an identity. It becomes the foundation of your discipline, energy, and momentum.

But if you take nothing else from this section, let it be this: **Every day, break a sweat.**

Not sometimes. Not when it's convenient. Every. Damn. Day. That one decision will transform everything: your body, your confidence, your energy, your focus, your productivity, your joy.

So here's your challenge: **Break a sweat for the next 30 days straight and activate the napping beast inside of you!**

EVERY. DAMN. DAY.

☐ **Reflect**

- On days you break a sweat in the morning, how does it impact the rest of your day?
- What usually prevents you from working out in the morning? What can you do to get around this?
- If the day got away from you and you only had 10 minutes, what could you do to get your Heart Rate star for the day?

☐ **Take Action**

- Download the Win The Day app to join the 30 day challenge and track your progress each day.
- In less than 30 short days, you'll be exploding with more power, purpose, and productivity! **You'll be looking good and feeling even better!**

CHAPTER 16
EAT RIGHT

"Let food be thy medicine and medicine be thy food."

— Hippocrates

Cheat Code #8 - Bright Lines

I remember exactly where I was the moment I discovered the concept of bright lines. It was the summer of 2022. Each month in our Morning Hero accountability coaching programs, we focus on a different theme. We pick a book of the month, dissect its concepts, and work together to implement the tools in real life. In the summer, the focus is always health and fitness, to help people get "summertime fine" so they can look good in their bathing suits.

I take the book selection seriously. I wouldn't prescribe anything to my community that I don't personally subscribe to. So I read. A lot. I'll go through ten, sometimes fifteen books just to find that one gem that's not just hype but truly transformational. As we approached June, I was looking for something revolutionary. Health and fitness is such a noisy space, full of gimmicks, magic pills, weight loss hacks, and nonsense designed to sell supplements but not actually change lives. I didn't want hype. I wanted truth. I didn't want a diet. I wanted a lifestyle.

And that's when I found it.

I did a Google search for "top books on health and fitness," and among the hundreds of titles, one book stood out like a neon light: Bright Line Eating by Susan Peirce Thompson. The reviews blew me away. People weren't just losing weight. They were keeping it off, for years. This wasn't another plan; this was a permanent shift. And the core idea of Bright Line Eating immediately clicked for me because it mirrored everything I believe as a Morning Hero: success doesn't come from what you do sometimes, it comes from what you do every damn day.

The book is built on one simple yet powerful truth: to have lasting success with your eating habits, you must establish bright lines.

So what's a bright line?

A bright line is a clear, unambiguous rule you never cross. It's a hard boundary. There's no maybe. No sometimes. No just this once. It reminded me of the third rail of the train tracks back in my hometown of Chicago. On the L, the third rail is called the hot rail. It's where all the electricity flows. You touch it, you die. No second chances. No gray area. That's a bright line.

In her book, Susan breaks down four bright lines for eating: no sugar, no flour, no snacking between meals, and controlling your portion sizes. But the real power, the magic sauce, is in the first two: no flour, no sugar. Ever.

Now, before you roll your eyes or clutch your cookie in panic, let me break this down. Susan isn't a nutritionist, she's a neuroscientist. She studied the brain's response to food and found something staggering: most of us are food addicts. And the addiction we have to food, especially flour and sugar, looks exactly like the addiction patterns of hardcore drug users. I'm talking heroin and cocaine.

EVERY. DAMN. DAY.

She proved it by showing how those drugs are made. Cocaine is just a cocoa leaf, processed into white powder. Heroin is just a poppy seed, processed into white powder. Sugar is sugarcane, processed into white powder. Flour is a wheat germ, processed into white powder. Same exact process. Same end result: white powder that hijacks your brain. The only difference is that two of those substances are illegal, and the other two are in nearly every single food we eat. And the craziest part? Flour and sugar kill more people every year than cocaine and heroin ever will because they're legal and they're everywhere.

So when Susan said you need a bright line, an unbreakable boundary to protect yourself from these addictive substances, it hit me hard. I knew she was right. But man, it didn't mean I was ready.

Let me tell you how addicted I was.

We live across the street from a 7-Eleven in San Diego, and I was a regular. I mean celebrity status regular. Everyone in that store knew me by name. They knew my schedule. They knew I'd show up at 7:37 p.m. every night for my fix of donuts and cookies. Rain or shine. Hail or high water. After dinner, I'd rush the kids into bed just so I could sprint across the street and get my sugar hit. It was a problem.

So imagine my horror, reading this book telling me I could never eat sugar or flour again. My first reaction? Hell no. But then I remembered one of my favorite quotes from Jim Rohn: "If you want different results, you have to be willing to do something different." So I committed to trying it for just thirty days. No sugar. No flour. Just to see. The first few days were rough. My body expected dessert after every meal. It was muscle memory.

But after three days, something shifted. The cravings started to vanish. After one week, I stopped thinking about donuts. After two weeks, I went to a birthday party with three cakes and didn't even want a bite. I didn't even crave the icing.

That's when I realized that Susan was right…. sugar is an addictive drug! And once you're off of it, the spell breaks.

I kept with the no flour, no sugar lifestyle after the thirty days, and in less than three months, I dropped from over 215 pounds down to 195. And I did it with zero intense workouts. All I did was walk or run and eat clean. That's it.

And here's the best part… I've kept the weight off without even trying. I now float between 193 and 195 with ease. No stress. No obsession. And it all came down to those bright lines.

Why do bright lines work, especially for me?

Because I've tried everything: Atkins, keto, paleo, vegan, vegetarian, pescatarian, Whole30…you name it. But nothing stuck. Why? Because most plans leave wiggle room. You can eat this sometimes or in moderation. Have a cheat day. Just track your calories.

But for someone like me, that doesn't work. Give me a cheat day and I'll eat fifteen thousand calories and erase six days of discipline. I need hard rules. I need boundaries that I don't cross. When you give me that, I can lock in. I can commit. I can win.

That's why Bright Line Eating works. It's not a diet, it's a discipline. A new identity. A new operating system. And it's why I prescribe it to all Morning Heroes.

If you want to live with more energy, more clarity, and more freedom from food drama, you need to establish a bright line: never eat sugar or flour again. Ever.

Because your energy, your clarity, and your health depend on it. And once you master this cheat code, you'll feel like a brand new human.

EVERY. DAMN. DAY.

Cheat Code #8 - Skip Breakfast

Let me start by saying this loud and clear: I'm not a nutritionist. I'm not a health coach. I'm not a personal trainer or some fitness guru. I'm a professional tinkerer. I experiment. I test. I optimize. I'm always tweaking my habits to find new ways to unlock more energy, clarity, and productivity in my day. So while this isn't medical advice, it is personal experience, and what I'm about to share has worked wonders for me and millions of others like me.

And it starts with one truth that might ruffle some feathers: you don't need to eat breakfast first thing in the morning.

Yeah. I said it.

I know it goes against everything you've been told. I used to believe it too. I was all in on the classic mantra: "Breakfast is the most important meal of the day!" So I made sure to load up every morning with a big, hearty meal. I'm talking eggs, sausage, bacon, hash browns, syrup, butter, gravy. I need to stop because I'm making myself hungry.

And then I'd crash hard. About thirty minutes later, I'd slam headfirst into a wall. A fog would roll over my brain. My eyes would glaze over. I'd still be there, but nothing was computing. It felt like my brain had frozen, like a computer program that's still open but locked up. I could hear you talking, but I couldn't process a thing.

So I started digging. Why does this happen? Turns out digestion requires a massive amount of energy. While your brain normally consumes about twenty percent of your body's energy, once you eat, your body shifts its focus. Now, your stomach becomes the main event. Blood, oxygen, and energy all rush to your gut to handle that big meal, and your brain gets put on the back burner.

That's why you get sleepy after breakfast or lunch. It's not in your head. It's in your gut, literally.

Enter fasting.

While researching how to beat that dreaded post-meal crash, I stumbled on a strategy that changed everything for me: intermittent fasting. The concept is simple. Fasting is just a stretch of time where you don't eat. And the truth is, you already fast every single day. You just don't think about it because most of it happens while you're asleep.

The trick is to extend that fasting window by skipping breakfast. Instead of eating at seven or eight in the morning, you "break your fast" around lunchtime. The most popular structure is called sixteen-eight fasting. You fast for sixteen hours and eat during an eight-hour window, usually from noon to eight p.m. This way, your body stays out of digestion mode longer, and that freed-up energy gets rerouted to your brain.

You think faster. You focus better. You make sharper decisions. Your mood lifts. You feel lighter and clearer, like your brain just got a tune-up.

I started skipping breakfast over five years ago, and I've never looked back. Now, I'll admit, I was skeptical at first. I thought, there's no way I can get through my morning without food. I'll be sluggish. I won't have energy to work out. My brain will stall. But then something crazy happened. When I didn't eat, I actually had more energy.

It's counterintuitive, but it works.

On fasting mornings, I feel lighter, sharper, and more productive. I power through my workouts and then dive into work with laser focus. That's when I coined the phrase #DoneByLunch. Because that's exactly what happened. I was knocking out my most important task before noon. And by the time I finally sat down to eat lunch, I had already won the day.

EVERY. DAMN. DAY.

The rest of the afternoon? That was for family time. Playtime. Chill time. Whatever I wanted. The pressure was off because the heavy lifting was already done.

One of my favorite fasting hacks is using food as a reward. Every morning, I write down my one big action, the most important task for the day. The one thing that, if I get it done, moves my life or business forward. And then I make a deal with myself: I don't eat lunch until that one thing is done.

No lunch. No exceptions.

Sometimes it's writing. Sometimes it's making twenty-five cold calls. Sometimes it's filming content or having a hard conversation. Whatever it is, lunch becomes the prize. And let me tell you, hunger is a powerful motivator. Something that normally takes two hours suddenly gets done in thirty minutes when you know a chicken bowl is waiting on the other side. That's the magic of #DoneByLunch. Fasting sharpens your brain, and the promise of food gives you fire.

I get a full day's worth of results in half the time.

Now, a few important notes. Fasting isn't for everyone. If you're pregnant or nursing, you need steady fuel for your baby. If you're training like a bodybuilder or doing intense early-morning lifts, you may need extra fuel in the morning to power those workouts. So as always, listen to your body. Do your research. Experiment. Try it for yourself and see what happens.

But for many Morning Heroes, especially those who crave more focus, more energy, and more time freedom, this strategy is a game-changer.

When I fast, the only thing I consume in the morning is coffee. Because coffee is a hunger killer. It suppresses your appetite and helps you cruise through the morning without the grumblies. And because there's no food in your stomach, the caffeine hits harder. It's like a brain boost on steroids.

Empty stomach plus black coffee equals samurai focus.

If you're doing more intense workouts, like running or strength training in the morning, you may need something to help your body recover. In those seasons, like when I was training for a half-marathon, I kept it light. Instead of a full breakfast, I'd make a smoothie or a protein shake. That way, I got energy and recovery without going into full digestion mode.

Pro tip: add a shot of espresso or cold brew to your smoothie and turn it into a protein coffee frappé. Tastes amazing. Fuels your body. Boosts your brain.

Fasting may not be a bright line, but it's one of the most powerful tools in my Hero arsenal. It's how I stay energized, focused, and laser-sharp every morning. And it's a big reason why I can consistently say:

"I get more done before lunch than most people do all day."

Give it a shot. You might just unlock a new level of time freedom that you didn't realize was possible. Super productive mornings equal super fun afternoons.

Cheat Code #9 - Zero Calendar Meal Planning

One of the greatest weapons you can wield in your quest to eat right is surprisingly simple: be intentional. That's it. That one word… intentionality…can change everything. Because the truth is, most people don't fall off track because they're lazy or lack discipline. They fall off because they get caught off guard. They don't have a plan in place.

EVERY. DAMN. DAY.

Here's how it typically plays out: you're grinding through your morning, knocking tasks off your to-do list like a productivity machine. And then suddenly, BOOM! You look up and realize you're starving. Not hungry, starving. And when you're starving, you don't think. You don't pause to ask, "What's clean and healthy?" You ask, "What's fast and nearby?" That's how you end up in the drive-thru ordering a Big Mac or scarfing down a leftover donut in the break room. Not because you're a failure. Not because you're undisciplined. But because you didn't make the decision ahead of time.

You can't rely on willpower to eat right. Willpower is not infinite. It fades. It drains. It runs dry, especially as the day wears on. In the morning, you're strong, sharp, focused, disciplined. But after a full day of emails, meetings, clients, and unexpected fires to put out, by the time lunch rolls around, your mental reserves are toast. So when it comes down to a choice between a leafy salad and a greasy slice of pizza, you choose the pizza. Not because you're weak, but because your brain is exhausted and your discipline is running on fumes.

So what's the fix? Simple. Make the decision when your discipline is highest. That means early in the morning before the whirlwind hits. Before stress, fatigue, and cravings show up at the door. When you're calm. When you're clear. When you're still in control. You make the decision then, and from that point forward, you're just executing. No second-guessing. No negotiating with yourself. The decision is already made. All that's left is follow-through.

That's the power of meal planning.

During your morning Power Hour, when you're setting your intentions for a 5-star day, include one intention to eat right. And don't stop there. Take it a step further. Plan your meals for the entire day. Get specific. Don't just write "eat healthy." Actually ask yourself: what am I eating for lunch today? What are we cooking for dinner tonight? Maybe it's grilled steak with sweet potatoes and green beans. Maybe it's a chicken bowl with brown rice and broccoli. Whatever it is, lock it in.

Then, zero-calendar it. Open your schedule and actually block off time for your meals. In those blocks, write exactly what you plan to eat. It may sound silly, but it's a powerful move. Because once it's on your calendar, it's locked in. It becomes part of your day. From that point forward, you're not improvising. You're not battling temptations. You're not scrambling at the last minute. You gave your subconscious the orders in the morning, and now it's just following the route.

It's like giving your brain a GPS. You set the destination at five a.m., and when you get hungry at 12:47 p.m., your mind doesn't even flinch. It already knows: we're having the chicken bowl today. You drive right past Burger King because there's nothing to debate. You're not hungry and stressed and deciding at the same time. You already decided. That's the beauty of this system. That's how you win.

This cheat code isn't just about food. It's about decision lock. It's about taking one small but powerful action during your Power Hour that keeps you from having to wrestle with yourself later. When you plan your meals early, you don't have to fight yourself at your weakest. You made the choice during your strongest moment. Now it's just execution.

That's what Morning Heroes do.

Go ahead and give it a try right now. Pull up your calendar and schedule time blocks for each of your meals. But instead of giving those time blocks generic labels like "Lunch" or "Dinner," actually put what you are eating as the label of that block. So "Lunch" becomes "Chicken salad from Chipotle" or "Dinner" becomes "Steak and broccoli with the family." When you get this specific, you'll be surprised how you won't get cravings for anything else. Your subconscious will lock this in and you won't want to deviate from the plan.

This is how you live with intention.

This is how you eat like a Hero.

Conclusion

So there you have it… three powerful cheat codes to help you dominate your day with discipline in the kitchen:

1. **Establish Your Bright Lines** – No flour, no sugar.
2. **Skip Breakfast** – Unlock your mental clarity and focus.
3. **Zero Calendar Your Meals** – lan it, lock it in, and follow through.

When you put these strategies into motion, you're no longer just *trying* to eat right. You're stacking the deck in your favor. You're giving yourself a system to *guarantee* a gold star every single day in this category. You take food out of the chaos column and move it firmly into the control column.

But if you take nothing else from this section, let it be this:

> Bright Lines are the foundation. No flour. No sugar. No exceptions.

This lifestyle will not only transform your energy. Your cravings. Your waistline. Your confidence. Your productivity. Your focus. Even your sex life. Yeah… *all of it*. Because when you set that boundary, you take back your power.

So here's your challenge: **No flour. No sugar. For 30 days straight and see how amazing you feel!**

- ☐ **Reflection — Expose the Real Problem**

  - On a scale of 1 to10, how "non-negotiable" are your health standards right now? What would make it a 9 to 10?
  - Who else suffers when your energy crashes… your partner, kids, clients, team?
  - What will you commit to starting today, to get things back on track? (Bright lines? Fasting? Meal Planning?)

- ☐ **Take Action — 30-Day Challenge**

  - Go download the Win The Day app to join the 30-day challenge and track your progress each day.
  - In less than 30 short days, you'll be exploding with more power, purpose, and productivity! You'll be feeling light on your feet and bright in your mind!

CHAPTER 17
READ

"The man who does not read has no advantage over the man who cannot read."

— Mark Twain

Cheat Code #11 - Audible

In order to earn a gold star in the "Read" category, the rule is simple: consume something that feeds your mind every single day. Now, I know this one might sound obvious. Everyone talks about the benefits of reading. But let's take it a layer deeper.

Tony Robbins once said, "Reading is the fastest way to turn ten years into ten days." Think about that. Someone spends an entire decade grinding, failing, experimenting, succeeding, struggling, and learning, and then they bottle up all that wisdom into a single book. And you? You get to consume it in ten days. You get to stand on their shoulders, dodge their mistakes, leverage their experience, and use it to fast-track your own growth. That's the real power of reading. It compresses time. It collapses decades into days. It gives you access to lives you haven't lived and lessons you haven't yet earned.

But even though most people know the value of reading, they still don't do it. Why? Because who has time to sit down and read when we have a whirlwind to deal with?

Enter Audible.

Audible is the ultimate cheat code for busy lives. It lets you listen to books instead of reading them. And for those of us juggling work, family, responsibilities, and a thousand daily distractions, it's a game changer. Because let's be honest, while we'd all love to sit in a quiet space with a cup of coffee and flip through pages for an hour a day, life rarely gives us that luxury. But Audible doesn't ask for silence. It doesn't require a cozy nook. All it needs is your ears.

Listening to books allows you to multitask your way to mastery. You can be reading while you're driving. Reading while you're working out. Reading while you're washing dishes, folding laundry, walking the dog, or waiting in line at the grocery store. And yes, when I say reading, I mean consuming. Listening counts. Your brain doesn't care whether the information comes through your eyes or your ears. What matters is that you're feeding it.

And here's the kicker: studies show that the average person spends enough time in the car each year to equal the classroom hours required for a four-year college degree. Let that sink in. If you spent your commute listening to books instead of zoning out to talk radio or music, you could graduate from what Earl Nightingale once called Auto University. You could earn a "degree" in whatever specialty you want just by repurposing your drive time.

That's the real magic of listening to books. It transforms dead time into growth time. It converts the ordinary into the extraordinary. Suddenly, the drive to the grocery store isn't wasted; it's a seminar on leadership. The walk around the block isn't idle; it's a lesson in wealth building. The dishes don't just get cleaned; your mind does too.

Reading, whether with your eyes or your ears, is the gateway to your next level. So make it a daily habit. Make it part of your morning routine. Make it something sacred. Because the more you feed your mind, the more powerful your life becomes.

Cheat Code #12 - Reading Run

One of my all-time favorite things to do is combine reading and running.

Since you can listen to books on Audible, I knock out two wins at once. I feed my mind while I build my body. There's no greater feeling than that. Every morning when I go for a run, my endorphins start firing, my energy spikes, and I feel unstoppable. But it's not just a physical high, because while my body is moving, my brain is soaking up wisdom. I'm growing. I'm progressing. I'm feeding my mind and spirit, not just my muscles.

It's a full-body, full-soul experience.

It's like a sensory overload. My growth engine is revving. My physical engine is ignited. My mind is being tickled by new ideas, while my body is burning through calories. And when I get back from that run? I feel unstoppable! I've conquered something hard, I've challenged myself, I've learned something new, and I feel great!.

And *that* momentum carries into the rest of my day.

This simple combo… running while "reading" (aka listening), is my secret weapon. It's the ultimate hack. You kill two birds with one stone. You get two stars for the price of one. Body and mind. Momentum and mastery. Growth and grind!

Cheat Code #13 - Learning Sprints

Imagine what would happen if you committed to reading just one book every single week. How much faster could you become an expert at anything you wanted? Truly think about that. What could you master in a year if you absorbed 52 books filled with wisdom, strategies, and life experience?

This is where I stumbled onto one of my favorite personal growth strategies. I call them learning sprints. Whenever I decide there's an area of my life I want to radically improve, I don't just dabble in it, I immerse myself in it. I pick a topic and go all in for one to two months, consuming a book a week until I've built a deep, almost instinctive mastery of it.

When I wanted to dial in my health, I committed to an eight-week sprint where I listened to nothing but health and fitness books, eight of them, back to back. Each one had its own gems, a handful of principles that resonated with me, and over time, I stitched those pieces together into my own personal health philosophy, the very one I now teach inside The Morning Hero.

I've done the same for finance, marketing, business, mindset, sales, you name it. Every month or two, I choose a new domain of mastery and dive deep. The beauty of this method is that it's shockingly doable. The average audiobook is about seven hours long, which means at 1.5x speed, you can finish one in less than five hours. That's just 45 minutes a day. Between my workouts, walks, drives, and idle moments where I might otherwise scroll my phone, I can easily hit my listening time without even rearranging my life.

And here's where the magic happens. After a few weeks of deep focus, you're no longer just learning about something. You're starting to think like an insider. You see patterns. You start connecting dots others can't see. You're not just repeating what one author says, you're synthesizing perspectives from multiple experts, creating your own unique framework that's tailor-made for your life and goals.

When I first launched The Morning Hero coaching practice, I was incredibly skilled at helping people get results. Transformation came naturally to me. I knew how to guide people, shift their mindset, and unlock their full potential. But there was one big problem: I was terrible at marketing. I had no idea how to get my voice out there. I didn't know how to attract people, how to build a brand, or how to scale a business. I had the gift, but I had no idea how to get that gift into people's hands.

That's when I hired my first business coach. I'll never forget what he told me: "Being a good coach isn't enough. You also have to become a good marketer." I had never considered that before. I always thought, if you build it, they will come. That couldn't be further from the truth. They can't come if they don't know about it. So at that moment, I launched my first intentional learning sprint on marketing.

I devoured everything I could get my hands on: Russell Brunson, David Ogilvy, Seth Godin, Dan Kennedy, Donald Miller, you name it. I dove deep into the psychology of storytelling. I learned how to build funnels, craft compelling messages, create irresistible offers, design lead magnets, and architect entire client journeys from social media post to paid program.

Over the course of just a few months, I consumed more than ten books, and by the end of that sprint, I knew more about digital marketing than many people who had spent four years getting a marketing degree. In fact, I had friends who had gone to school for marketing, and suddenly, I was the one teaching them how to build digital brands, write persuasive copy, and design client acquisition systems, things they had never even touched in class.

All of that came from one simple, consistent habit: reading every single day. That's the superpower. That's the unlock. That's how you go from clueless to confident. From unsure to unstoppable. From hidden to high-performing.

You want to become world-class at something? Read every day. You want to learn a new language? Read every day. You want to master a new skill? Read every day. You want to be a better leader, communicator, entrepreneur, or parent? You already know the answer. Read every day.

Because if you want to level up your life, I guarantee you, the blueprint you're looking for is already sitting inside of a book.

Cheat Code #14 - Book in Bed

Your subconscious never sleeps. Even when your body shuts down for the night, your subconscious mind is wide awake, continuing to process whatever you fed it just before you drifted off. You've probably experienced this without even realizing it. Ever watched a horror movie late at night and found yourself waking up in a cold sweat, haunted by nightmares? That's no accident. It's because your subconscious stayed on the job, marinating in the last images and emotions you poured into it before closing your eyes.

And that's where so many people go wrong. They're unintentionally feeding their subconscious straight-up toxicity every night without even realizing it. Be honest, you probably fell asleep last night with your phone still in your hand. Most people do. They scroll endlessly through Instagram, binge-watch random YouTube videos, or let the algorithm drown them in a flood of content. Comparison, envy, fear of missing out, imposter syndrome, insecurity, it all comes rushing in during those last precious minutes before sleep. And guess what? That's exactly what your subconscious will fester on all night long.

This is why I swear by one simple cheat code: read a book before bed. It's one of the easiest and most powerful ways to hijack your subconscious and give it a focused, positive assignment to chew on overnight. Think of it like giving your brain a closing shift task list. You're telling your subconscious, "Here, work on this while I sleep."

One night, I remember I was reading a book on how to write a book. That's actually how this book was born. I had just finished a chapter on how to craft captivating titles. I didn't brainstorm. I didn't force anything. I just read the chapter, closed the book, and went to sleep with that idea lingering in my mind.

The next morning, BOOM! I woke up with five solid book title ideas, just like that. They hit me out of nowhere, fully formed, like little gifts from the mental night shift. I grabbed my journal and wrote them down before they evaporated. That's when it really hit me: your subconscious is like a full-time employee working the graveyard shift. The only question is, what kind of work are you giving it? Are you tasking it with obsessing over the chaos and comparison of your social feed? Or are you asking it to soak in the knowledge of a good personal development book?

That's why I keep a stack of books right on my nightstand. It's not just aesthetic, it's a strategy. When I crawl into bed, those books are sitting there like little guards, silently daring me to choose growth over garbage. They trigger something in me. A reminder. An invitation. A choice. I reach for one, flip through a few pages, and slowly drift off. And you know what? It works like magic.

First of all, books are boring, and that's exactly why they work. Your phone is designed to stimulate. Every notification, every reel, every flashy color and sound, it's engineered to hook you and hijack your brain. That's why your mind can't settle down. Every swipe is a jolt. But a book? A book soothes your nervous system. It slows the rhythm. It tells your brain it's time to relax, to downshift, to let go. It's like putting your mind in airplane mode.

And more than that, a book gives your subconscious something valuable to marinate in. It feeds it with insight. It plants ideas. It installs upgrades while you sleep. And that's what I want simmering in the background of my mind at night, not some influencer's highlight reel or a rage tweet from someone I don't even know. I want wisdom. I want fuel for the life I'm building.

So here's the move: put yourself to sleep with a book. Every night. No phone. No noise. Just words, ideas, and your mind slipping into its next level. That's how you turn your nights into fuel for your future. That's how you win, even while you sleep!

Conclusion

Alright, let's bring it home.

Reading isn't just something "smart people" do. It's not a luxury. It's not a hobby.

It's a *weapon*.

Reading is how you download decades of wisdom in days. It's how you sharpen your mind, upgrade your thinking, and fuel your goals with firepower.

We broke down four powerful Reading Cheat Codes:

1. **Listen to Books on Audible** – Turn your dead time into growth time. Commutes, workouts, chores... they all become classrooms. No excuses.
2. **"Read" While You Run** - Get two stars for the price of one by combining your exercise and learning habits. This one move will 10x your vibration for the day!

3. **Learning Sprints** – If you want to become an expert in anything, just read about it daily and watch how fast you evolve.
4. **Read Before Bed** – Give your subconscious a powerful assignment before you sleep. Let your mind solve problems and unlock ideas while you rest.

Every book you read adds another brick to the empire you're building.

Now, here's the challenge:

"Read" for 45 minutes per day for the next 30 days. That will amount to one book per week.

Again… "Read" is in quotations because it just means consume one book per week, which means you could also listen to it on Audible.

One book per week. That's four books this month. They can be on mindset, leadership, marketing, health… whatever area you want to master next. Pick the books. Schedule the time. And get after it. And if its true that "the more you learn, the more you earn"… not only will your mind expand, so will your bank account!

☐ **Reflection**

- What topic do you need to become an expert in to take your work, career, or life to the next level?
- Where can you find time in your day to listen to an audio book to become an expert in that area?

☐ **Take Action**

- If you haven't already done so, download the Audible app and sign up for an account.
- Then scan the QR code to join the 30-day challenge and track your progress each day for your reading habit.
- In less than 30 short days, you'll become an expert in any area that you've been stuck in. **Next book... next breakthrough!**

CHAPTER 18
ONE BIG ACTION

"The man who chases two rabbits catches neither."

— Confucius

Cheat Code #14 - The One Thing

In the book The ONE Thing by Gary Keller, he makes a compelling case that every big goal, every audacious dream, can be boiled down to just one specific action, the one thing that has the greatest impact on bringing it to life. This concept is deeply rooted in the 80/20 Principle, which states that 80% of your results come from just 20% of your efforts. The trouble is, most people spend their time spinning their wheels in the 80%, doing tasks that feel productive but don't actually move the needle. They procrastinate or avoid the 20% of actions that would truly make the difference. He takes it a step even further. He says that within that 20% of activities that make the most difference… there's the ONE. The ONE is the single activity that has the highest impact toward hitting your goal. That's your ONE Thing. And more often than not, it's the very task you dread most, the one that stretches you, challenges you, and forces you out of your comfort zone.

If you put your full focus on that ONE Big Thing every single day, you won't just make progress... you'll create life-shifting momentum. You'll move from stagnation to acceleration. From stuck to unstoppable. Let me show you what this looks like in real life.

When I was working in commercial real estate, I set one bold goal for myself: I wanted to become the number one agent for restaurant retail space in downtown San Diego. Now, that's not a small goal, but I've always believed I was built for greatness! So I got licensed, joined a brokerage, and set the intention that within three months, I'd have 20 listings. (Spoiler alert: I had no idea what I was doing.)

What I quickly learned was that commercial listings don't fall into your lap. You have to earn them. You have to build relationships with property owners, people who have something to lease or sell. And there are a thousand ways to try to do that. I tried it all: sending out flyers, joining networking groups, running social media ads, buying email lists, hiring marketing agencies, and passing out business cards like they were Halloween candy.

But after months of noise and activity, I realized there was only one method that consistently worked, and had always worked in the industry: picking up the phone and making the damn calls.

That's it. That's the secret. Not flashy. Not sexy. But wildly effective. The only reason more people don't do it is that the phone feels like it weighs a thousand pounds. On the other end of that line is the risk of rejection. The potential to feel small. The fear of being told no. But it's also where the real progress lives.

Gary Keller asks a simple question in The ONE Thing:

"What's the ONE thing you can do, such that by doing it, everything else becomes easier or unnecessary?"

EVERY. DAMN. DAY.

For me, the answer became obvious: Make 20 calls a day to property owners in my territory. That was it. That was my non-negotiable. So every morning, I was the first one in the office by 7 a.m. I didn't check email. I didn't scroll. I walked straight to the call booth, pulled out my call list, and went to war with that phone. I didn't let myself move on to anything else until I'd finished those 20 calls. That was my ONE Thing. And the results were staggering.

After just two months of doing this consistently, I started getting a flood of return calls. The voicemails I'd left were finally paying off. Before long, people were calling me, wanting to work together. All of a sudden, everything changed. I didn't need email campaigns. I didn't need social media posts. I didn't need fancy flyers. Because my phone was ringing off the hook with inbound business.

And it all stemmed from doing that one uncomfortable thing every single day.

That experience taught me something I'll never forget: If you can identify the one action that has the greatest impact on your goal, and you pour your energy into that one action, everything else becomes easier, or even irrelevant. You don't have to hustle harder. You just have to focus smarter.

So now, let me turn the question to you.

What's your biggest goal or ambition right now? Is it growing your business? Launching a passion project? Getting in shape? Writing a book? Starting a nonprofit?

Now, ask yourself:

What's the ONE thing you could do today that would have the biggest impact on making that goal a reality?

That's your ONE Thing.

And here's what most people won't tell you: your ONE Big Thing will likely be the same action, day after day after day. Just like it was for me: make 20 phone calls. That was it. Every single morning. It never changed.

Yes, there may be seasons where your ONE Thing evolves as your goals shift. But most of the time, the answer remains consistent. There aren't five or six "top" priorities. There is only one. That's why it's called The ONE Thing.

And let's be real, your brain will fight you on it. It will distract you. It will try to convince you to work on things that feel productive but aren't. It'll say things like:

"Oh, today, my ONE Thing is to work on my Instagram strategy."

"Today, I should go play golf… maybe I'll meet a new client."

Those aren't bad things. But they're also not the main thing. And if we're being honest, they're just cleverly disguised ways to avoid the hard thing, the real work.

So you have to be ruthlessly honest with yourself. Every single morning, ask:

"What's the ONE thing I could do today that would make everything else easier or irrelevant?"

Then go do it. Relentlessly. Without compromise.

Because when you pour your full effort into that ONE Big Thing, day after day, your life won't just change gradually. It will change exponentially.

EVERY. DAMN. DAY.

Cheat Code #16 - Get Dressed

I know it's comfortable to just roll out of bed, shuffle to your laptop, and work in your pajamas. Or maybe you throw on those old college sweats you've been wearing for the last decade. It feels easy. It feels cozy. And hey, nobody on Zoom really sees what's going on from the waist down anyway, right?

But here's the thing: your brain is always watching. It's picking up cues from your environment and your appearance all day long. Those cues become mental triggers. And when you look in the mirror and see yourself in baggy pajamas, hair pointing in 12 different directions, what do you think that's telling your brain? Exactly, it's whispering, "We're not in work mode. We're in lounging mode. We're in lazy Sunday mode."

And your brain believes it. When your brain sees leisure, it becomes leisure. It slows down. It gets comfortable. You might still knock out a few tasks, but you won't attack them with the urgency, sharpness, and precision that your most important work deserves. It's like showing up to run a marathon in flip-flops. You might eventually cross the finish line, but it's going to be slow, sloppy, and way harder than it needed to be.

Now, let's flip the script. Imagine walking past a mirror in the morning and seeing yourself dressed like someone about to conquer something big. It doesn't have to be a suit and tie, unless that's your thing, but it should be something that signals, "We mean business today." The moment you gear up, your brain shifts gears too. You stand taller. You speak with more authority. You start moving with more intention.

You don't have to go overboard, but you do need to cross that invisible line between "at home chilling" and "ready to go slay dragons." For me, that line is a crisp blazer and a pocket square. Even if my calendar is wide open, even if I'm just heading to the coffee shop to write or strategize, I throw it on. Because when I see that guy in the mirror, I see a man on a mission. I see someone who's not just dabbling; he's building something that matters.

And here's the magic, this isn't just about clothes. It's about creating an identity shift every morning. The moment you "suit up," you're stepping into your role. You're telling yourself, "This is who I am, and this is how I show up." It's the same reason athletes wear uniforms, firefighters gear up, and superheroes have capes. The outfit isn't just for style; it's a trigger that tells the mind and body, "It's go time."

So what's your cape? Maybe it's a blazer. Maybe it's a pair of killer heels. Maybe it's a favorite watch or a fresh polo shirt. The point is, it should be something that, when you put it on, you can't help but feel dialed in. It should make you look at yourself and think, "Oh yeah, this person gets stuff done."

Find your cape. Wear it every day before you face your One Big Thing. Do that, and watch how quickly your execution changes. You'll stop drifting into your day and start charging into it. You'll feel sharper. You'll work faster. You'll move through obstacles like they don't even exist.

You can't tackle big things in little gear. Gear up, step up, and go win your day!

Cheat Code #17 - Go to Work

In order for you to consistently hit your ONE BIG ACTION each day, you need to engineer your environment. We live in an age of remote work, a time when the office can be your kitchen, your living room, or even your bed. It's easy, almost too easy, to roll out of bed, stay in your pajamas, and set up shop wherever your laptop lands. You may not realize it, but your environment plays a critical role in your ability to focus and produce high-quality work.

EVERY. DAMN. DAY.

If there's one piece of advice I can give to anyone working remotely, it's this: Go to work! If your job or company offers a physical office space, even if they give you the flexibility to work from home, take advantage of it. Go into the office. If that's not an option, find a coffee shop, a coworking space, or even a quiet library. The point isn't just to leave your house. It's to create an environment with which your brain associates one thing and one thing only: work.

Your brain is constantly making associations between spaces and activities. Your home is associated with comfort, relaxation, and leisure. The kitchen is a space tied to eating and socializing. Your bedroom? Sleep and rest. So when you try to work in these spaces, your brain struggles to make the shift. Instead of dialing into a work mindset, it's pulled in the direction of what it naturally associates with that space.

During the height of the COVID pandemic, I set up my workspace in the kitchen. It seemed like a logical choice at the time; we had a large table, good lighting, and it was central to the house. But something strange started happening. I couldn't stop snacking. All day long, I was going to the refrigerator or peeking into the pantry grabbing handfuls of chips. Even after a full meal, I'd find myself compelled to check the fridge. Before I knew it, I'd gained 20 lb.

Why? Because my brain associates eating with the kitchen. Sitting there with my laptop didn't change that. My brain, stuck in its habitual wiring, kept nudging me, "Hey, we're in the kitchen. Isn't it time to eat?" And I'd comply, over and over again. It wasn't until I moved my workspace out of the kitchen that this pattern finally stopped. The change was almost immediate. Once I created a dedicated space for work, my snacking dropped dramatically. My brain stopped sending those signals because it no longer associated my workspace with food.

Here's the psychology behind it: your brain thrives on routines and associations. When you repeatedly do a specific activity in a specific space, your brain builds a connection between the two. Over time, this connection becomes automatic.

Think about your bedroom. You've trained your brain to associate it with rest. That's why experts advise against bringing work into the bedroom; it can disrupt your sleep patterns. The same principle applies to your workspace. When you create a dedicated work environment, your brain begins to associate that space with focus, productivity, and getting things done. As soon as you step into that space, your brain knows: it's time to work.

Conversely, when you mix work with spaces tied to other activities, like eating or relaxing, your brain becomes confused. It struggles to shift gears, leaving you distracted, unfocused, and, in my case, over-snacked.

So how do you set up an environment that primes your brain for work? Here are some simple but powerful steps:

1. **Define Your Workspace** - Designate a specific space for work... a place where that's all you do. It doesn't have to be fancy or large. A corner desk in a spare room or even a specific table at your local coffee shop can work wonders. The key is consistency. Use the same space every day, and let it become your productivity sanctuary.
2. **Eliminate Distractions** - Your workspace should be free from distractions associated with other activities. Keep snacks out of sight if you're near the kitchen. Turn off the TV if you're in the living room. Remove anything that tempts you to break focus.
3. **Make It Inviting** - Create an environment that energizes and inspires you. Add a plant, hang an inspiring quote, or position your desk near a window for natural light. Your workspace should feel like a place you're excited to enter.
4. **Stick to a Routine** - Just like you have a morning routine to kickstart your day, develop a pre-work ritual to ease into

your work environment. This could be as simple as getting dressed, making a cup of coffee, and walking to your designated space.

At the end of the day, productivity isn't just about willpower or discipline. It's about creating the conditions for success. When you design your environment to support your goals, you remove friction and make it easier to stay focused and effective.

Cheat Code #18 - Grind Time

Now that you are dressed and you are at a designated location that's designed specifically for your work, it's time to actually **get to work!** It's time to start working on your ONE BIG THING. This is the single most important thing that you have to accomplish today that's going to maximize your wealth, work or mission. The time that you are working on this ONE BIG THING is called "grind time." You will need at least one… preferably two hours blocked off every morning for your #GrindTime.

If you don't grind, you won't shine!

Most people want to avoid the grind. They want the shortcut. They live in a fantasy where they can get instant results and reap all the rewards without putting in the work. But that's not reality. Anything that's worth getting will require an extraordinary amount of work. It will require you to grind. It will require you to focus. It will require you to become obsessed with your ONE THING. Every day you need to have designated time where you are undistracted and you have intense focus on doing the ONE THING that's going to lead to extraordinary success for you.

For some people it is obvious what that ONE THING is. If you are a writer, maybe it's writing your next book. If you are a programmer, maybe it's writing code. But if you're an entrepreneur or you own your own business where you have 1,000 things on your plate every day, it can be hard to say which one of those 1,000 things is "The ONE THING" because all of them can feel important. Here's a simple rule of thumb... your ONE THING is your biggest money-making activity. What's the ONE THING that brings in the most leads, sales, business, opportunities, revenue (aka, money in your pocket!). Maybe that's calling prospects to gain new clients. Maybe that's marketing. Maybe that's networking. Maybe that's writing or producing content for social media. For each person, it's different. But ask yourself, "What daily activity has the biggest impact on me growing my finances?" That activity is your ONE THING, and it should be the first thing you do when you begin your work.

In the book *Eat That Frog!* by Brian Tracy, he states that every day, you should eat the frog first. The frog is the most important thing that you need to work on. It's also the big, hairy, ugly action that you don't want to take. Everyone avoids the frog. But if you eat the frog first, then the rest of your day is easy and delicious! Once you tackle the hardest thing you have to do for the day, the rest of the day is easy and joyful.

There's also science behind why you should do the hardest thing first in the morning. That's when your brain is at its highest cognitive functioning. According to research, your brain's peak performance is somewhere between 8 a.m. and 10 a.m. You haven't yet suffered from fatigue and you're still firing on all cylinders. Your energy and focus are at their highest, and it is during that time that you should be doing the ONE THING that's going to require your best thinking. It's the ONE THING that's going to require your greatest decision-making. It's the ONE THING that requires your greatest discipline to complete. It's The ONE THING that demands your best problem-solving.

I often see people push their ONE THING to later in the day. They claim that they need to build up momentum. Or if they were really honest with themselves, they're just procrastinating. They start with doing small things like checking email and replying to things that don't need their immediate attention. They read newsletters that don't need to be read.

EVERY. DAMN. DAY.

They check stats that don't need to be checked. They research topics that don't need to be researched. They use their highest brain power to work on the smallest things. They spend their biggest energy on the tiniest tasks. They use their tall thinking on short actions. They are wasting the best time of the day. Between 8 a.m. and 10 a.m. is when they can produce the best work, yet they waste it away on meaningless, trivial nonsense. That time should be dedicated to your #Grind!

By establishing a grind time… a black-out period where you completely focus and concentrate on doing your ONE THING… you can compress 4 hours worth of work down into a 2-hour window. When you are using your overworked, exhausted brain to do a very intensive task, it takes you twice as much effort and time to complete that task. So pushing things off to later in the day means that you are doubling the time that it will take you to do that thing. However, if you know how to leverage your brain's firepower early in the day, you can complete hard tasks in half the time. You essentially cut your work time in half just by moving it to earlier in the day!

I remember when I was in commercial real estate, making cold calls was the hard part of the job. Every day, I was supposed to make 25 phone calls to prospects, and I avoided it like the plague! I would justify pushing it to later in the day because I had to start checking emails and responding back to people first. Then I would work on marketing materials. Then I had to do industry research to make sure I had all my talking points down. By the time I got down to do the real work, it would be 3 p.m. or 4 p.m. At that point, I'd be pretty exhausted. I would have every excuse in the world why I shouldn't make the calls. "It's too late to make calls now. No one is going to answer the phone." "I don't have enough time to make all of the calls, so I should just start fresh tomorrow." Even if I decided to make some calls, I would only do two or three before giving up for the day. My brain was running on fumes by that point.

I finally recognized that I would never be successful unless I blocked off time to do that ONE THING each and every morning. Doing research, working on new marketing materials, reading email newsletters, none of that was going to help me hit my goal. Making cold calls every day was the ONE THING that was going to help me get deals (aka, money in my pocket) the fastest. So I put a hard boundary around the time block from 8 a.m. to 10 a.m. and turned it into an appointment with myself to do this ONE THING. I guarded that time block with my life. I didn't check emails. I didn't talk to friends. As a matter of fact, I wouldn't even have my phone with me. I would lock my cell phone in my desk drawer, and I would go into a conference room in our office that had a landline phone to make calls. I didn't want to be distracted by dings and notifications trying to pull me back into low-level activities. That time was dedicated solely to making money… That time was solely for my #Grind.

As soon as I walked into the office, I went straight to that conference room to make calls. I didn't fire up my computer. I didn't check my inbox. I just went straight into my #Grind. I had already made a list of all of my prospects and printed it out so that I didn't need to look at a computer to see who I needed to call. Once I was in that conference room, I wouldn't leave until every call was made. After finishing my ONE THING, I would emerge and go to my desk, boot up my laptop, and check my emails for the first time of the day.

This was my grind. After executing this ONE THING consistently, something magical happened. Instead of me calling people, people were calling ME! People had listened to my voicemails, and they started calling me back to discuss selling their properties. I got so many inbound phone calls, that I never had to make another cold call again! All because I established a #GrindTime… a two-hour block of time in the morning where I focused on my ONE THING and didn't let any distractions get in the way.

Your success is dependent on your ability to focus on your ONE THING. For you to be able to focus on your ONE THING, you have to have a designated block of time where you have a scheduled appointment with yourself to work on that thing every single day. That time is your #GrindTime. Protect it with your life because your destiny depends on it.

Cheat Code #19 - Establish Firm Boundaries

In that last cheat code, I talked about how you need to block yourself off from the outside world for two to four hours each day to work on your ONE THING. This is your #GrindTime. That's the only way that you will build the consistency needed to hit your wealth goal. When I first implemented my grind time. I would turn my cell phone on airplane mode and lock it away in a drawer so no calls or notifications could interrupt me. I needed that time to be absolutely focused on finishing my ONE THING as fast as possible.

One day, my boss was trying to reach me. He called several times during my grind time. Since my phone wasn't ringing, his calls were going straight to voicemail. After I finished my ONE THING (which was making cold calls to prospects), I turned my phone on and saw that he had left several voicemails from him. My heart sank! I knew that he was going to be furious with me for not answering his calls. I called him back in a frenzy.

When he first answered the phone, I immediately started apologizing. He said, *"Jarvis, what the hell were you doing for the last two hours!?"*

I told him about my #GrindTime. I explained that every day, I went straight into the office and I started making calls without any distractions. I told him about how I lock my phone away so that I could completely concentrate on making calls.

I'll never forget what he said to me. He said, *"Jarvis, that's exactly what I want you to do! I didn't hire you to sit around all day and wait for my calls. I hired you to bring in new business, and if that's what you were doing, then I'd rather you ignore my call!"*

His response gave me freedom. His response gave me permission. Permission to not be available. Permission to not respond to people immediately. Permission to go into a black hole without the guilt of having to be accessible for others.

That day showed me that it's OK to set firm boundaries and protect my time. When I'm doing my highest-leverage activity, it's OK to go dark. It's OK to hide my phone and shut down my inbox so that I can't be distracted. That day, my boss gave me permission. He said that doing my ONE THING was even more important than addressing his needs, and he was the person signing my paychecks! That day, he gave me freedom to ignore everything and everyone while I was doing my most important, most critical, highest-leveraged activity… my ONE BIG THING!

Then he said something else that rocked my world. He said, "Jarvis, I respect you more, now that I know you have discipline with your time." He actually looked up to me because he saw that I was a person of discipline. He saw that I was a person that had boundaries. That I was a person that lived up to my word and my commitment to myself. He saw that I didn't just let other people pounce all over my time.

When I started respecting my time, he started respecting me. People respect people with boundaries (remember, my vegan friend who firmly established his non-negotiable?) People will respect you more when you show that you value your own time. If you are available to everyone all the time, then they know that they can drag you around and they won't respect you or your time. But when they see that you put yourself on a pedestal, then they will put you on a pedestal too!

People respect people who respect their own time. So now, I want to give you the same permission that my boss gave me that day. From this point forward, I give you permission to not be available to everyone all the time. Turn your phone off, close down your inbox, and work on that ONE BIG THING every morning as soon as you start working.

Everyone else will be fine if they have to wait an hour or two before they get a response from you. The world won't end if they get your email response at 10 a.m. as opposed to 8:30 a.m. But if you consistently put off your ONE BIG THING to address other people, then your income won't be fine. It will stay average. You weren't built for average. Have firm boundaries with your time and watch your wealth skyrocket!

Cheat Code #20 - Go Dark

Your inbox is a Pandora's box of distractions, non-urgent emails, trivial tasks, and fires that don't need putting out immediately. Once you open that door, it's almost impossible to close it.

That's why I recommend that you avoid opening your inbox until your ONE BIG THING is finished. If you can build this one simple discipline to safeguard yourself from your biggest distractor, your productivity will skyrocket! I check my email at three strategic points in the day: after my grind time, after lunch, and before I finish work for the day. I have three email blocks scheduled on my calendar.

You control the day; don't let the day control you. And your email is the biggest way that you will lose control of the day. It has everyone else's intention for your time. Free yourself from these shackles and you'll restore your freedom. Odds are, there's nothing urgent waiting for you anyway. They can wait. Your ONE BIG THING can't!

Your next biggest distractor from doing your most critical work is your phone. Every ding, every notification, every ring, every chime. It has us trained like a starving dog hearing the dinner bell. We will stop everything and dive for our phone just to see who messaged us or liked our latest post.

What you don't realize is that every time you break your concentration, it takes 15 minutes to get back into a state of flow again. It's like a big, heavy locomotive, one of those old-school steam engine trains. Once it gets up to speed, it can move. However, it takes a long time for it to build up to full speed. Your brain is the same way. Every time you grab your phone, it's like slamming the breaks and coming to a dead stop. And then you have to put coal in your engine and fire it back up to get your wheels to slowly start moving again. You probably lose three to four hours of productivity just from grabbing your phone every 15 minutes all day long.

Try this: Move your phone out of your vision. When your phone is in your line of sight, your brain will constantly yearn to grab it. Even if it doesn't ring or chime, we are obsessed with knowing if there is a notification waiting that we missed, so we will reach for it without even being prompted. Also, our brain doesn't want to focus on hard work (remember the prehistoric brain), so it will search for ways to distract itself, and your phone is public enemy number one. So move it out of your line of sight so your brain won't even be tempted to grab it. I put my phone on silent mode and tuck it away in a desk drawer or deep into my laptop bag before every #GrindTime session.

When you can focus on one singular task for one to two hours without distractions, you'll notice that you get the same amount of work done that you probably accomplish in a full day. Establish your #GrindTime as an "email and phone black-out period," and you'll be an action-taking machine!

Cheat Code #21 - Be a Robot

Your ONE BIG THING is a big hairy frog. You won't want to do it. Right now, it probably takes a lot of effort, energy, willpower, and motivation to hype yourself up to do that ONE BIG THING. Your brain probably resists it because it's hard. The easiest way to go from resisting something to making it your autopilot where you just do it every day without even thinking about it is to turn it into a routine. A routine is something that you do the exact same way every day until you get to the point where you can do that thing without thinking. It has been transferred from your conscious to your subconscious where your automaticity lives. When you can successfully transfer an activity from your thinking mind to your unconscious mind, then it becomes a part of your autopilot.

The question is, how do you get something to become your subconscious autopilot? Repetition and routine! My kids hate to brush their teeth. Every single night, it's a battle to the death. I have to fight them tooth and nail to get them to brush their teeth before bed. I'm sure I was the same way as a child. But guess what? Eventually, I got to the place where I got up and brushed my teeth without even thinking about it. There are days when I get to work and say, "Damn, did I brush my teeth this morning?" I seriously don't even remember doing it. That's because it's a part of my routine. I just get up and do it unconsciously now. It's a part of my autopilot, so I execute it in such a flow that it just happens without me even realizing that I'm doing it.

So how do you establish a routine so that an action can become your autopilot? It has to happen at the same exact time and in the same exact way every single day. Your morning routine probably has very little variation. You wake up (hopefully after zero snoozes!) You go to the bathroom, take a pee, wash your hands, look at yourself in the mirror, grab your toothbrush, brush your teeth, wash your face, etc. Your brain is still in a zombie state, yet you can execute all of these things robotically because it's been done in this order for so long that it's burned a neural pathway into your brain. It's done at the same time, in the same place, in the same order every single day. That's how a routine is established.

As best as you can, schedule your #GrindTime block on your calendar at the exact same time every day. My original #GrindTime was from 8 a.m. to 10 a.m., and I didn't let anything get in the way of that. I didn't let other people schedule meetings at that time. That time was an appointment on my calendar that was locked in every day for me to meet with myself to do my ONE THING. When other people asked for a meeting at that time (like when clients wanted to meet), I would politely say, "Oh shoot, I'm not available at 9 a.m., could you do 1 p.m. instead?"

You don't have to make yourself available to everyone at all times. It's OK for you to have time on your calendar where you are unavailable. It actually makes you seem more respectable and exclusive. People shouldn't have unlimited access to you because then you seem needy and easy. It should be an honor for them to get time on your calendar, and therefore, you shouldn't present yourself as having unlimited availability.

The hottest restaurants in town have very limited seats, and if you can snag a reservation on a Friday night, you've hit the jackpot! You'll bend over backwards to go to that restaurant if you're lucky enough to get a reservation. However, you can go to McDonald's anytime and get a meal in 10 minutes. You don't see people jumping for joy to go to McDonald's (unless they are high at 2 a.m. on a Saturday night!)

Be exclusive. Don't let people control your calendar. You control your calendar. Therefore, don't ever prioritize anything else over your #GrindTime window. That means clients. That means admin work. That even means your boss. Because if you don't grind, pretty soon, you won't have a boss anyway!

Be a robot. Do your #GrindTime at the exact same time, in the exact same way every day. Create a recurring calendar appointment labeled #GrindTime. This is the most important appointment of your entire day. It's where you will make all of your money!

Cheat Code #22 - #DoneByLunch

I briefly touched on the #DoneByLunch strategy in the "Skip Breakfast" cheat code. #DoneByLunch isn't just a hashtag; it's a mindset, a productivity

EVERY. DAMN. DAY.

hack, a declaration of freedom. At its core, it's simple: finish your most important work, the one big thing, before lunch. That's it. That's the rule.

When you wake up early, skip breakfast, and break a sweat, your body enters a peak state of focus. Your mind sharpens, your energy spikes, and suddenly, you've got this sacred window where your best brain is on fire. And instead of wasting that energy on emails or scrolling Instagram, you lock it on the single most important thing that will move the needle in your life or business. Get that done, and the rest of the day is gravy.

Here's the personal deal I make with myself: no food until I finish. No snack. No shake. No lunch. Fork doesn't hit the plate until my one big thing is done. And since I love food, trust me, whatever stands in the way of that first bite doesn't stand a chance.

That's habit stacking, discipline meets dopamine. James Clear popularized it in Atomic Habits, but I live it daily. Stack the pain of doing hard things with the pleasure of eating lunch, and suddenly, the resistance disappears. The work gets done. The habit reinforces itself.

But let me tell you where this really clicked for me. When my son was born, I made a vow to be a super-present father. I didn't just want to provide for him financially; I wanted to be there. Every day, I'd finish my work and pick him up from preschool around 1 p.m. Some days, we'd hit the park. Other days, the beach. It wasn't about working less or coasting; it was about working smarter in the morning so I could buy back my afternoons.

That urgency to finish before pickup transformed me. My mornings became supercharged. I worked with intensity. I cut distractions. And because of that, I unlocked extraordinary afternoons… afternoons filled with memories, laughter, and moments I can never get back.

So I'll ask you: what would you do if you had extraordinary afternoons? What would you do more of if you had your time back? What's been neglected? Your hobbies? Your health? Your relationships? When was the last time you had the margin to golf, hike, play pickleball, or simply sit in silence without guilt?

See, I don't believe you need to grind 14 hours a day. I believe you can strategically design your day so you get the most important work done and still live an extraordinary life. That's exactly what the #DoneByLunch lifestyle is about. That's what it means to be a Morning Hero.

Start early. Finish early. Live an extraordinary life. Welcome to the #DoneByLunch life..

Conclusion

So there it is, the cheat code for explosive progress: focus on your ONE Big Action.

Not the dozen tasks screaming for your attention. Not the easy stuff that makes you feel productive but doesn't actually move the needle. Not the social media posts or shiny distractions. Just one action, the one you've been avoiding, the one that actually matters, the one that changes everything.

This is how you stop spinning your wheels. This is how you break through the plateau and start building real momentum again.

It's not about doing more.

It's about doing what matters most, and that starts with ruthless clarity and relentless follow-through on your ONE Big Action.

So here's your challenge:

EVERY. DAMN. DAY.

1. **Wake up and identify your ONE Big Action** which is the single move that would have the biggest impact on your wealth / work goal.
2. **Do it first.** Before email. Before calls. Before distractions creep in.
3. **Don't eat until it's done #DoneByLunch**

No excuses. No avoidance. Just decisive, focused execution.

Do this for one week and you'll feel the shift. You'll feel the momentum. You'll feel your confidence rise and your results multiply.

Do this for 30 days straight? Your business, your income, your impact will explode through the roof!

☐ **Reflection**

- What's the ONE THING that you need to focus on daily to accelerate your wealth, work, or career goal?
- How can you block out one to two hours each day to work on that thing (#GrindTime)?
- What usually prevents you from doing your ONE BIG THING?
- How can you protect yourself and establish boundaries so you can focus on doing your ONE BIG THING every day?

☐ **Take Action**

- Scan the QR code and join the 30-day challenge and track your progress each day on your ONE BIG THING.
- In less than 30 short days, you'll be more focused, more organized, more accomplished and **more wealthy!**

CHAPTER 19
SPREAD JOY

"A generous person will prosper; whoever refreshes others will be refreshed."

— The Bible (Proverbs 11:25)

Cheat Code #23 - Make Someone Smile

I remember one day during the pandemic, I picked up the phone and called my friend and mentor, Karl Gorman. Let me tell you a little bit about Karl. He's one of the most business-minded, financially savvy, and successful people I've ever met. At the time, Karl was the number one sales rep at a major insurance firm, selling corporate benefit packages to Fortune 100 companies. He was pulling in over half a million dollars a year and drove a Maserati. He was that guy, the one who walks into a room and instantly commands attention. The kind of presence where everyone turns and whispers, "Who is that?" His energy was magnetic. You just wanted to be around him. And when he spoke, people listened, because they knew whatever came out of his mouth was going to be gold.

In 2021, the world was in full-blown crisis mode. The pandemic was raging, the economy was spiraling, and panic was in the air. Every headline screamed disaster. People were losing jobs left and right. Companies were folding. It felt like the entire global system was on fire. Now, I'm normally a very optimistic person, but even I was feeling the weight of it all. I needed some grounding, so I called Karl, hoping he'd have some words of wisdom like he always did.

We hadn't spoken in a few months, and I wasn't sure how he was holding up through all the chaos. As soon as he picked up, I asked him, "Hey Karl, how are you doing?" I'll never forget his response. He said, "Jarvis, I couldn't be doing any better!" I paused. "Wait, what?" I said. "Karl, what do you mean? The economy's collapsing. People are getting laid off. The world's in a state of emergency. What do you mean you couldn't be doing any better?"

That's when he told me something that stopped me in my tracks. He said, "Jarvis, I've got so much business right now I'm actually turning clients away! Every time my phone rings, it's another company wanting to sign a new policy. I can't keep up, so I'm referring business out. I'm making more money than I've ever made. My family's thriving. Honestly, life's never been better."

I was stunned. "How?" I asked. "How is that even possible? Most people are scrambling to stay afloat. What are you doing differently?" I was expecting him to tell me about his marketing strategy or some deeply strategic business plan. He paused for a moment and then said the sentence that would tattoo itself on my heart:

"Jarvis, I don't know how to explain it… all I can tell you is, the more I give, the more I get."

And just like that, it all clicked.

Karl wasn't just a powerhouse in business; he was also the most generous human I've ever known. He sat on the boards of three nonprofits. He gave away 20% of his income every year to help minority

EVERY. DAMN. DAY.

kids get into college. Anytime we went out to dinner, he'd tip the waiter $100 without fail. He told me that everything in his life changed when he stopped chasing income and started focusing on impact. Every single day, he made it a point to leave a positive mark on someone's life. He told me his secret was simple: he asked himself one question every morning, "How can I put a smile on someone's face today?"

The moment he shifted his mindset from "How do I get what I want?" to "How can I help others get what they want?" everything in his world expanded. His relationships deepened. His business exploded. And the joy in his life multiplied.

That conversation cracked something open in me. I realized that if I wanted to receive more joy, more love, more fulfillment, I had to become a source of it first. I had to go first. Because the truth is, joy is a boomerang. The more you throw it out into the world, the more it comes flying back to you.

And it doesn't take much. Spreading joy isn't some grand, heroic act. It's simple. It's small. It's everyday kindness. It's giving a sincere compliment to the barista at Starbucks. It's bringing home a bouquet of flowers for your wife just because. It's sending a random text to a friend that says, "I miss you. I'm thinking about you."

Every single day, we are handed dozens of opportunities to reach out, to lift someone up, to leave the world better than we found it. These moments may seem small, but over time, they plant seeds. And when you keep planting seeds of joy, generosity, and impact, they grow into a forest of abundance.

The more you give, the more you get.

And the more smiles you create in the world, the more your life will be filled with them. So let me ask you this…

How can you put a smile on someone's face today? Seriously. Write their name down, and go spread some joy!

Cheat Code #24 - Text Roulette

I want to introduce you to a little game I play often, one of the simplest, most powerful ways I've found to spread joy. I call it Text Roulette. It's incredibly easy, wildly effective, and it always puts a smile on someone's face, including mine.

Here's how it works. I open the text messaging app on my phone, flick my thumb a few times, and let my messages scroll like a slot machine. Conversations fly past the screen, threads from weeks or even months ago, until it finally slows down and lands on one at random. That's where the magic begins.

I pick someone I haven't spoken to in a while, usually someone who's drifted a bit into the background of my life. Before I send anything, I'll hop over to their social media page and scroll through their latest updates. Most people post every few days, so it doesn't take long to catch up on what's new. I look for something I can comment on. A new job, a family trip, or a tough season they're navigating. Then I jump back to my text messages and write something thoughtful and kind.

It might be as simple as:

"Just saw your latest post. Huge congrats on the new job! So proud of you. ☐"

Or maybe:

"Hey, I saw what you shared about your dad. Just wanted to say I'm thinking of you. Sending love. ☐"

EVERY. DAMN. DAY.

That's it. A 15-second message. But what happens next is often magic.

That one small act, just a few heartfelt words, can completely brighten someone's day. And here's the best part: if you do it in the morning, it creates this ripple effect that echoes through the rest of your day. You feel incredible sending that message, knowing you sparked a little light in someone's world. Then, maybe five, ten, thirty minutes later, they respond. Their joy becomes your joy. You reply. They reply. And suddenly, you've got this joy tennis match bouncing back and forth, infusing your day with connection, gratitude, and good energy.

What started as a random scroll becomes a spark, one small moment of intentional kindness that multiplies. That's the power of Text Roulette. It's not just about sending messages. It's about reconnecting with the people in your life, even if just for a moment, and choosing to be a source of joy. You never know who needs to hear your words today.

Go ahead and do it right now. Pull out your phone, go to your messages app, scroll, stop, and send the love. Then just sit back and watch how it creates a chain reaction that will uplift your whole day!

Cheat Code #25 - The Love Bomb

Earlier in the book, I shared how my wife and I went through a rough patch. We separated for a period of time. Eventually, we found our way back to each other. And during that season of reconciliation, what I like to call our courtship 2.0, I was on a mission to win her heart all over again.

Every single day, I'd wake up and set a clear intention for what I wanted in my relationship. And I'd ask myself one simple question: "What can I do today to spread joy to Jane?" At the time, we were living in different cities. I was in Chicago, and she was in San Diego. So I couldn't show up physically, but I could show up with my words.

Every day, without fail, I sent her a message. Some days it was something short and sweet like, "You light up my world." Other days it was a long, heartfelt poem, just to express emotions I would've normally had a hard time saying out loud.

Now, I'm not saying those text messages are the reason we're married today. But I am saying this: Most relationships fail because people stop affirming each other. They assume their partner knows how they feel. Or they think that just because they live under the same roof, love is implied. But nothing replaces good, old-fashioned words of affirmation.

To this day, I make it a point to send my wife a love bomb every single day. Just so she never forgets she's the centerpiece of my world. The star of my universe. The honey to my bee. The peanut butter to my jelly. (Yeah, I know... corny.)

But you know what? These little three-minute messages are the reason we haven't had a fight in over seven years. They're the reason we have one of the happiest, most joy-filled marriages I've ever witnessed. We're not pretending. We're not performing. We're genuinely, deeply, authentically happy, and that joy overflows into our home, into our kids, and into everything we do.

So if you're serious about spreading joy, start at home. Don't take your partner for granted. Ask yourself this one question every morning: "How can I spread joy to the person I love today?" If you answer that question every day, you won't just be putting up with each other... you'll legitimately enjoy every second that you're together!

Cheat Code #26 - S.E.C.

One afternoon my family and I went out for lunch. From the moment we sat down, we could tell something was off with our waitress. It took her forever to greet us, and when she finally showed up, she had an obvious attitude. No smile. No warmth. It was like our presence in her section was a personal inconvenience. I used to wait tables all through college, so I've got a deep appreciation for good service, and nothing gets under my skin more than bad customer service. I was two seconds away from giving her a piece of my mind when suddenly, my cousin walked in.

Now, let me tell you about my cousin. She's notoriously late, but she's also the bubbliest, most joyful person in our family. She had just finished flight attendant school to work for Southwest Airlines, so that should tell you everything you need to know about her energy. She walks through the door beaming, and as she arrives at our table, I immediately start venting about how terrible our waitress has been. And right on cue, our waitress walks up. Before I could say a word, my cousin turns to her and says with a huge smile, "Girl, those are some awesome shoes! I love those. They look so cute on you!"

The waitress froze. Then, slowly, you could see her entire being shift. Her stiff posture relaxed. Her frown melted into a big, blushing smile. She and my cousin started chatting about shoes, fashion, and who knows what else. In a matter of seconds, my cousin had turned this grumpy, closed-off waitress into a radiant ball of light. She layered compliment after compliment, and you could literally see joy taking over her body. Five minutes later, that same waitress came back with a free appetizer, telling us it was on the house. She was all smiles. We couldn't believe it.

I turned to my cousin, still stunned, and said, "What did you just do?! We were about to ask for a new waitress because of her attitude, and you just completely flipped her mood in five seconds!" She smiled and said, "That was intentional. We learned this in Southwest flight attendant training. It's called the S.E.C. method, Smile, Eye Contact, Compliment." She went on to explain, "Everyone wants to be acknowledged. Everyone wants to be validated. When you compliment someone, you're affirming a decision they made, whether it's the shoes they put on that day, the way they styled their hair, or something they chose to wear. That validation fills them with joy, and the beautiful thing is, once they light up, they reflect that joy right back onto you. It becomes a ripple of energy."

She told me she practices this everywhere she goes. The moment she walks into a space, she looks for something to compliment. Not fake praise, but a sincere, thoughtful observation. It sets the tone for the entire experience. I thought it was brilliant. So the next day, I decided to try it myself. I walked into Starbucks and set a very clear intention: I'm going to compliment my barista today. But I wasn't going to just throw out a fake compliment; I was going to look for something real, something genuine I could appreciate.

As I approached the counter, I noticed the barista had a special pin on his apron. When I got to the register, I said, "Hey, that's an awesome pin you've got there. It looks really special. Where did you get it?" The look on his face was priceless. It was like no one had ever noticed that pin before. He lit up and started telling me the story of how he earned it. Apparently, it's one of Starbucks' highest honors. He was a "Master Roaster," which only 1% of all baristas achieve. He had gone through an intensive training program, attended a special school, and passed rigorous tests. He was so proud. He talked my ear off for five straight minutes while a line formed behind me, and I didn't mind one bit.

And ever since then, every time I walk into that Starbucks, he lights up like we're old friends. All because I took a sec to acknowledge him. That's all it takes. Just a sec. Everywhere you go, every single day, set the intention to see people. Not fake flattery, not manipulation, but real, intentional, authentic appreciation. Look for something they chose. Something you can genuinely admire.

1. Smile.

2. Make Eye contact.

3. Give a Compliment.

It only takes a SEC. But that one tiny moment can ripple joy through someone's entire day.

And the best part? When you give out joy bombs, the universe has a funny way of blessing you right back… with more joy, more favor, more magic than you can imagine.

Cheat Code #27 - Intentional Downtime

I get this question all the time. "Jarvis, do you schedule your personal things on your calendar?" The answer is emphatically yes. I set an intention for every hour of the day, which includes planning for family, friends, and fun. I believe that you should be just as intentional about your personal life as you are about your work life.

Your calendar shouldn't only be filled with work-related things. You should also block out the time that you're going to do things for yourself and for your family. I call this "intentional downtime." I always say that **your calendar is where your commitments are**. I should be able to look at your calendar and see everything that's important to you. It has all your priorities. So if you have a non-work-related goal that is a priority to you, then it should be reflected on your calendar. You should have appointments for family and fun just like you have work appointments.

Your personal life shouldn't just be an afterthought. And that's what happens to most people. They are very intentional about their work life, and they put no effort into planning their personal life. Next thing you know, their entire life starts to crumble because they only have a one-legged stool. Remember, the three pillars of success and fulfillment: health, wealth/work, and relationships. These three pillars make up the legs on your stool, and a stool can't stand on one leg alone. It needs other supports.

Your life is the same way. Your life can't stand on one leg. That's why wealth/work shouldn't be the only thing you set an intention for in your calendar. Your calendar should also reflect your health and relationship priorities as well. Every day, I schedule my downtime and it's reflected on my calendar. This goes for my workouts and fitness routine, my meal times, my family time, and even intentional time to binge Netflix (yes, I do this, but notice, I do it intentionally). Here are four reasons why you should plan out your downtime just like you plan out your up-time:

#1 - It deepens your commitment to those activities.

For me, when I see an appointment on my calendar, I am committing to it subconsciously. Once I put something on my calendar, I've made an agreement with myself to do that thing. Even if it's something like taking my wife on a date or playing with my kids, I schedule that time on my calendar. Some people may think that's too rigid. To those people, I say, "I'm not rigid. I'm committed." I'm committed to show up for my family. I'm committed to show up for my health and fitness. I'm committed to showing up for my mental well-being. Your calendar shows your commitments, and when you look at my calendar, you can clearly see that I'm committed to not only building a successful business but also a strong body and an amazing home life. What does your calendar say about you? If you aren't blocking out time on your calendar for health and relationships, then you aren't fully committed to them.

#2 - It puts boundaries on your day.

Every day, I schedule what time I'm leaving work and what time I'm having dinner with the family. It's blocked out time on my calendar. Therefore, as I am going throughout my day, my day has a hard stop boundary. I know that at 5 p.m., I need to go to the grocery store to get the ingredients for dinner so it can be ready by 6 p.m. All day long, I have a sense of urgency to close out my day at 5 p.m. because I know that I have a dinner appointment with my family at 6 p.m. I have added motivation to finish my work as quickly as possible so that I'm not late for the appointment. Otherwise, if I don't have that dinner time blocked off on my calendar and it is just left blank, my work would easily fill up that void. My work would easily linger late into the evening if I let it. There's always work to be done. Therefore, I have to put a hard stop on my day, or else, work takes over and I become a one-legged stool.

#3 - It gives you something to look forward to.

Each morning when I set my intentions, I ask myself, "How am I going to show up as a HERO for my family today? What fun thing am I going to plan for us to do this evening?" And then I schedule it and put it on my calendar. Oftentimes it'll be something like, "Take the kids to the park," "Family game night after dinner," or "Give my wife a foot rub while watching our latest Netflix series." When I actually schedule it as an appointment on my calendar, I see it all day long. So as I'm doing hard things throughout my day, each time I pull my phone out to glance at my calendar, I see the fun thing that I have planned for that evening, and it gives me something to look forward to. It actually makes my #GrindTime a little more enjoyable and motivating. I know that I have a reward coming at the end of the day. I have something fun planned. I'm going to put a smile on someone's face. And that brings me joy in the moment. So if it's 11 a.m. and I'm making phone calls, I might be feeling a little drained and defeated, but then when I see on my calendar that I'm going to take my son to the park that afternoon, I start smiling. It makes my phone calls more enjoyable, knowing that I have a reward waiting for me later. The hard thing that I'm doing in that moment doesn't feel as hard anymore. Don't fill your calendar with only heavy, hard things. Put fun, joyful things on your calendar too. It will keep you in high spirits even when you are doing your heaviest tasks.

#4 - It gives your brain permission to be present.

Oftentimes we plague ourselves with overthinking and over-processing things. This usually is about work or things that stress us out, and our brain continues to process those things even though we're not physically at work anymore. We can be sitting at the dinner table with our children trying to talk to us, and we just sit there with a blank stare because we're thinking about something that happened at work or something that we still have to get done. Our spirit is not there. You might as well not physically be there at all because it has the same effect. You have to be able to give your brain permission to shut off. You have to give your brain permission to switch to a new activity. Your calendar tells your brain what to focus on at that moment. While I'm grinding, I see it on my calendar. It triggers my brain to start grinding. And when I'm supposed to be present at the dinner table with my family, it's on my calendar, and it triggers my brain and gives me permission to be there with my family. I'm not thinking about other things. Essentially, your calendar gives your brain its instructions of what it should be processing at any point in the day. And so if you don't put downtime on your calendar, your brain won't know that it has permission to turn off. Your brain doesn't naturally have any boundaries, so you have to put your brain in a box, and the way you do that is by scheduling everything on your calendar. Including downtime. This extends to weekends too. I schedule out my entire weekends. Of course, it looks a little different. I'm not scheduling work. I'm scheduling fun things.

One day, I was showing one of my CEO clients my calendar, and they saw on my calendar that I had "Netflix and Chill" time scheduled for me and my wife that evening. At the time, we got really into a murder mystery series, and it was part of our bonding time. After we put the kids down, we would sit and watch one episode of the series. So I actually had it scheduled on my calendar. My client noticed that block of time scheduled on my calendar, and she asked, "Why do you schedule time to watch TV with your wife?"

I told her that if I didn't schedule it in my calendar, I might try to do some work after dinner instead of sitting on the couch and being present with her. I told her that I had to schedule it to give my brain the opportunity to warm up to the idea all day long so that by the evening time, my brain could be fully committed to that activity and not try to work or think about other things at that time.

After explaining why scheduling downtime is important, she said she was going to try it. I saw her a few weeks later and she had a whole different spirit about herself. "Jarvis, you would never believe how good things are going with my husband! That little trick you told me about scheduling downtime has made all the difference in the world."

As a busy executive, she said that their family time would be an afterthought. She would just rush through dinner, put the kids down, and then pull out her laptop work through the night. She shared with me that her marriage was on the rocks, and she never realized how unhappy her husband was. They had grown very distant from each other.

After I showed her how to start being more intentional with her downtime, she started planning fun things for her and her husband to do together each night. Every morning, when she was setting her intentions for the day, she would ask herself, "What creative way can my husband and I connect tonight?" And then she would schedule it on her calendar. Some nights, it would be a game night. Some nights, they would have a glass of wine after they put the kids down. It changed from night to night, but every night she had a block of time scheduled for her and her husband to connect. She said, "Jarvis, it's like we have a new marriage. We enjoy each other again. Planning our downtime has become the best part of my day, and all day long I'm looking forward to it. He's no longer an afterthought. I have him committed to my calendar just like I have my business commitments on there. And to be honest, he's more important than my business. And there's no reason that my business should get all of me and he gets the scraps."

The takeaway: Be intentional about every hour of your day **INCLUDING** your downtime. This ensures that you have all the legs on your stool and it's a strong foundation that can withstand anything that life throws at you.

Cheat Code #28 - Date Night

When it comes to spreading joy, the place where you should exert the most energy, the first place you should pour joy into, is your marriage or relationship. Your relationship is the foundation. It's the starting point of all happiness. The joy you feel in your life is directly rooted in the energy you generate at home. If your home life is broken, no amount of success can override that. No amount of money can soothe that pain. In fact, a broken home can become the biggest detractor from your success.

Napoleon Hill once said that one of the greatest demises of a person's potential is a poor choice in a partner. If there's constant turmoil at home, it will limit your ability to produce at a high level. That's why I put extreme focus on my marriage. Earlier in the book, I shared that when my wife and I got married, we made a non-negotiable commitment: weekly date night. It is locked in stone on our calendar every single week, without fail. It's the highlight of our week. It's sacred time where we focus on rekindling our relationship.

And now that we have children, date night has become even more important. Because let's be real… parenthood is beautiful, but it's also stressful. Over time, the stress of raising kids can wear on a marriage. You start to lose connection. You become more like business partners managing schedules and logistics, just trying to keep the children alive, and somewhere along the way, you forget how to truly know and enjoy each other. That's why we protect our connection like our lives depend on it. And here's another powerful reason: your children are watching

They're forming their impressions of what love looks like based on what they see between you and your partner. If your relationship lacks affection, playfulness, or connection, they won't know what a healthy relationship is supposed to feel like. Your daughter won't know what kind of love to expect. Your son won't know how to treat a woman. They model everything, so if you want to raise kids who thrive in love, they need to witness two parents who are in love. That's why date night for us is not a luxury… it's a religion.

All week long, we're texting each other ideas, scouting new restaurants, and coming up with fun things to do. It doesn't have to be expensive, it just has to be intentional. Some of our favorite dates are simple, like taking a walk on the beach with our sports bottles filled with wine. We call them "wine walks." It's free. It's playful. It's magic. We laugh, we reminisce, we connect. Because a date isn't about how much money you spend. A date is about quality time, presence, and attention. You need time outside the house, outside the whirlwind of family life, where you can truly see each other again.

Make date night a ritual. Make it a priority. Make it a religion. Because when your marriage is strong, your life will be too.

Conclusion

By now, you've seen the power of intentional joy. Not the kind that happens to you, but the kind you create on purpose. Joy isn't a random emotion that drifts into your life when the stars align. It's a habit. A skill. A muscle you can flex every single day.

We've talked about the cheat codes, simple tools to create ripple effects of happiness in your relationships, in your work, and within yourself. You learned about Text Roulette, a quick and easy way to light up someone's world with a thoughtful message. That 30-second act of kindness can echo throughout your entire day, sparking connection and joy in ways you didn't even expect.

You learned about the practice of daily love bombs, intentional words of affirmation for your partner. A simple text, a poetic message, or a kind word can rebuild bridges, ignite intimacy, and breathe life back into relationships that have quietly settled into autopilot.

You heard the story of Karl, and how he shifted his entire mindset from chasing income to chasing impact. How his daily goal became not to make money but to make someone smile. And how, ironically, the more joy he gave away, the more abundance he received in return.

Because that's the secret. The fastest way to receive joy is to become the source of it. If you've ever felt stuck in a rut, burnt out, or disconnected, here's your way out:

Don't wait for joy. Create it. Every day. On purpose. With intention.

So here's your final challenge:

For the next 30 days, do one intentional thing each day to spread joy.

- Send a random compliment.
- Write a love note.
- Buy a stranger a coffee.
- Reconnect with someone you've lost touch with.
- Text your kid and tell them how proud you are.
- Tell your barista they have an awesome smile.
- Leave a sticky note on your partner's pillow with a simple "I love you."

Be the reason someone smiles each day and you'll find more joy than you ever imagined.

EVERY. DAMN. DAY.

☐ Reflection

- Who deserves more of your attention?
- If someone looked at your calendar, would they be able to tell that your relationships are a priority to you?
- What's the simplest way for me to put a smile on someone's face? (Text message? Voice note? Compliment?)

☐ Take Action

- Scan the QR code and join the 30-day challenge and track your Joy-Spreading habit each day.
- In less than 30 short days, you'll become a **magnet of joy and blessings** that you won't have room enough to receive!

PART IV
YOUR HERO'S JOURNEY

CHAPTER 20
IT'S YOUR TURN

"Your playing small does not serve the world. There is nothing enlightened about shrinking so that other people won't feel insecure around you."

— Marianne Williamson

Answer the Call

This is the moment. The call you've been hearing, The truth is, you've always known it was there. You've known you were meant for more. You've known there was another level of energy, focus, and impact waiting for you. And now here you are, with a decision to make.

You've read the stories. You've seen the framework. You've learned the cheat codes. But none of that matters unless you step forward. Unless you decide to act.

Tomorrow morning, the alarm will go off and you will be faced with the same choice you've faced every morning of your life. You can roll over, hit snooze, and fall back into the same life that you've been living. The life that's beneath the best version of you. Or… you can decide to WIN. You can swing your feet to the floor, step into the quiet stillness of the morning, and dominate the day!

That single choice matters more than you realize. Because every morning you choose to stay small, the world misses out. Every time you surrender to the whirlwind, every time you hide behind comfort, every time you sleep in instead of showing up, we all lose.

You see, this isn't just about you anymore. It's not just about your goals, your habits, your productivity. It's about the people who are watching you. Your kids, your partner, your team. They don't need you half-alive, stumbling through your days and escaping through your nights. They need you lit up. They need you focused. They need you at your best.

And beyond them? The world needs you. Your gifts, your ideas, your potential, those aren't yours to hoard. They were given to you for a reason. They were entrusted to you to serve others. When you play small, when you don't step fully into who you were called to be, you're not just cheating yourself. You're cheating all of us.

So understand this: Hiding your greatness is selfish. The world deserves to see you unleashed! Your community deserves to benefit from your creativity and leadership. Your family deserves to experience you fully alive, present, and purposeful. Your colleagues deserve to be inspired by your example. Every morning you waste is another morning you've kept that light locked away.

But when you rise, when you commit to the way of the Morning Hero, you don't just win the morning. You ignite a ripple effect that touches everyone around you. You show your children what discipline looks like. You give your spouse a partner they can lean on and grow with. You model to your team what focus and consistency can achieve. And you contribute your fullest self to a world starving for leaders who live with passion and purpose.

So yes, this is your call to adventure. But it's bigger than that. This is your responsibility. The world needs you. The world deserves you. Not the half-hearted, tired, burnt-out version of you. The full, unleashed, all-in you.

EVERY. DAMN. DAY.

Tomorrow morning, the alarm will ring. And in that moment, you will decide: Will you roll over, or will you rise?

This Is Your Life as a Morning Hero

Now that you have fully committed to answer your call for greatness and embark upon your hero's journey, let me paint the picture of what your new life will be like. Here's a snapshot of a day in your life as a Morning Hero.

Time	Activity	Description
5 a.m.	Power Hour	You wake up into the calm peace of the morning. No kids screaming. No frantic rush to start the day. You have time and space to be proactive instead of reactive to the day. You spend some time setting your 5-star intentions and "zero-ing out" your calendar. You feel planned, organized and ahead of the day.
6 a.m.	Activate	Your family is still sleeping so you take advantage of the margin by going for a "reading run." The sun is rising, your heart is pumping, your mind is stimulated, your vibration is rising. You feel on top of the world! You feel unstoppable! Your HERO has officially been activated for the day! You just got 2 stars (**Heart Rate** and **Read**), and most people aren't even awake yet. You are officially WINNING the day before it even begins!

7 a.m.	Skip Breakfast	Now, your day can officially begin. You get the kids ready, check your inbox for anything urgent, and have your morning coffee. You opt to skip breakfast, allowing your brain to get into a hyper flow state. Instead of dragging through your morning, you feel super charged and super focused!
8 a.m.	Get Dressed and Go to Work	You've got some BIG things on your plate, so you get dressed and you go to battle. Instead of working from home, you go to a dedicated place to "eat your frog" with minimal distractions.
9 a.m.	#Grind Time	You put your phone on airplane mode, you close down your email inbox, and you go to war with your ONE BIG THING. You've made a deal with yourself that you can't have lunch until it's done, so you move with a sense of urgency and purpose. You are no stranger to the #Grind. You actually look forward to it now. You've been so consistent that now it's your autopilot. And the results are showing. Your business is growing, and it doesn't seem hard anymore. Things actually feel easy!
11 a.m.	Admin Work	Congratulations! You've accomplished your **ONE BIG THING**! It feels good getting it out of the way so early in the day. The rest of the day is just bonus! Since you were disconnected from your phone and email while you were doing your ONE BIG THING, now you catch up on texts, respond to emails, and tie up loose ends. You spend an hour cleaning the slate before rewarding yourself with a well-earned lunch.

12 p.m.	#DoneBy Lunch	Three stars down and you are on fire! There's no way that you're going to mess up that momentum with a crappy lunch! You swing by Chipotle and get a brown rice bowl with loads of chicken and veggies. You stick to your Bright Lines by avoiding flour and sugar. You get a glimpse of your reflection in the mirror and you like what you see. You look good and you feel even better!
1 p.m.	Meditation Walk	You've been going 1,000 miles an hour, so you decide to hit the pause button and go for a walk. but instead of listening to an audio book, you choose to just be present with your thoughts. You start getting some clarity. A new idea for something at work. A resolution to a problem that had you stuck. Then someone pops into your mind and you pull out your phone and send them a text message. They popped into your mind for a reason, so you just let them know that you were thinking about them. They respond with a heartfelt message of appreciation. That little joy bomb made their day... and it made yours too. It also earned you a star for **Spreading Joy.**

2 p.m.	Bonus Block	This is the moment where your day feels like it opens up. Because you dominated the morning, you've created a pocket of freedom in the afternoon, a bonus block of time that feels like a second wind. You use this time for meetings, appointments, and all the little admin tasks without stress weighing on your shoulders. The pressure's gone because the big domino, the task that actually moves your life forward, was already knocked down before lunch. Now you've got margin. You can even turn it into you time. Hit the gym, take a fitness class, pick up a hobby, or do anything that you "never have time for." This block is your reward, an extra slice of life you earned by winning the morning.
6 p.m.	#Salad4 Dinner	You've been making healthy choices all day. You started the day with a great workout. You had a delicious brown rice and chicken bowl for lunch. There's no way you're going to mess that up with a crappy dinner. You make a fancy salad with double protein. It's beautiful, it tastes amazing, and it leaves you completely full and satisfied. You'll be able to fall asleep easy without your stomach turning from a big heavy dinner. Congratulations… You've earned your **Eat Right** star for the day!

7 p.m.	Intentional Downtime	You planned some quality time with your partner. They love murder mysteries, so you blocked out some time to "Netflix and Chill" after dinner. You have a shared Google calendar so when you scheduled it, they got a notification and they've been looking forward to it all day! Your brain doesn't try to flip back into work mode after dinner. You intentionally planned to lay on the couch and enjoy this time, so your brain sinks into being present. It's a great way to reconnect and rekindle after a long productive day.
8 p.m.	Power-Down Hour	Your Power-Down Hour alarm goes off and that's your cue to start bringing your night to a close. It's your warning sign that you have 60 minutes to get to bed. But in reality, you didn't need the warning signal. You are exhausted! You had a wildly productive day and you can barely keep your eyes open at this point. You finish that episode of the murder mystery and you turn off the TV, along with all other devices. You plug your phone in the charger that's positioned across the room away from your bed, and then you complete your night routine. The calm peace of this last hour has allowed your brain to wind down and now, it won't resist sleep. It actually welcomes it.

9 p.m.	Book in Bed	You crawl into bed and grab a book from your nightstand. A few pages in and your eyes grow heavy. You smile. The day was everything you wanted it to be. Five stars earned. Momentum built. You leave nothing undone, nothing unsaid, nothing wasted. You close your eyes knowing one thing for sure: You didn't just survive this day, you won it. Another Day, Another W.

Declare Your New Identity

Being a Morning Hero isn't just about a morning routine. It's a lifestyle. It permeates into every hour of your day. It's not something you have to think about or consciously do. It defines who you are. It's a new identity. And the moment you shift from this being something you do, to someone you are, that's when everything shifts.

Earlier, I mentioned that I took on running as my preferred method to raise my heart rate (and I recommend it for you as well). I knew running a half-marathon was going to be hard because I never considered myself a runner. I have a pretty stocky build, and I don't look anything like a runner. In my mind, I was just someone who was trying to run. I struggled with it at first. I hated it. I never wanted to go for runs. I had to constantly fight my mind as it came up with every excuse in the world to stop. "Jarvis, your ankles hurt. Maybe you should take today off!" "Did you hear that? You might have broken a bone in your foot. You better slow down!" That inner voice was relentless!

But then one day, I saw a guy on the running trail and he looked like a seasoned marathon runner. He had all the gear, he had the perfect body type, he had the look, he had the technique…. he WAS a runner! You can tell that running was his life!

EVERY. DAMN. DAY.

And then I looked down and saw that he was wearing the same shoes that I was wearing. Then I scanned upward and noticed that he had the same running gloves that I had on. Then I noticed that we were the only two people on the running trail at that time at 6 a.m. I said to myself, "I must be a runner too! I AM A RUNNER!" That moment changed everything for me.

I stopped looking at myself as someone who was attempting to run and started calling myself a runner. That day, I stepped into a new identity as a runner. From that day forward, everything was automatic. I just naturally did what runners do. I ate what runners ate. I trained how runners train. I didn't even have to think about it because it became a part of who I was.

When we went to Chicago that year and it was 10 degrees outside, I naturally woke up at 5 a.m. and put on my running gear to go for a run. My mother said, "What are you doing? It's freezing outside! You can't go out there!" I said, "Of course I can… I'm a runner!" It hadn't even crossed my mind to not go for a run that day. It was automatic. I wake up… I run. That's what runners do.

And that year, I completed a life-long goal of mine to run a half-marathon. I defeated this nearly impossible goal for me not because I learned how to run… not because I tried this running thing… but because I BECAME a runner! The moment I shifted my identity, I no longer had to force myself to take the actions. The actions were automatic to fit my new identity.

Right now, you might be saying to yourself that this morning thing sounds cool and maybe you'll give it a try. Maybe you've even set your alarm to get up one hour earlier for a power hour and you're excited to WIN tomorrow morning. But this isn't something you do… this is someone you BECOME. From this day forward, you have to believe that you ARE a Morning Hero. You wake up an hour earlier than your whirlwind… You set your 5-star intentions… And you do it EVERY. DAMN.DAY!

The moment you say to yourself "I AM A MORNING HERO," you send instructions to your subconscious autopilot, and it will transform all of your habits and behaviors to match your new identity. And once your new identity is locked in… there's no turning back!

The Oath

Every great transformation begins with a vow. The soldier swears allegiance. The athlete declares commitment. The couple takes their wedding vows. A Morning Hero is no different. If you are going to rise, if you are going to live every damn day with intention, then you must stake your claim with words. Words that etch themselves into your identity. Words you can return to on the mornings when comfort whispers and mediocrity claws for your attention.

So here is your oath. Read it slowly. Say it out loud. Write it in your journal. Let it burn into your soul.

The Morning Hero Oath

I am a Morning Hero.I am no longer asleep to my potential.I am no longer reactive, distracted, or scattered.I wake up with power. I wake up with purpose.I command my time. I lead my life.I am the example my family has been waiting for.I choose discipline over comfort.I choose action over excuses.I am not trying anymore.**I am a Morning Hero.**And from this day forward…I wake up, and I WIN.Every. Damn. Day.

This is not just a set of words. It is who you are now. When the alarm rings tomorrow morning, you will not wonder what to do.

You will rise because that is what Morning Heroes do.

You will sit in silence with your journal because that's what Morning Heroes do.

EVERY. DAMN. DAY.

You will plan your calendar with precision because that's what Morning Heroes do.

You will exercise, eat right, read, spread joy and attack your biggest "money-making activity" with aggression because that's what Morning Heroes do.

You will dominate every. damn. day because that's just what Morning heroes do!

This is your oath. This is your declaration. This is your line in the sand.

Welcome to the Morning Hero Movement

Join the Movement

This world is divided. There are the few, and then there are the many. The few wake up with purpose. They rise before the world and plant their flag in the ground, declaring, "Today, I will WIN!" The few live a life *of* purpose, *on* purpose. The few fight every damn day to become the fullest version of themselves. That's us. That's the Morning Heroes.

And then there are the many. The sleepwalkers. The drifters. The coasters. The ones hitting snooze again and again, trading away their dreams for just a little more comfort under the covers. They wake up already behind, already overwhelmed, already consumed by the noise. They live on autopilot, content with an average life. They drift through the motions. They are stuck, stagnant, plateaued, living life half-asleep.

But not you. Not anymore.

You've officially joined the movement! This is not just *you versus you* anymore. This is *us versus them.* This is the few against the many.

This is the committed against the complacent. The awake against the asleep. The heroes against the herd. And we are in the fight of our lives.

Sleep Walkers	Morning Heroes
Wakes up late into chaos	Wakes up early with intention
Constantly distracted	Laser-focused on purpose
Scattered and unorganized	Structured, centered, in control
Burned out and overwhelmed	Energized and *done by lunch*
Stuck in reaction mode all day	Proactively designs the day
Wastes time scrolling and drifting	Wins the day by 9 a.m.
Makes excuses	Makes moves
Lives for weekends and vacations	Lives fulfilled *every single day*
Feels stuck, stagnant, coasting	Feels alive, aligned, and *ascending*
Fears change and stays comfortable	Chooses courage and consistency
Consumes inspiration	*Becomes* the inspiration

When you start waking up at 5 a.m., or even earlier, people are going to look at you differently. They'll think you're crazy. They'll question you. They'll mock you. They'll laugh at you for saying no to late nights, for protecting your mornings, for living with a discipline they can't imagine for themselves. And if you aren't careful, their mediocrity will start to bleed into you. Their comfort will start to feel contagious. Their excuses will start to sound reasonable.

We are at war. Not with people, but with mediocrity. We are at war with average. We are at war with a culture that says that it's OK to coast through life doing the bare minimum and not truly stretch into our full power. When you wake up and WIN every day, you are not just winning for yourself. You are striking a blow against mediocrity. You are standing as a lighthouse in a world swallowed by fog. You are the living, breathing proof of someone living a big life. That we don't have to settle. That we don't have to coast. That we don't have to sleepwalk through our best years.

That's the power of a movement. It's not about you anymore. It's about us. Each time you win your morning, you don't just elevate yourself, you elevate everyone around you. Your energy becomes contagious. Your discipline becomes magnetic. Your results become inspiring. And people will start to ask you, "What's gotten into you?" That's when you look them square in the eyes and say, "I am a Morning Hero!" You are now the recruiter. You are the example. By living as a Morning Hero, you will light the path for others to follow. You will pull them into their own greatness. You will slay the sleepwalker in them and ignite them on their own Hero's Journey.

This is how movements spread. Not by slogans or speeches, but by ordinary people choosing every day to stop playing small and live extraordinary lives. By one hero at a time, stepping forward, saying, "I refuse to drift. I refuse to coast. I will rise. I will fight. I will WIN." And those who witness your transformation will want it for themselves.

So welcome. You are no longer just a reader of this book. You are no longer just an individual chasing goals. You are part of a tribe, a family, a collective of Morning Heroes around the world. We fight for our lives, for our dreams, for our families, for our future. And we fight together.

From this day forward, you carry the banner. You are not just waking up early. You are standing on the front lines of a revolution against the status quo. You are proof of what's possible. You are the spark that will ignite others.

Together, we will change the world!

Every. Damn. Day.

We finally arrive at why this book has such a provocative title. Let me take you back to when I first became a Morning Hero. My wife and I had just gotten married and we were trying to have our first child. I didn't realize how hard it is to have a kid when you actually want one. I had spent most of my life trying to avoid having kids, but now that I wanted one, it was not easy! Month after month would pass by and we would go through the ritual. We had my wife's ovulation dates mapped out on a calendar with the exact days highlighted where she was "most fertile." We had apps on our phones that alerted us of the exact moment one of her eggs would drop, and it was "go time!" We researched the proper techniques and strategies to increase the chances of getting pregnant. Then came the waiting period. That four-week period where you have to see if she gets her period. Month after month passed. We would be so disappointed when her period came. It was so frustrating. I was thinking to myself, "How are all of these people on earth having unwanted pregnancies, and here we are, the perfect couple to bring a child into this world and we can't get pregnant?" I started to curse God because it didn't make sense.

After two years of trying and failing to get pregnant, a friend of ours said, "You guys need to just stop trying. Take a vacation and just enjoy each other." They were right. We had been so busy trying to get pregnant that our marriage had just become a formality. We weren't enjoying each other. We had just become robots trying to execute this mission of bringing a baby into the world. Outside of that, we had lost all connection.

We took our friend's advice and went to Hawaii (as I mentioned before, we go every year!) This was going to be the first time that we were going to relax and just enjoy being with each other instead of being so maniacally focused on ovulation calendars and conception strategies. We got to Hawaii, and it was magical! The flowers, the sunsets, the colors of the ocean. It was the most beautiful place that we had ever been.

We were staying at a Waldorf Astoria and it blew my socks off! The level of detail, the quality and care that they put into maintaining the property, the level of enthusiasm and professionalism from everyone on the staff… you truly feel like royalty during your entire stay.

Our first evening there was like heaven. We went to dinner at a restaurant on the beach where we could hear the waves crashing as we ate some of the freshest fish that we have ever tasted. Then we walked along the beach and contemplated what our dream life would be together while gazing into the water, which had the most elaborate hue of blue and turquoise that I've ever seen in my life. The water is so clear, you can actually see all of the colorful fish swimming around like they're in a glass bowl. Then we hopped into the hot tub and enjoyed some wine while watching the sunset. It was truly a magical evening.

The next morning, my eyes sprang open, and it took me a minute to realize where I was. My beautiful wife was lying in my arms. I was lying in a bed that was as soft as a cloud. It was seriously like lying on a big pillow of richness. "OK, so that wasn't a dream. I'm actually in Hawaii at the Waldorf Astoria." My wife was cuddled into my chest in a deep, comfortable sleep. I gently tried to un-wedge myself from her loving grasp and sit up in the bed. I looked at the clock and saw that it was only 4:47 a.m.

Just at the moment, I heard a soft whisper, "Babe, we are on vacation. Can't you just sleep in with me?"

At that moment, the internal negotiations began. "Jarvis, she's right. You are on vacation. You deserve to sleep in!" "Jarvis, you are supposed to be enjoying this time with your wife!" "Jarvis, get your ass back in bed."

But then something happened. My instincts took over. My leg muscles elongated and I stood up. It was almost like I was on autopilot. I told her that I'd be back in about an hour and I got dressed and left the hotel room. I walked down to the beach and sat in the sand while the moonlight was still dancing on the ocean surface. No one was out there. It was just me. It was peaceful. It was tranquil. It was a sanctuary. I closed my eyes and started my intention-setting practice. I started with a gratitude prayer, then a meditation to listen for answers from God. In that silence, I heard a voice. That voice said to me, "Let go." I was just overwhelmed with this sense of peace knowing that everything was happening according to "His" plan and that I didn't have to force anything. Just let go and let him do his magic.

Then I journaled my goals and brainstormed an agenda for having the most amazing and fun-filled day in Hawaii. After about 30 minutes of quiet time sitting in the sand all by myself, I stood up and started running along the beach. I was the first person to touch this sand since the tide had come in. It was so pure. It actually sparkled like I was running on little tiny crystals. At this time, the sun was just rising, making an unbelievable display of colors in the sky. It was the most beautiful feeling I've ever experienced in my life. It truly was a "miracle morning."

After my beach run, I stopped by the coffee shop and got my wife an extra-large non-fat latte, which is her love language. I came bursting back into our hotel room with coffee and a bright, vibrant energy that was unreal. It was the perfect way to start the most amazing vacation with my amazing wife. This was the first day of the best vacation that we have ever had together.

One month after the Hawaii vacation, my wife said, "Babe, I'm late." I couldn't believe it. We rushed to get a pregnancy test and our suspicions

EVERY. DAMN. DAY.

were confirmed. WE WERE PREGNANT! We had gotten pregnant in Hawaii. I can't help but believe that starting each day with peace, hearing a word from God, and raising my vibration every morning led to us having the most amazing, relaxing, and enjoyable time, which put us in the right mental and emotional state to conceive and receive our son.

Being a Morning Hero isn't something you do… it's someone you are!

Even on vacation.

Even when you don't feel like it.

Even on holidays.

Even when it's your birthday.

Even on the weekend.

Even in Hawaii.

It's a mindset… a lifestyle…. and people may not understand it. They may fight you on it. They may want you to be normal. But you don't have normal-sized goals. You weren't built for average. You weren't designed for mediocrity. You were created to have a BIG life and leave a BIG impact. And that mission will require a bigger version of you. One who has discipline. One who does what's right, not what's convenient. One who straps on their cape every day and carries the weight of the world. Your calling will require you to be a Morning Hero.

On Mondays

On Tuesdays

On Wednesdays

On Thursdays

On Fridays

On Saturdays

And yes… on Sundays too!

This is just who you are now.

You Wake up, and you WIN…

Every. Damn. Day!

Next Steps

I'm proud of you. You're still here. That means that something I said resonated with you. Congratulations. You've taken the first step on your Hero's Journey. But nothing changes just because you finished reading this book. If you stop here, you'll fall right back into the old rhythm. The snooze button will creep back in. The whirlwind will swallow you up. The old you will come knocking at the door, and if you're not careful, you'll let them right back in.

Information without implementation is pointless. As the Bible says, "Faith without works is dead." So now, it's time to get to work! This is where you cross the line from knowing into doing. From coasting to committed. From dabbling to dominating. From trying to transformed. From a boring life to a BIG life! So here are your *Next Steps*.

Step 1: Download the 'Win The Day' App This book gave you the foundation. But the app is your toolbox, your accountability partner, your daily coach in your pocket. Inside, you'll find everything you need to actually live the Morning Hero life, not just read about it. You'll set your 5-star intentions, track and score your day, compete in challenges, and stack your WINS to keep you consistent. Think of it as your command center. Before you even put this book back on the shelf, go download the app. Don't wait. Don't "mean to get around to it." Do it now. That's your first act as a Morning Hero.

Step 2: Start the 30-Day Challenge The fastest way to lock in everything you've learned is to *practice it every single day* for 30 days straight (#NoDaysOff). That's what the 30-Day Challenge is for. It's not a test. It's your launch pad. By the end of 30 days, this won't be something you're trying to do anymore. It will be who you are. It will be automatic. The challenge is your rite of passage. If you can make it 30 straight days, you will officially earn your cape as a Morning Hero!

Step 3: Join a Tribe Unfortunately, many people never make it to the 30-day mark. They never hit their "tipping point" where everything becomes effortless, easy, and automatic. That's why we created accountability tribes. Inside the app, you can join a "Tribe" and do the Morning Hero Routine together each day. This is the best way for you to stick with your new habit until it becomes your new identity. Accountability = Consistency... and that's what will happen when you join a tribe. You will have rock solid consistency. No more "falling off the wagon." You will Wake up early... You will set your Intentions, and you will do it EVERY. DAMN. DAY!

Step 4: Conquer Your Life This is where it all comes together. This isn't about mornings anymore. It's about the life you're building full of health, wealth, happiness, family, impact. It's about living bigger than your excuses. It's about finally becoming the person you've always known you could be. Every morning you WIN is another brick in the mansion of your life. Stack enough wins together, and you won't just transform your mornings... you'll transform your entire existence!

So here it is. Your line in the sand. Your moment of decision. Are you going to close this book, nod your head, and slide back into the old pattern? Or are you going to take the next steps, download the app, start the challenge, join the tribe, and rise up as a true Morning Hero?

Don't wait. Don't hesitate. Don't "start tomorrow." Tomorrow is for drifters. Today is for heroes.

Your next step is simple: **Act now.**

Download. Start. Join. Conquer.

Final Words

You don't need more information.

You've got everything you need right now.

You don't need more motivation.

You just need to start.

Because when you win the morning,

You win the day.

When you win the day,

You win your life.

And when you start winning your life,

You make the world brighter for everyone around you.

So go…

Wake up.

Rise strong.

EVERY. DAMN. DAY.

Lead loud.

Serve big.

Smile wide.

Love hard.

And WIN…

EVERY. DAMN. DAY!

This is your time.

This is your season.

This is your life to win.

Another day, another W.

Now, go claim it.

Scan the QR code, Download the WIN The Day app, and let's begin your HERO'S Journey!

ABOUT THE AUTHOR

Jarvis Leverson is on a mission to wake up the world. Known as *The Morning Hero*, Jarvis has helped thousands of professionals, entrepreneurs, and leaders reclaim their mornings, install rock-solid habits, and win every damn day.

After spending 15 years as a top-producing sales executive in technology and real estate, Jarvis hit rock bottom. He was burned out, stuck, and coasting through life. That personal crash became his wake-up call. By engineering a simple morning routine, he rebuilt his health, his business, and his life. Today, he teaches that same system to audiences across the globe.

Jarvis has trained sales teams at companies like Google, Accenture, Keller Williams, Berkshire Hathaway, and Sun Life Financial. He is the co-author of the #1 Amazon Bestseller *Peak Performance: Mindset Tools for Sales* and the founder of *The Morning Hero* community and coaching programs. His signature keynote, *Win Every Day*, inspires professionals to master their mornings and unlock their full potential.

A devoted husband and father, Jarvis lives in San Diego with his wife and two children, where he practices what he preaches: family first, mornings sacred, and life lived at full throttle.

Contact Jarvis for interviews, speaking, or coaching.

Jarvis@themorninghero.com

https://www.instagram.com/the.morninghero/

ACKNOWLEDGMENTS

This book would not exist without my wife, Jane. You are the heartbeat of my life and the true original Morning Hero. From the very first page to the very last, your patience, encouragement, and unwavering support carried me through this process. While raising our two kids and managing the whirlwind of daily life, you gave me the space, energy, and belief I needed to bring this book into the world. This isn't just my book … it's ours.

To **Erik Seversen**, thank you for your guidance and coaching. Your steady hand and wisdom were instrumental in turning scattered ideas into a finished book that I am proud to share with the world.

To **Karl Gorman**, you've always been the model of living big and stepping fully into greatness. Your example inspired me to stop playing small and start living life all out.

To **David Brownlee**, thank you for being a cheerleader every step of the way. Your encouragement lifted me when I needed it most.

To **Hal Elrod**, your book *The Miracle Morning* convinced me that I could become a morning person. That single belief sparked the journey that has now transformed not only my life but also the lives of thousands of others.

To **Anthony Trucks**, thank you for pushing me onto bigger stages and helping me share this message with the world.

To my **mother, Sweetie Ann**, who constantly affirmed me and gave me the confidence to do hard things, and to my **mother-in-law, Mary Jane**, who gifted us family trips to Hawaii, a place where much of this book was written. Your love and generosity made this dream possible.

To **Rick Chatham**, thank you for being an incredible Morning Hero coach and for helping me bring this movement to life with passion and excellence.

To the **Morning Hero Tribe** — thank you for listening to all of my "dumb ideas," for experimenting with me, and for proving over and over again that this system works. Your wins are my greatest joy and my constant reminder that this work matters.

To the authors who shaped me — **David Goggins, Grant Cardone, Darren Hardy, and Brendon Burchard** — I've studied your words, your cadence, and your conviction. You gave me a model for how to share my story boldly and unapologetically.

And finally, to **you, the reader**. You are why I wrote this book. My hope is that, as you turn these pages, you don't just gain a few new habits … you step into a new identity. That you claim the title of Morning Hero, and that you wake up and win… every damn day.

DID YOU ENJOY THIS BOOK?

If you enjoyed reading this book, you can help by suggesting it to someone else you think might like it, and **please leave a positive review** wherever you purchased it. This does a lot in helping others find the book. We thank you in advance for taking a few moments to do this.

THANK YOU

You might also like other Thin Leaf Press titles:

The Successful Body: Using Fitness, Nutrition, and Mindset to Live Better
The Successful Spirit: Top Performers Share Secrets to a Winning Mindset
Winning Mindset: Elite Strategies for Peak Performance
Winner's Mindset: Peak Performance Strategies for Success
The AI Advantage: Thriving Within Civilization's Next Big Disruption
The AI Revolution: Thriving Within Civilization's Next Big Disruption
The AI Mindset: Thriving Within Civilization's Next Big Disruption
AI: Work Smarter and Live Better Within Civilization's Next Big Disruption
Peak Performance: Mindset Tools for Managers
Peak Performance: Mindset Tools for Sales
Peak Performance: Mindset Tools for Leaders
Peak Performance: Mindset Tools for Business
Peak Performance: Mindset Tools for Entrepreneurs
Peak Performance: Mindset Tools for Athletes
The Life Coach's Tool Kit, Vol. 1
The Life Coach's Tool Kit, Vol. 2
The Life Coach's Tool Kit, Vol. 3
Ordinary to Extraordinary
The Magical Lightness of Being
Explore.

www.ingramcontent.com/pod-product-compliance
Lightning Source LLC
Chambersburg PA
CBHW050853160426
43194CB00011B/2140